# MULTICULTURAL EDUCATION:

## A CROSS CULTURAL TRAINING APPROACH

### MARGARET D. PUSCH
Editor

Intercultural Press, Inc.

Library of Congress Catalogue Card Number: 79-92379
ISBN: 0-933662-06-8


Printed in the United States of America

This manual was originally prepared under a contract with the Bilingual
Higher Education Program, New York State Education Department.

MULTICULTURAL EDUCATION:
A CROSS-CULTURAL TRAINING APPROACH

CONTENTS

# PREFACE

There are a large number of people who helped make this book a reality. Some of their names appear throughout the text as they are credited for their contributions. Others generously discussed their ideas and shared materials that helped crystallize our thoughts. The diversity of their professional interests and personal origins helped us consider each topic from more than one perspective. They taught us much and we are grateful.

Special thanks goes to Daisy deJesus who initiated a project in the Bilingual Higher Education Program, New York State Education Department to develop materials for training teachers in multicultural education. We are indebted also to Barbara Sjostrom of that department who provided assistance and suggestions as the material was developed, and to Armando Cotayo, Marietta Saravia-Shore, and Gladys Wolff, educators in bilingual teacher training programs, for carefully critiquing early drafts of a manual developed for the project.

Finally we would like to thank Irene Kruka, Carol Friis and Mary Ann Recht for their patience and skill in typing all that follows in this book.

Margaret D. Pusch
LaGrange Park, IL.
September, 1979

v

INTRODUCTION

This is a Manual designed primarily for use by faculty in teacher education programs. It will of course be of interest to a wider audience because it touches on a number of central educational concerns. The specific intent, however, is to provide education faculty with a useful resource for building multicultural education training into the teacher education curriculum. It is further intended to be both practical, something that is usable in the classroom, and broad enough in scope to escape the opprobrium of being a book of mere technique.

It unites two important streams in contemporary national affairs. One flows out of the new role the nation assumed in the world after the Second World War. The other emerges from the struggle of the society to deal with its own irreversible pluralism. As different as these two developments appear, they had in common the need to understand better the nature of culture and its effect on individuals and groups. To prepare people to cope with a culturally diverse world, cross-cultural training was spawned. To prepare them to deal with a culturally diverse nation, multicultural education was fought through the courts and legislatures. Each thrust developed its separate perspective, one principally in the research and training worlds, the other in the streets, the communities and the schools.

They were irresistibly drawn to each other as living in a culturally pluralistic world became less and less distinguishable from living in a culturally pluralistic society.

Now we offer the full integration of these two approaches.

This Manual begins with definitions in order to establish a common ground, to assure that we are all talking about the same thing.

Chapter 2 is on the theory of intercultural communication which provides the conceptual framework for cross-cultural training.

A history of multicultural education (Chapter 3) with a strong focus on linguistic diversity is followed by a discussion of multicultural education curriculum, (Chapter 4) including consideration of how existing courses can be infused with multicultural perspectives.

The question of training teachers for multicultural education competencies is taken up in Chapter 5. Methods of teacher training are reviewed and cross-cultural training is examined in detail. Specific applications in teacher education are listed and succinctly described.

Chapter 6 consists of 30 teaching strategies drawn from the cross-cultural training literature and adapted for teacher pre-service and inservice training. It includes exercises such as role plays, critical incidents, case studies, simulations, group discussion, etc. It is expected that teachers and trainers will select those which fit best their own teaching styles and weave them into pre-existing courses and training programs.

Chapter 7 outlines procedures for the evaluation of cross-cultural training and education. The chapter is long and detailed. It is our feeling that evaluation is one of the most neglected aspects of teaching and training -- often for the want of a clear and full description of what it provides and how to go about it.

Finally, we have included a very select annotated bibliography and film list to provide the basis for exploring further without getting lost in a thicket of unfamiliar names and titles.

CHAPTER 1

DEFINITION OF TERMS

## CONTENTS

# CHAPTER 1

## DEFINITION OF TERMS

David S. Hoopes and Margaret D. Pusch


The intercultural and multicultural fields are of sufficiently recent development to be suffering from the multiplicity of tongues and prolixity of jargon that are almost inevitable when new concepts are discussed. Nothing about intercultural or multicultural human relations is really new, but by putting certain ideas about communication, culture, society, education and human psychology together, a different way of looking at and learning about interaction among cultures has emerged. This approach explains things that until now have been somewhat of a mystery. It also gives us new conceptual tools which can be used in achieving social aims.

One of these social aims is multicultural education. It is the intent of this work to demonstrate how the concepts developed in the intercultural communications field and the methods and strategies of cross-cultural training can be applied to multicultural educational efforts. Yet multicultural education too is a new phenomenon, at least as something consciously conceptualized, planned and promoted within the educational system. It is imperative therefore to deal also with its terminology.

Finally in doing this we inevitably encounter and use old terms. Many of these -- like "culture" and "race" for instance -- are terms that have complex meanings which change with context and evolve over time. These too will be defined to clarify their use here. We will start with the basic terms.

# BASIC TERMS

Culture is the sum total of ways of living; including values, beliefs, esthetic standards, linguistic expression, patterns of thinking, behavioral norms, and styles of communication which a group of people has developed to assure its survival in a particular physical and human environment. Culture, and the people who are part of it, interact, so that culture is not static. Culture is the response of a group of human beings to the valid and particular needs of its members. It, therefore, has an inherent logic and an essential balance between positive and negative dimensions.

A subculture is a group of people within a larger sociopolitical structure who share cultural (and often linguistic or dialectical) characteristics which are distinctive enough to distinguish it from others within the same society.

Race is a somewhat suspect concept used to identify large groups of the human species who share a more or less distinctive combination of hereditary physical characteristics. Within a society racial identification may be used to separate out a culture group for special priviledges or disabilities.

Class refers to a stratum of people within a society who share basic economic, political or cultural characteristics; for example: wealth or its absence, "life chances" in a market situation, kind of labor performed, tastes, family background, linguistic characteristics, or sets of special attitudes and behaviors. Class membership may provide access to power and priviledge or other benefits within a social, economic or political structure.

An ethnic group is a group of people identified by racial, national or cultural characteristics. Ethnic group membership is normally determined by birth. Most commonly, ethnic groups are seen as interdependent sub-units of larger cultural or political entities. The term "ethnic group" is often applied to groups which have a minority status in the larger society.

Identity group (or role group) is any group of people who share enough characteristics, interests, attitudes or behaviors to provide an ease of communication and a satisfying sense of relatedness. Identity groups may be based on profession or vocation, family status, avocation, special skills, etc. Cultures are identity groups but identity groups are not cultures. (A role group is an identity group based on a professional, vocational, familial or some other role.)

Language is the systematic, structured verbal and, in most cases, written code used for communication among a group of people. Language and culture are determining factors in the way people think, the way they communicate and the way they behave.

Dialect is a variety of a spoken language which differs from the standard form of the language and is used by a group of speakers who are set off from others geographically or socially.

**Communication** is the transmission of messages from a sender to a receiver in any one of a variety of codes -- language, gestures, signs, written symbols, etc. -- to which the sender and receiver attach meaning. The aim is to transfer the message with as little loss of meaning as possible. Communication is also a transaction that generates new meanings. Communication through means other than spoken or written language is generally referred to as non-verbal communication.

**Education** is the process of growth in intellectual and emotional skills which equip people to cope with human existence individually and as members of groups. Education occurs in many ways and under many different circumstances during most of one's life, though much of it is dictated by the culture to which one belongs.

**Schooling** is formally structured education designed to provide the knowledge and intellectual and emotional skills which established governing bodies in society deem most important.

**Cultural conditioning** (socialization) is the learning provided by a cultural/social group designed to fit the growing child to the ways of thinking and behaving developed by the group over time to assure its survival.

**Cultural Relativism** suggests that cultures cannot be judged or evaluated from a single or absolute ethical or moral perspective. Evaluations are relative to the background from which they arise. No culture's values, ethics or morals as a whole may be judged as inherently superior or inferior to another's.

**Prejudice** describes hostile and unreasonable feelings, opinions or attitudes based on fear, mistrust, ignorance, mis-information -- or a combination thereof -- and directed against a racial, religious, national or other cultural group.

## THE TERMINOLOGY OF MULTICULTURAL EDUCATION

**Multicultural education** is a structured process designed to foster understanding, acceptance, and constructive relations among people of many different cultures. Ideally, it encourages people to see different cultures as a source of learning and to respect diversity in the local, national and international environment. It stresses cultural, ethnic and racial, in addition to, linguistic differences. It is often broadened to include socio-economic differences (urban, rural, age/youth, worker/middle class), professional differences (doctor/nurse), sex and religious differences. Multicultural education refers first to building an awareness of one's own cultural heritage, and understanding that no one culture is intrinsically superior to another; secondly, to acquiring those skills in analysis and communication that help one function effectively in multicultural environments. Stress is placed on experiencing cultural differences in the classroom and in the society rather than simply studying about them. Multicultural education is not just a set of ethnic or other area study programs but

-4-

an effort to demonstrate the significance of similarities and differences among culture groups and between individuals within those groups.

A basic premise of multicultural education is that in some degree all people, especially Americans, have experienced a variety of cultural influences and are therefore multicultural. The implementation of multicultural education may be seen as the appropriate adjustment of the educational process to the realities of the American experience.

Bilingual education is designed to create a learning environment and program which will enable students to take the fullest advantage of their educational opportunity by learning in their first language while at the same time becoming thoroughly proficient and skilled in a second language. For example, to American students who are deficient in English, basic subjects are taught in the student's first language while English is studied intensively as a second language. The aim is to help students become fully fluent in English without being academically penalized by the fact that it is their second language.

Monoculturalism, biculturalism and multiculturalism are terms which characterize a continuum along which people may move in expanding their cultural identities. There is some question, however, as to whether the words "monocultural" and "bicultural" are either accurate or useful. It can be argued that virtually no one is purely monocultural or bicultural. All people are multicultural.

It is our belief that "monocultural" and "bicultural" are in fact useful terms when referring to the experience of individuals. There are people whose cultural experience is so limited that, despite the presence of other cultural influences in them, they can be considered monocultural. Similarly, there are those who have had intensive experience in two linguistic/cultural environments but upon whom other cultural influences have had no apparent effect.

We will therefore make discreet use of the terms "monocultural" and "bicultural" though we recognize them to be oversimplifications. Biculturalism is the more ambiguous term. Many who reach a state of functioning easily in two languages and cultures report experiencing an uncertainty of norms and values which gives them a sense of anxiety and insecurity. Biculturalism may also produce a feeling of having a dual or split personality with attendant psychological stresses. Careful management of the bicultural experience reduces the difficulties of making the transition from culture to culture.

At the same time, bicultural people share what is sometimes called a "Third Culture" experience. This is the experience of bridging two cultures. There is a potentially valuable sociopolitical role for people with this experience as mediators or links between cultures during times of cross-cultural stress.

Cultural/linguistic diversity refers to the existence of two, three or more cultures (or commonly spoken languages) among people who live within a single sociopolitical structure.

Cultural/linguistic pluralism refers to cultural or linguistic diversity within a given political or social structure.

Cultural pluralism is the central encompassing concept. For most thoughtful people, cultural pluralism has replaced the "melting pot" in describing the multiethnic and multicultural character of American Society. Ideally, members of a pluralistic society recognize the contributions of each group to the common civilization and encourage the maintenance and development of different life styles, languages and convictions. Equally important is a commitment to deal cooperatively with common concerns. An interest in providing an education for children that enables them to realize personal goals and contribute to community life is a common concern that calls for such collaboration. Education for a plural society includes intercultural, bilingual and multicultural dimensions. It strives to create the conditions of harmony and respect within a culturally diverse society.

## TERMINOLOGY OF INTERCULTURAL COMMUNICATION
## AND CROSS-CULTURAL TRAINING

The two principal terms in this field are "intercultural" and "cross-cultural." There are other pertinent words which attach various prefixes to the word cultural -- such as transcultural, supra-cultural, intra-cultural, etc. but which will not concern us here (transcultural is more or less a synonym for cross- and intercultural.)

Both "intercultural" and "cross-cultural" refer to interaction, communication and other processes (conceptual analysis, education, the implementation of public policy, etc.) which involve people or entities from two or more different cultures. There has been some effort to limit "intercultural" to that which is interactive between cultures and "cross-cultural" to that which is comparative or conceptual, but the distinction doesn't hold. In fact, they are used more or less synonymously and tend to vie with each other for predominance.

As for specific terms:

Intercultural communication refers to the communication process (in its fullest sense) between people of different cultural backgrounds. It may take place among individuals or between social, political or economic entities in different cultures, such as government agencies, businesses, educational institutions or the media. This includes non-verbal as well as verbal communication and the use of differing codes, linguistic or non-linguistic. Culture is viewed as having a major influence on the communication process.

Intercultural (cross-cultural) education is educational activity which fosters an understanding of the nature of culture, which helps the student develop skills in intercultural communication and which aids the student to view the world from perspectives other than one's own.

Intercultural learning (sometimes "cross-cultural learning" or simply "culture learning") may refer to either (1) learning the principle characteristics of another culture, or (2) the way in which a learner progresses from ethnocentrism to an acceptance and appreciation of another culture.

Cross-cultural awareness (sometimes "cultural awareness" or "cultural self-awareness") refers to the basic ways of learning that behavior and ways of thinking and perceiving are culturally conditioned rather than being universal aspects of human nature. In this learning, unconscious, culturally-based assumptions and values held by individuals are brought to the surface.

Cross-cultural training refers to all kinds of programs that train people to live, work, study or perform effectively in a cultural setting different from their own. Several other phrases are sometimes used, such as "race relations training" or "cultural awareness training." The techniques of cross-cultural training are normally experiential though they may include comparative cultural studies or the study of specific target cultures. In most cases, consideration of the theoretical framework for cross-cultural experiences and intercultural learning is included. Simulations, case studies, role plays and the like are used extensively, along with some formal presentations and general discussion.

Cross-cultural perspective refers to the process of looking at cultural phenomena from the perspective of both the culture in which they occur and another culture.

Intergroup is a general term for relationships and interactions between and among groups of any kind. It is especially used for the diverse cultural and ethnic groups in the U.S.

Interracial refers to relationships between different "racial" groups. In the United States, it most commonly refers to relationships between Blacks and Whites, though relationships involving Asians and Native Americans are appropriately included. "Interracial" is frequently used more loosely to include other ethnic and culture groups, sometimes to the point of attaching it to any minority/majority relationship. We will use it only in its narrower definition as referring to relationships between biologically defined racial groups.

Inter-ethnic is broader and refers to relationships between individuals and groups with not only racial but with national and linguistic differences as well.

Despite the emphasis here on American society and American culture groups the concepts and processes defined are universal. They are as critical to understanding interaction that occurs in an international context as they are to understanding interaction within a multi-ethnic community. Indeed, the great majority of research in intercultural communication has been on interaction between people of different national cultures. Yet the same problems exist within as between countries and the same principles apply.

One of the promising aspects of the intercultural communications field is that it is linked inescapably to the problem of survival in a culturally diverse and conflict-ridden world. To deal with intercultural issues at home is, in a sense, to deal with them globally. Thus to the immediacy and dynamism involved in working on linguistic, ethnic, racial, cultural, and educational issues in the United States is added a transcendent perspective on human history and human survival on earth.

CHAPTER 2

INTERCULTURAL COMMUNICATION CONCEPTS
AND THE PSYCHOLOGY OF INTERCULTURAL EXPERIENCE

## CONTENTS

CHAPTER 2


INTERCULTURAL COMMUNICATION CONCEPTS
AND THE PSYCHOLOGY OF INTERCULTURAL EXPERIENCE


David S. Hoopes


Intercultural communication as a field in itself is relatively
new. Anthropologists, political scientists and linguists have for a
long time, of course, been concerned with the various dimensions of
culture and communication, but, until recently, none put them together
in a broad framework of intercultural relations. Academically, the
stage was probably set when "communication" was distinguished from
"speech" and became a subject of specialized concern, and when
anthropologists began studying the patterns of modern as well as
ancient and "primitive" cultures. It is most easily dated, however,
from the publication in 1959 of Edward T. Hall's Silent Language.
This book gave us the first comprehensive analysis of the relationship
between communication and culture.

Intercultural communication is one of those fields which emerged
from immediate experience and was built upon practical need, rather
than being the off-spring of abstract intellectual inquiry (as
occurred, for instance, in the development of demography). The needs
were fairly explicit: (1) to train Americans to function more effectively abroad during the post World War II period when they were
swarming overseas in vast numbers to live, work or study; (2) to aid
in the adjustment of foreign students and trainees who began in the
same era to come in large numbers to this country seeking the keys to
industrial and technological development; and (3) to understand and
manage the more explosive dimensions of inter-racial and inter-ethnic
relations in the United States as the civil rights movement gained
momentum in the early 1960s.

The people most affected by these events and forces sought answers wherever they could. They read Hall, including his second book, The Hidden Dimension, in which he analyzed the cultural use of space and demonstrated vividly the practical value of cross-cultural analysis. They read in communication theory, especially David Berlo's Process of Communication which was used as the theoretical framework for international communications training programs at Michigan State University. They read Herskovitz on cultural relativism and Gordon Allport on prejudice. They studied the results of Rokeach's world-mindedness research and began to explore kinesics and other aspects of non-verbal communication. They read anthropologists Clyde Kluckhohn and Margaret Mead and were particularly influenced by Florence Kluckhohn and Fred Strodbeck's Variations in Value Orientations. Many turned to humanistic psychology and human relations training, studying the work of Carl Rogers and Abraham Maslow.

Then the Peace Corps began sending thousands of young Americans to the far corners of the earth. These Peace Corps volunteers had to be trained. Materials were gathered in bits and pieces -- exercises, mimeographed readings, bibliographies -- and used in the training process, ultimately to appear in the first cross-cultural training manual (Wight and Hammons, 1970).

In the mid-1960's a cluster of scholars, students and program officers at the University of Pittsburgh began to study the subject with some care. A series of intercultural communication workshops were sponsored by the Regional Council for International Education and the Intercultural Communication Network to explore the process in a multicultural laboratory setting. Funding for these workshops and other activities that furthered the development of the field was provided by the National Association for Foreign Student Affairs. Marshall Singer, a political scientist at Pittsburgh, wrote his seminal essay, "Culture: A Perceptual Approach" in which he used the Whorfian hypothesis as his take off point, except that he substituted "perception" and "perceptual systems" for "linguistics" and "linguistic systems" as the arbiters of culture. Singer's essay appeared in the first of a series of Readings In Intercultural Communication edited by David Hoopes and published by the Network. The Readings were designed to make more easily available to people in the field articles, essays and educational materials that had not yet found their way into normal publishing channels.

Edward Stewart was working on an elaboration of the Kluckhohn-Strodtbeck value orientations model, analyzing American mainstream culture from a cross-cultural perspective, though his book, American Cultural Patterns: A Cross-Cultural Perspective, did not appear in print until 1971. Stewart's work was particularly important because it not only compared and contrasted cultures but examined them from the perspective of cross-cultural interaction. Stewart had been part of a research team at the Human Relations Research Organization in Washington where a complicated technique for training American military and technical personnel going overseas was developed. It was an elaborate "contract American" role-play for which Stewart's analysis served as the theoretical framework.

-11-

At about the same time, a psychologist at the University of Illinois, Harry Triandis, was heading a team working on the development of a self-instructional training device called a "culture assimilator." Somewhat later Triandis wrote The Analysis of Subjective Culture, a complete comparative study on the nature of culture.

An anthology of readings (Samovar and Porter) was published in 1972, but it wasn't until 1975 that the first substantial basic text on the subject came out (Condon and Yousef). Two thin books attempting to analyze communication in inter-racial terms also appeared about this time (Smith, 1973; Rich, 1974).

By now other developments had taken place. The Culture Learning Institute of the East-West Center had become an important source of new research. Courses were being introduced in colleges and universities around the country. The Training Institute of the Business Council for International Understanding was gaining a foothold in business for cross-cultural training. The Center for Research and Education in Denver refined the techniques of Peace Corps training and served as a focal point for the early efforts of cross-cultural trainers to identify themselves as professionals. In the military, the Navy had long sponsored intercultural research and now inter-racial training was instituted in several sectors. The State Department and U.S. Information Agency (USIA) began to recognize the significance of intercultural communication in American foreign relations. By 1978, USIA and the Bureau of Educational and Cultural Affairs, Department of State, would be combined into the International Communication Agency.

The Society for Intercultural Education, Training and Research was established in 1975 to bring together people in a variety of disciplines with a special interest in intercultural relations. The organization soon launched a major state-of-the-art study in the intercultural field with funding from the Department of State.

Cross-cultural and ethnic issues were getting attention in education. One of the major events that focused attention on these issues was the civil rights movements and its culmination in the riots of 1967. Many old concepts went up in flames along with the cities that year. One of them was the "melting pot." The inherent culturally pluralistic nature of American society could no longer be ignored. The demand for minority and ethnic group rights coupled with an assertion of cultural identity brought intercultural communication home to the United States. This was especially true in education where integration, special programs for the economically disadvantaged and, finally, bilingual/bicultural and multicultural education programs were initiated. As a result of these efforts, the influence of students' cultural and linguistic backgrounds on learning patterns became increasingly obvious. It became equally apparent that understanding the cultural dimensions of communication and human relations processes as well as differences in cognition is critical in making a successful transition to a genuinely pluralistic society.

By this time too the literature of black and ethnic protest had turned into an analysis of ethnicity and inter-ethnic relations. Glazer and Moynihan published Beyond the Melting Pot and then a second book on ethnicity; Kenneth Clark studied the psychology of the black ghetto; Ramirez and Casteneda wrote on cultural democracy and bicognitive development. Among the ethnically oriented, "communication" was not a key word. More often one heard "cultural pluralism," "ethnic identity," and "cultural democracy."

One of the most significant problems in the field has been its division into two parts which have remained unnecessarily separate -- the international intercultural and the domestic inter-ethnic. The international has found its focus of interest in higher education and in training personnel for overseas service while the inter-ethnic interest has been located in elementary and secondary education and has concentrated on teacher education at the university level. Interest in the latter is increasing among other professionals in, for example, the areas of health care delivery and social work. Further, internationalists tend to come from mainstream American culture and use intercultural communication terminology while the domestic concern arises most strongly out of the minority groups and expresses itself in terms of "cultural pluralism." There is thus, almost a cross-cultural division inherent within the field. There is an understandable volatility and immediacy of conflict in domestic inter-ethnic relations. This lends to it a different character, and sometimes those pressures act to impede cooperation between the two in dealing with ethnic issues either conceptually or in practice. But the thrust of both communities, domestic and international, should be in the same direction, toward the development of the knowledge and the skills needed to manage cultural diversity and bring about a more equitable distribution of the social good.

What follows is an effort to provide a theoretical framework for this manual. It recognizes that the manual is a tool for practitioners. It will therefore not attempt to review the literature beyond the brief survey given above or to pursue every idea in its fullest complexity. Instead it will focus on those selected concepts which are felt to be the most relevant to educators with the responsibility for training teachers to deal with the challenges of multiculturalism.


PERCEPTION

A major theme of this manual is that the key to achieving effective cross-cultural relations is to become functionally aware of the degree to which our behavior is culturally determined. By functionally aware, we mean with an awareness that translates into an ability to alter or manage our behavior in intercultural contexts.

One of the simplest and yet most difficult ideas to internalize is the concept of perceptual difference -- the idea that everyone perceives the world differently and that members of one culture group share basic sets of perceptions which differ from the sets of perceptions shared by members of other culture groups. It is not that the idea is difficult to understand, it is that it is hard to impose upon ourselves, to internalize so that it affects our behavior. The way we perceive the world, what we expect of it and what we think about it,

-13-

is so basic and so ingrained, is buried so deep in us and in our unconscious that we continuously act and react without thinking why -- without even realizing that we might think why (Singer, 1976).

In our daily lives we are bombarded with vast quantities of sensory data (which later in this chapter will be called "communication from the environment" as we look at its implications for the communication process). Sights, sounds, smells, tactile sensations, tastes are continuously presented to us. This bombardment goes on all our waking hours, so much so that we are forced to screen most of it out. This screening process, called "selective perception," is critical to our mental health. Without it we would quite simply go mad. But what criteria do we use for this screening? How do we decide what to hear, see, smell, taste or feel of all the myriad possibilities? For the most part, our culture or our cultural environment tells us.

If we live in the city, we are unconscious much of the time of the urban noise and clatter. We hear it only when it becomes so intrusive that we cannot ignore it. The visitor from the country, however, will tend to be much more aware of the noise, because of a perceptual system more accustomed to quiet and open to nuances of sound. As the linguist knows, we hear certain distinctions in some spoken sounds and not in others. We focus on certain aspects of dress -- color, style, neatness -- and not others or we focus on dress at certain times and not others. We smell that which tells us something about our food or our surroundings or about another person and ignore smells that do not. Again, the stranger will often detect odors that the native resident does not.

Clearly many things affect the selection process: environment, personality, and immediate need; but the basic framework is provided by culture. We learn to make these distinctions, to select out what we do from our experience, principly according to the instructions we receive from our culture. Those instructions come from all the spoken and unspoken norms we begin learning from the moment we are born.

Another thing we do to deal with this mass of sensory data is to classify or categorize it. These categories are the means by which we sort, define, understand and store our experience. As with selective perception, we establish the categories within a system of values and value judgments based largely on the dictates of culture. This is one way in which values become operational and indeed comprehensible. We categorize events. We also categorize the physical world. "Teaching" is a category. "Building" is a category. By establishing categories and by defining our experience within them, the mind is provided a mechanism for rapid if not instantaneous processing and storing of information. In this way, our experience becomes manageable. We can store and forget most of it, reacting to and dealing with only that which is important. But what is defined as important depends on value judgments and varies according to the values of the individual.

If I pass a school building on the way to work, I am likely simply to classify it as "building." Someone who teaches there will probably ascribe more importance to it. It may be a "pleasant building" or an "unpleasant building", or, perhaps, a "source-of-income building." It may be a "source-of-love building" for the teacher who is romantically involved with another staff-member or "fear building" if there is disruption in the student body. The students will have a whole set of classifications too, as will parents. But for me, one for whom it is not directly relevant, the original simple classification is enough even though I may be aware of and have strong opinions about education. (There is, of course, a possibility that I will stereotype it as "blackboard jungle," thereby projecting some of my fears and prejudices into it.)

Two problems arise which are particularly important in intercultural communication. One is that when our experience doesn't fit into our categories, it produces ambiguity. Our response may be to force it into an inaccurate category, thereby distorting our perception of reality; or we may feel insecure and uncertain. Those feelings affect our relationship to the world around us. When we encounter values, behaviors, communication styles, ways of thinking which don't fit our categories of meaning but fit, instead, the categories of some other culture group, communication is likely to break down. An American mainstream male who is touched and hugged by a male from another cultural background will probably classify that behavior negatively, respond with discomfort if not anger, and have difficulty relating to the person who hugged him.

Since categories of meaning are defined largely by culture, someone who becomes bicultural has learned another set of categories of meaning by which to judge experience.

The second problem is that categorizing can lead to stereotyping. In our own culture we make a vast assortment of distinctions among people; distinctions in the way they look, in the way they dress, in the way they move, in the way they sound. These subtleties of distinction are necessary because members of our own culture are those, normally, on whom we most depend for physical, social and economic security. We must distinguish carefully in order to provide for ourselves. This is not so with people from other culture groups. If we don't encounter them very much or don't depend on them, our tendency is to categorize them in the simplest way possible. We classify them according to certain traits of dress, behavior or mein (skin or hair color, shape of face, salient features, stature, etc.) and ignore all else about them (later to be convinced or, at best, puzzled by the fact that "they all look alike!"). It becomes stereotyping when we confuse our categories with reality. This is compounded by a tendency to invest those categories, because they constitute the unknown, with negative or destructive emotions. These are emotions to which, as humans, we are all subject - fear, envy, mistrust, etc. They are emotions all too often reality-based, arising out of competition for limited resources, territory or power, but the important point here is that from a natural and necessary function of the human organism, a major barrier to intercultural communication may emerge.

The data and the categories are, in most societies, assigned meanings. The perceptual system and the culture as a whole thereby become both embodied in and shaped by language (if I don't have a name for something, it may be difficult for me to perceive). Language then is a reflection of culture and one of the principle vehicles by which culture is transmitted to and reinforced in members of the group. Yet it is not the whole of culture. Much of our perceptual system is manifest in the ways in which we behave and organize our environment which, contrary to the suggestion above, may be perceived without the intervention of language. Learning the language or the linguistic code is therefore important but almost equally important is learning the culture or the cultural code.

What data our perceptual system selects may depend on temporary or immediate need, personality or culture, though we would argue that culture and the value system it embodies is the strongest and most pervasive influence. However it takes place, it provides order and structure to the world and in this order and structure we find our security as vulnerable human beings. Our perceptual system, therefore, is the foundation on which we build our relationships to the rest of the world.

## CULTURAL SELF-AWARENESS

One of the major sources of intercultural misunderstanding and conflict lies in the clash of these deeply rooted and culturally conditioned perceptions of reality. It is to the unconscious nature of these perceptions that intercultural specialists lay much of the blame. As long as our way of perceiving the world -- on which our communication styles and behavior patterns are based -- is "out of awareness," it is not accessible to being deliberately changed, managed, understood or influenced. It will continue to contribute to misunderstanding and conflict. This condition alters only as the individual becomes more aware and has more knowledge of the degree to which his perceptions and his behaviors are culturally conditioned -- that is, as he develops "cultural self-awareness."

Achieving cultural self-awareness, however, is not a simple process. In fact, the inclination is to resist it. Among the reasons:

1. Awareness is an emotional event derived from experience rather than an idea attained through an intellectual process. Yet we have generally been taught that the intellect is our principal avenue of learning.

2. We like to think of ourselves as autonomous and not subject, against our will, to forces buried within us by our cultural heritage.

3. We are all vulnerable. Anything that probes the nature of our identities is threatening.

Even for those who pursue it, cultural awareness is elusive. One of the striking experiences intercultural specialists have is of suddenly being caught in some kind of crosscultural insensitivity, trapped behind their own perceptual blinders unaware of the cultural biases they are manifesting. No matter how much we experience, how skillful we become, how conscious we are of the cultural dimension of human relations; with distressing frequency we find ourselves imprisoned in our own limited perceptions. We miss the point of some statement, event or behavior; we respond emotionally and in a way so natural that even when our own ethnocentrism stares us in the face, we fail to see it and fail to realize that we have missed or grossly misinterpreted something or responded inappropriately. Yet once our error is made clear, we are startled by how obvious it is.

Our tendency is to recognize the problem in others and deny it in ourselves. Our resistance to self-learning lies at an emotional, unconscious level. If we are going to come to grips with the concept of cultural relativity and take significant steps toward cultural self-awareness, we have to become fully engaged with our own perceptions, our own behaviors and our own communication patterns. Only then will we be able to break through the cognitive defenses, the inherent disbelief, and the simple incomprehension that cross-cultural misunderstanding relates to us here and now rather than to "them" out there.

It is the function of cross-cultural training to provide the framework and content for that kind of learning.

There is a tendency, particularly in cross-cultural relations in this country, to identify the need for cultural awareness training as existing primarily among members of the majority or mainstream culture. It is argued that members of minority groups already have cross-cultural skills by virtue of having survived in the hostile context of majority culture. While basically sound this argument ignores two things;

1. The more minorities understand and master the skills of intercultural communication and cross-cultural human relations, the more effective they will be in managing and manipulating mainstream society. The experience of having survived is simply not enough.

2. There is no guarantee that these skills, developed to meet needs in a majority-minority bicultural relationship, are transferable to the multicultural relationships which characterize culturally pluralistic societies. The evidence, in fact, suggests the opposite.

Cross-cultural training or training in cultural awareness should be seen as a potentially valid experience for anyone, regardless of cultural background.


## THE INTERCULTURAL LEARNING PROCESS

Developing cultural awareness is a process of looking inward. "intercultural learning," as we use the term here, is a similar and parallel process but is focused outward on the learning of other cultures. By that, we do not mean gathering information about other culture groups. We mean instead learning another culture so as to be able to experience what it is like to be part of it and to view the world from its point of view; learning it so as to be able to function effectively and comfortably within it.

Intercultural learning can be seen to take place along a continuum, running from ethnocentrism at one end of the spectrum to some form of adaptation or integration at the other. In outline form, the continuum looks like this:

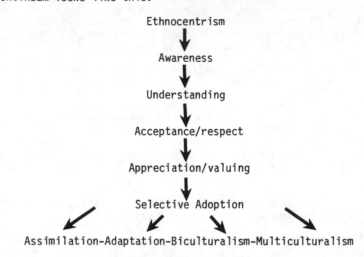

Ethnocentrism

↓

Awareness

↓

Understanding

↓

Acceptance/respect

↓

Appreciation/valuing

↓

Selective Adoption

Assimilation-Adaptation-Biculturalism-Multiculturalism

Ethnocentrism is a basic human survival response. From birth we begin identifying with and affirming that which gives us sustenance, our parents, our families, our culture groups. To believe that one's group is right and must be defended provides or has provided human beings with one of their most effective defenses against the depredations of nature and of other human beings. Strength lies in the group. Yet as civilization becomes more advanced and complicated, as the population increases and as culture groups become more accessible to each other, another, more negative aspect of ethnocentrism becomes a threat -- conflict intensifies and annihilation of the species becomes a real possibility as humans develop more and more sophisticated methods of destroying each other.

The principle characteristic of the ethnocentric is the relatively blatant assertion of personal and cultural superiority ("my way is the right way") accompanied by a denigration of other cultures and other ways. The ethnocentric impulse is to divide the world into two parts -- us and them (the "we-they" conflict).

It could be argued that the answer to ethnocentrism is not progress on the intercultural learning continuum but movement outward on what might be termed an "identity continuum," from parents to family, to community, to culture group, to nation, to globe. Movement along the identity continuum, in fact, does occur. It results from the broadening effect of education and experience. Yet it does not tell us much about the process of relating to specific other cultures or individuals from those cultures. To identify with a nation or the world as a whole is too general to help us understand our culturally different neighbor or the nation across the border. It also tends to serve best as a conceptual ideal rather than something that provides a useful framework for understanding real intercultural relationships and how one deals with them.

Awareness refers here to an awareness of other cultures, not to self-awareness. The first step out of ethnocentrism is to become aware that other culture groups exist as something other than the enemy -- even if they are still classified as peculiar.

Understanding (not to be confused with "liking") follows when one begins to sort out the nature of other groups and recognize that culture is a complex process which can be understood in terms more rational than one's emotional response to "them." Emphasis is still likely to be on the strange and different, however, and the other culture will get the short end of any comparison with one's own, if there is not outright antagonism.

Acceptance/respect begins when the person recognizes and accepts the validity of the cultural differences he or she encounters. It is possible at this point to accept other cultures as they are without comparing them to or judging them against one's own. It is also possible to respect those very things that are so different and that may, at an emotional level, produce negative reactions in us.

Appreciation/valuing comes when you have put into perspective the strengths and weaknesses of a culture and can invest yourself in appreciating and valuing specific aspects of it.

Selective Adoption of new attitudes and behaviors can now occur as the individual consciously or unconsciously responds to character-istics encountered in the other culture which are felt to be useful or desirable to emulate. This may take the form of adjustment or adapta-tion with the practical aim of enabling the person to function more effectively in the other culture. It may also be that the individual finds aspects of the other cultural pattern simply more comfortable or satisfying in personal terms.

At the end of the spectrum we have four theoretical states. We emphasize "theoretical" since none will be encountered in its pure form. Indeed, for this reason the last, multiculturalism, has to be seen as a process rather than a state of being. They should be seen as directions in which people can go as they reach an advanced stage in the intercultural learning process, not as fully defined final states of being.

Assimilation/Acculturation. It has been argued that no one who has had a substantial dose of a primary culture and language (let's say, arbitrarily, ten years) can ever wholly assimilate to another. Conceptually, assimilation has been a process associated more with generations than individuals. For individuals, acculturation is probably the better term. In our use, it suggests the adoption of the second culture, language and behaviors as primary and the rejection either by choice or by external pressure of the primary language and culture. The person who has assimilated or acculturated is not likely to lose, in very large measure, the original cultural conditioning.

-19-

Adaptation is the more calculated response to intercultural learning. In the adaptive process the individual adjusts to the stresses and challenges of experiencing another culture and adapts his or her mode of behavior in order to feel comfortable and to function effectively within it. During this process, however, the person does not attempt to absorb and incorporate the new behaviors. There is a role-playing quality to adaptation. The person learns the language and the gestures, attempts to understand and empathize with the perspectives of the second culture but resists as much as possible the encroachment of the second culture on his or her own.

There is thus a major dilemma at the heart of the process of cross-cultural adaptation.

If adaptation is in some significant degree role-playing, then where does that leave genuineness of response in intercultural relations? One develops skills in fitting into and functioning within a different cultural setting by learning new behaviors. In the degree to which these behaviors are contrary to one's primary behavior pattern, they might be judged insincere.

On the other hand, if one throws oneself fully into intercultural learning, the new behaviors may encroach on the old. The person may experience a cultural loss -- an unwanted acculturation and a movement toward a psychologically precarious position between cultures where confusion of identity is a real and constant threat.

Biculturalism, in a sense, is an answer to the latter problem. The fully bicultural person develops a dual cultural personality. Yet some sacrifice, wanted or unwanted, of the primary culture is involved. To many, biculturalism is seen as the ideal end to the intercultural learning process. To others, it may seem to be forced semi-acculturation. Adapation may be considered preferable. This preference may be particularly strong among some minority groups who know they must be able to function biculturally if they are to succeed in mainstream society, but who prefer to see themselves role-playing rather than internalizing a culture that has to a greater or lesser degree been oppressive.

On the other hand, if you use the term to define the background influences which have gone to make up the personality of the individual, most if not all people -- certainly in modern American society -- are at least bicultural if not multicultural.

Multiculturalism is a more complicated concept. Like assimilation, it may, in fact, not be realizable if you define it as being fluent in more than two cultures. The depth and breadth of experience required to learn a culture fluently is probably too great to be repeated many times. Defined differently, however, multiculturalism becomes a central idea in the context of this manual. The critical element in the expansion of intercultural learning is not the fullness with which one knows each culture, but the degree to which the process of cross-cultural learning, communication and human relations have been mastered. In other words, multiculturalism is achieved as the person learns the framework of intercultural communication and cross-cultural human relations and then applies it successively to new cultures encountered. It may further be applied to multicultural situations. For example, knowing the dynamics of intercultural communication and the significance and pervasiveness of perceptual difference based on cultural conditioning, a person is equipped to deal more effectively with situations (a multicultural classroom, for instance) in which more than two cultures are represented.

Thus multiculturalism is that state in which one has mastered the knowledge and developed the skills necessary to feel comfortable and communicate effectively (1) with people of any culture encountered and (2) in any situation involving a group of people of diverse cultural backgrounds. (By "comfortable," we mean without the anxiety, defensiveness and disorientation that usually accompany the initial intercultural experience.) The multicultural person is the person who has learned how to learn culture -- rapidly and effectively. Clearly it is an ideal.

Another way of looking at culture learning or cultural development is offered by James Banks (1977). He calls it a "Typology of the Emerging States of Ethnicity" and breaks the stages down as follows:

1. Ethnic Psychological Captivity: This is a pre-ethnocentric stage in which members of an ethnic group accept the negative self-perceptions imposed upon them by others.

2. Ethnic Encapsulation: This is closer to ethnocentrism.

3. Biethnicity: Having the capacity to participate in both one's own and another ethnic group.

4. Multiethnicity or Pan-Humanism: The ability to identify with an ethnically pluralistic nation.

There are two further points that must be made about the intercultural learning process.

One relates to the special role in society the bicultural or multicultural person may play. People who have had extensive experience in and have learned another culture, it is argued, have undergone cultural change or growth to the degree that they cannot simply be considered members of their primary culture. It is suggested that these people constitute a "third culture" (Useem, Useem and Donahue, 1963). Members of this third culture, regardless of their background or where they live, constitute a distinct identity group based on shared learnings and perceptions derived from an intercultural experience. Further, people of the third culture constitute a mediating resource among the world's societies.

Thus the individual who is bicultural or multicultural has the potential to become a "mediating man" (Bochner, 1973), one who is able to bridge the gap between cultures in the process of working out global cultural relationships. If we live in a plural rather than an assimilationist world, this becomes a critical function since cultures will not, as the old ideal hoped they would, grow together and become one -- even under the leveling impact of technology. As the earth becomes increasingly crowded, the need for more extensive and sophisticated mediation of differences is apparent.

Consequently, the skills that members of the third culture have are extremely important to human society and will become more so. Yet many who have those skills do not realize it. This is true, for example, in the intercultural profession of foreign student advising. It is our experience that most of the several thousand people who work in this profession and deal continuously with people from all over the world are surprisingly unaware of the practical importance and potential of the multicultural experiences and skills they possess.

The mediating role which bicultural members of minority groups can play in cross-cultural relations is increasingly appreciated by those who accept the inescapability of cultural pluralism in this country.

Another problem is that the intercultural learning continuum as described here is based on the assumption that the person moving along it starts out being conditioned by a discreet and separate culture; that the culture stands distinct from other cultures and is the dominant cultural factor in the individual's social experience. While this is the experience of many millions of people throughout the world, for millions of others it is not. Indeed it has been argued that experiencing such purity of cultural conditioning is rare -- certainly in the U.S. -- and that everyone from the beginning experiences a multiplicity of cultural influences. It is suggested, therefore, that multiculturalism is inherent and universal.

## IDENTITY AND CULTURE SHOCK

Members of minority, ethnic, racial and culture groups exist, by definition, within a larger majority and usually dominant culture group. From the day they are born (or arrive), their environment is in some degree inescapably bicultural and it becomes more so as they grow up. In other words, the ethnocentric beginning is not so strong in minority groups, if only because they do not dominate the larger social, economic and political environment. Biculturalism is often necessary for survival. Rather than being the end point in the learning process, biculturalism is built in from the outset.

This is one of the reasons why identity is such a critical issue for many minority groups. The dominant culture in a society does not normally reinforce the identity of minority groups. Indeed, as we know, where there is prejudice, discrimination and exploitation, the reinforcement is negative, tending to keep minorities in Bank's state of "Ethnic Psychological Captivity." Ethnocentrism may be less of a problem for minorities, therefore, than the other side of the ethnocentric coin: cultural self-affirmation. In contrast to ethnocentrism, which is normally seen as negative, cultural self-affirmation has positive connotations and may be considered important to group mental health. Where minorities live in oppressed circumstances, however, this kind of affirmation may be difficult to achieve. Those who are concerned with intercultural communication and bi- and multi-culturalism should take care to distinguish between the need of the dominant culture to resist an excess of ethnocentrism and the necessity for minority cultures to remedy a deficiency of self-affirmation.

Identity is a problem too in individual intercultural experience. Unfortunately little has been written on the subject.

Hoopes and Althen (1975) suggest that people live within culture groups composed of personal and social relationships which define who they are, i.e. place them in roles and provide identities which are major dimensions of "self." Furthermore, these roles and identities are continuously supported and affirmed by the culture group, that is by the natural, social and personal environment in which the individual has been nurtured. It is within this environment, of course, that the vast majority of people feel most comfortable.

When we encounter a different culture, we are usually deprived of the supports and identity reinforcements that are available in our own group. Difference in language alone can be a significant source of anxiety since language is closely linked to identity. We are also deprived of many of the guides and cues which orient us to our social, cultural and linguistic environment and as a consequence are likely to experience a marked disorientation (Brein and David, 1974). The results, in terms of the impact on the individual, may range from mild discomfort to radical emotional dislocation and an inability to function in that environment -- the response often described as "culture shock." Heightened insecurity and attendant physical and emotional symptoms are the most common features of culture shock (difficulty eating or sleeping, mild paranoia, extreme reserve in social contacts, depression, irritability, fault-finding).

In cross-cultural training we often identify four basic responses to culture shock or the threat to identify encountered in a new cultural environment. These are:

Fight, which is the basic "we/they" response. The ambiguities and challanges of intercultural relations are reduced to group competition in which the ethnocentric impulse dominates. The other culture is seen in a negative light and one's own culture is defensively over-affirmed.

Flight, which involves a retreat from interaction with the other culture and an immersion in one's own culture group (abroad, this means a home-culture enclave).

Going native, in which the individual acculturates rapidly, superficially apes the host culture and attempts to slough his or her own cultural identity. This is often viewed as another form of flight, since it basically constitutes an escape from the complexities, difficulties and rewards of the intercultural experience.

Adaptation, which, as we have discussed in more detail above, consists of finding ways to comprehend and adjust behaviors to the other culture while at the same time affirming oneself and one's own cultural identity.

The most striking examples of culture shock lie in the experiences people have had in moving to live, work or study in another country. There is extensive literature on the adjustment of foreign students in the United States and on Americans living abroad. It can be experienced, however, right at home without going any further than from the suburb to the city. One study identified the reaction of White teachers suddenly transferred from suburban White to inner city Black schools as culture shock (Korn, 1972).

We don't have to go to a foreign land or even to the heart of another culture's territory (living space) to experience culture shock or at least some of the anxieties attached to it. It is our belief that anxiety can be experienced in the face-to-face encounter with anyone who is significantly different in language, values, attitudes and behaviors -- and even in appearance (there are those who are thoroughly disoriented by a nun in a habit!). The reaction may be less intense or complicated than in the foreign experience but it is something we may encounter frequently in our daily lives and is a factor in multicultural education. It is important for those who function in bi- or multicultural environments to be aware of responses occurring at an emotional level not within easy reach of rational assessment. These responses may include anxiety produced by encountering differences, which results in some of the behaviors associated with culture shock.

Minority racial and ethnic groups in the United States, both as groups and as individuals, have from the outset had to contend with the identity problem while relating to and functioning within the dominant culture. They have developed their own sets of responses and adjustments in achieving the success that they have in establishing ethnic identity. What may be more difficult is relationships between ethnic and racial minority groups. Common identities, such as sharing minority status and the struggle against prejudice, discrimination and economic exploitation, may help bridge the gap. As we come to grips with true multiculturalism, however, our ability to deal with a multiplicity of ethnic relationships will be put to the test.

A striking example of the complexity of the identity issue sometimes occurs when an American returns to the ancestral homeland for the first time naively expecting to establish more or less automatically some kind of close identification. The result all too often is a shock of non-recognition and a sudden encounter with just how "American" he or she is. This experience is less likely to happen if expectations are brought closer to reality before the journey is made.

Expectations are, in fact, a critical stumbling block in dealing with cultural differences. The further your expectations are from reality, the greater the problem will be -- with the rigidity of the individual's personality serving as the independent variable. Even if one develops a relatively accurate conceptual picture of the other culture or the people from it and is successful in cultivating flexibility of mind, he still has to deal with the fact that most of what he does, feels and thinks is based on assumptions and values deeply imbedded and often inaccessible to the conscious mind.

## CULTURAL ASSUMPTIONS AND VALUES

Our basic approach to values and value orientations has been taken from the work of Florence Kluckhohn and Fred Strodtbeck (1961). Applied to the value system of mainstream American culture, it was first used in cross-cultural research and training by Edward C. Stewart (1971). Taking the Kluckhohn-Strodtbeck model as a beginning point, Stewart divides cultural assumptions and values into four components.

1. Form of activity
2. Form of social relations
3. Perception of the world
4. Perception of self and of the individual

Each of these are then broken down into discreet values or assumptions and are analyzed from a cross-cultural perspective. That is, they are looked at in terms of how they compare with similar values in other cultures and, perhaps more important, how they are viewed by non-Americans when encountering behaviors based on them either in the United States or abroad.

Under "form of activity," for example, he notes that Americans are oriented toward "doing." To get things "done" is a virtue among Americans and has high value placed on it. This is apparent and has been noted by many foreign, especially non-western, observers. In other cultures, more value is often placed on "being," on the pure quality of the individual, or on "being-in-becoming," with stress on self-growth.

Stewart's analysis, based on the characteristics of mainstream culture in the United States, provides a useful guide to anyone wishing to understand it's dynamics. Some of the critical mainstream culture characteristics he identifies are:

. the separation of work and play (social activity);

. an orientation toward the future, with less emphasis or value placed on the present and, especially, the past;

. achievement motivation;

. competitiveness;

. informality and equality in social relations;

. directness or confrontiveness in communication;

. impersonality or objectivity (depersonalization) in relations with others;

. a need to be "liked;"

. the human being perceived as separate from and superior to nature.

. stress on the value of material possessions;

. a belief in progress (optimism);

. time conceived of as linear, flowing into the future and being subject to rigorous division and fragmentation;

. the concept of a distinct, separate, isolatable "self," resulting in an emphasis on individualism, self-reliance, independence, etc.;

. the ability to view people in fragments or react to them in terms of isolated parts or roles rather than as a total personality.

The above is a summary of a few aspects of American mainstream culture and should not be taken as an effort to fully characterize or stereotype it. Stewart argues that every culture group has within its members representation of a great variety of different and often opposing value orientations, but that some are found more often than others. For instance, in American mainstream society you are likely to find a pedominance of people who believe or assume that man can and should be the master or controller of nature -- able, within limits, to control, change or manipulate the physical environment as he wishes. In Japan, man is assumed to be integral with nature, the environment shaping human beings and in turn being shaped by them. Among Colombian Mestizos, nature is felt to be antagonistic to man, constantly threatening to overwhelm him (Stewart, 1977, pp. 62-63). The diagram on page 27 illustrates this concept.

The point is that while there will be a wide range of assumptions and value orientations represented in any given culture some will predominate. Further, predominance of one orientation does not always mean a weak manifestation of others. Asians tend to be predominantly "being" orientated, yet in Japan "doing" ranks high as a value too. Finally, individual value orientations may be shared by very different cultures. Friendship patterns, for instance, are similar in Russian and Arab cultures. An orientation toward the development of deep and demanding bonds exists in both.

The three diagrams below show on a continuum the <u>preponderance of belief</u> in three cultures on the question of man's relationship to nature. Though in each culture the whole range of beliefs may be found, the <u>preponderance</u> differs.

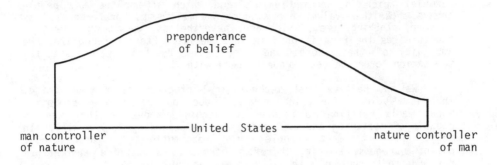

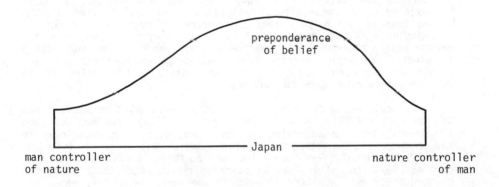

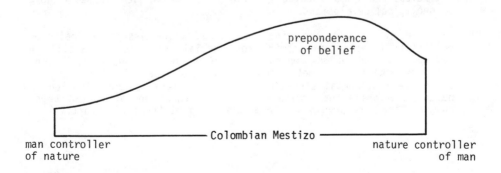

One of Stewart's important contributions is that he talks about "assumptions" as well as about values. Values are a statement of what should be, they have a quality of "oughtness" to them. Assumptions, on the other hand, are basic beliefs or perceptions of reality (that the external world is physical and without a spiritual quality, for example) which lie behind values and which affect the way people behave. (Neither values nor assumptions refers to "preferences," as in food, clothing, etc., which are, nevertheless, very much a part of "culture" as the term is used in this manual. Stewart recognizes the ambiguity of these words and ideas; but he happily resists the temptation to create new jargon to deal with it.)

We may believe that technological progress is a good thing. That is a value. The value, however, does not reveal the assumption about man's relation to nature as discussed above -- that man is capable of mastering and exploiting nature according to his will. In many, if not most people, the assumption is unconscious, out-of-awareness, and it, therefore, comes as a surprise when nature responds to technology with ugliness and pollution.

The contradictions and dynamics of technological progress are, of course, not quite that simple. It is, nevertheless, a basic proposition of cross-cultural analysis that values and/or the assumptions on which they rest are often if not normally out of consciousness -- they may be just below the surface or deeply buried -- and have a powerful effect on the way we behave, think and respond to others. We begin learning these values and assumptions from the minute we are born. The function of culture and learning is to reinforce them as we grow to adulthood.

But culture is not capricious. It is a survival mechanism, one of the most effective humans have devised as they have evolved from the trees. It is a mechanism for the survival of the individual in the context of the strength of the group. But a price is paid. Loyalty, conformity -- the price of culture is the ethnocentric person. That too, of course, is oversimplified. Ethnocentrism is the primordial thrust. Culture flowers, elaborates, decorates, explains, provides the context for human fulfillment. These are impressive fringe benefits. However, the primordial fears and primitive needs are there and are woven into the basic cultural fabric of the group, regardless of its "culture" (in the aesthetic sense) and/or technological development.

We can debate the great conscious value issues of religion, political ideology, economic and social structure. Still the assumptions and values which are buried beyond awareness in our everyday behavior are not accessible without special effort and are among the fundamental stumbling blocks to effective communication and human relations across cultures. Intercultural education and cross-cultural training provides a framework for that "special effort."

# COMMUNICATION

Communication is central to the cross-cultural encounter.

One of the definitions of communication that specialists in the field like -- and so do we because of its simplicity -- is: "Communication is the sending of a message from a source to a receiver with the least possible loss of meaning." In that simple definition, however, lies one of the most pervasive, complex and fallible of human functions. Coming to grips with the pervasiveness of communication is particularly difficult. Edward Hall, in the Silent Language, argues that culture itself is "communication," in that culture may be viewed as a continuous process of communicating and reinforcing group norms.

If the description of the perceptual system advanced above is accurate, then Hall may be correct. Culture is communication, or put differently, everything communicates. The reception of any sensory data is communication in the sense that at a very minimum it tells us it is there. It also tells us much more, especially as we build our perceptual world, from mother and the breast telling us we are loved and can expect nourishment to the flag or religious symbol that reconfirms nationality or religious identity.

This becomes even clearer when we think of all the characteristics of culture: dress, the patterns of male-female, youth-age and economic class relationships, language, family structures, marriage customs, living styles, behavior patterns, manners, cognitive processes, etc. Out of these cultural characteristics there develops, parallel to the linguistic code, a non-verbal system of communication which one might call a "cultural code."

The cultural code is more than simply non-verbal communication, which is associated with motions, gestures, body language, manners and the like. The cultural code is all -- with the exception of language -- that in the nexus of human interaction has meaning. Not doing something can often be as meaningful as some kind of action. In many Native American cultures, pure silence is immensely meaningful. Pure space has special significance in Japan. A failure to smile or to touch can communicate great meaning. Behavior communicates. The selection of dress and taste in music communicate. Teenage or youth culture in the United States is built on that kind of communication.

Unfamiliarity with the cultural code may result in disorientation. Culture shock in a new environment is due not only to identity anxiety, but also to the impact of trying to figure out and function within a new and different cultural code. The sounds, smells and other physical attributes of a new environment provide a constant and heavy barrage of sensory data that must be filtered and categorized. When we are in unfamiliar territory, this "communication from the environment" is not so easily or automatically sorted because our system for selection is not organized to deal with it. Those categorizing decisions that in a home culture occur with little effort suddenly become major and often exhausting events.

Despite its seeming simplicity, therefore, communication is a relatively complicated process by which meaning is translated into a code (language), fed into a transmitter (the voice box), sent over a channel (air/space), picked up by a receiver (the ear), decoded (translated from language to meaning) and fed into the mind of the receiver. Many things, often called "noise" or "static," can interfere with this process. A defect in transmission or receiving, an external distraction, or an internal distraction in the mind of the sender or receiver can produce "noise."

There are a number of built-in methods for counteracting these interferences. One is through redundance or repetition. Language and linguistic custom are structured so as to provide for the repetition or reinforcement of messages. (The English language is about one half redundant -- eliminate the underlined words, one-half of the total, and the message remains clear all the same.) Multiple channels may also be used; that is, communication through the other senses in addition to hearing. Signs, gestures, body movements (which are communicated through sight and are thus non-verbal) are a major part of communication. Touch communicates and in certain cases so do taste and smell.

Even more important is the feedback process, the response of the listener to the person sending the message. Feedback provides the speaker with an indication of whether the message has been received and received accurately. The effectiveness of communication is increased to the degree that it is a two-way process in which successive approximations of accuracy in getting meanings across are achieved. Communication specialists argue that exact communication is rare but that two-way communication enables us to get closer to exactness than one-way communication or talking "at" someone.

A simple model used in the communication field is:

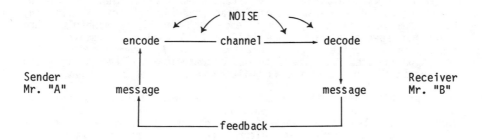

-30-

Mr. A sends Mr. B a message. It is in a code. It may be a linguistic code, verbal or written. It may be in the form of a picture or a symbol -- a smiling round face, for instance. It may be a grunt or a groan, a gesture, a frown, thoughtful silence or an almost impercept-ible twist of the body. Someone who sends you a box of candy as a gift is sending you a message which is supposed to be repeated each time you taste the sweetness. The message may be "I love you," "I think you're nice" (even "I think you're sweet!") or some other sentiment. The message lies encoded in the chocolates.

The listener, or the recipient of the message, Mr. B., decodes it and responds. The response is "feedback." In intercultural communication, feedback is especially important since so much of what is communicated may be non-verbal, unconscious and/or invested with the special meanings of the cultural code of the culture group. Is eye contact prohibited or expected in communication? What does a smile mean or a flick of the head? Does a grasping of the arm or the knee of someone of the same sex constitute responsiveness or improper behavior? What does it mean when you increase or decrease the social distance in a conversation ... disinterest? ... belligerence? When the feedback process is confused by differences in cultural codes, there is a breakdown in the automatic clarification it normally provides.

The noise or interference factor overrides almost everything else in intercultural communication. People who work with foreign visitors see it vividly. Professional interpreters often have to spend more time interpreting the culture than they do the language. The visitors see children speaking to their parents in ways that would not be permitted in their own countries; they see old people separated from their families; they find they are called by their first names immediately upon being introduced to someone; they are not given enough to eat when they are guests for dinner. Take this last experience as an example. American hosts and hostesses tend not to force food on their guests. They may offer but then forget it if the visitor declines. In many cultures, the serving of food and eating of meals are important rituals with carefully defined behavior. The host presses as much food on the guest as possible, insisting over and over that she or he eat, while the guest is expected to refuse many times before giving into the host's blandishments.

Visitors in American homes often go hungry because the food is not offered again after their first refusal and they don't understand or cannot accustom themselves to the acceptability of asking that food be passed to them. They are encountering differences that are confus-ing and disturbing. Those differences become barriers in the effort to understand the new culture and in the development of valuable relationships. They interfere with communication.

More pertinent here, the child who never hears his own language or a positive identification of his culture in school, who uses body language differently from the teacher, who expects authority to be exercised differently, or who verbalizes in an unexpected manner is going to experience or create static in the communication process.

That static will make teaching and learning difficult, if not impossible. This, of course, is simply another way of saying that cultural factors may interfere with communication in the teaching/ learning process.

It might be asked why we place so much stress on differences and relatively little on similarities. There are very good reasons but first let's look at the differences in a little more detail. They fall into four categories: (1) customary behaviors, (2) cultural assumptions and values, (3) patterns of thinking, and (4) communicative style.

1. Customary Behaviors. One culture expects children to be quiet and defer to adults while another encourages them to express themselves and to be independent. One culture reveres the past and venerates ancestors; another focuses on living for the present; a third looks to and plans for the future realization of it's goals. One culture places great stress on kin, family loyalty and interdependence; another on becoming independent from family and on self-reliance. All of these result in customary behaviors. They determine how you behave toward parents, children, cousins and others or how you act out your feelings about the past, present and future.

2. Cultural Assumptions and Values. Behind the behaviors, of course, are the assumptions and values a culture group holds. If mine are violated or contradicted when I'm with people of different cultural backgrounds, it is very difficult for me to suspend judgment. My response is automatic and unconscious. Those contradictions and violations will raise walls through which it's hard for me to "hear" what is being said. I am making interpretations and giving meaning to the communication that fit into my value framework. There are flashes going off in my head and feelings running through my body that I cannot prevent.

3. Patterns of Thinking. At an even deeper level, cognitive patterns differ from group to group. These are relatively familiar to educators. Do people think deductively or inductively? Do they admit or deny emotion in their thought processes? Are they more intuitive or reason-bound? Are they sensitive to their environment (field sensitive) or do they shut out environment (field independent) when they think? It is going to be difficult to communicate with someone if I start with a concrete fact and build my ideas on it (inductive) and the other person is accustomed to starting with an idea and using facts to flesh it out (deductive). More heat than light may be generated by the clash of my facts and his or her ideas.

4. Communicative Style. Each culture has developed it's own communicative style. A gesture, a smile or a touch on the arm may add emphasis to a message or communicate special meaning, but that emphasis or meaning is not the same for all groups. Some cultures encourage a wide range of tone and volume in speech, others do not. Bodily display varies radically from culture to culture. People from northern climates tend to display less emotion, speak quickly, and touch less than people from southern climates. The distance at which

people are comfortable when conversing varies; sometimes with marked effect. When you are accustomed to one style, encountering another can be confusing, disorienting or downright annoying. Languages, of course, reflect and/or have adapted to communicative style. When shifting to a second language, you may bring with you the communicative style of your first language. This may cause a negative reaction or discomfort in your listener that is distracting and serves as interference in the communication process.

Differences then are a cause of static, <u>but they do not constitute something wrong with the communication system.</u> Differences are inherent and natural but are perceived as the villain because we do not accept them as natural. In addition, we have not developed the skills to cope with them.

In basic communication theory, differences are seen as barriers while similarities provide the matrix in which communication is made possible. In pursuing effective communication the thrust is toward the identification of similarities. In intercultural communication, this is turned around. Differences are central and dealing with them is a fundamental cross-cultural skill. The argument that "we should emphasize our similarities rather than our differences" simply perpetuates cross-cultural communication difficulties. By failing to identify and appreciate differences at the outset, they are left in the path and unrecognized so that they almost inevitably become stumbling blocks. It is the ability to appreciate cultural differences that moves us along the culture learning continuum. Differences therefore constitute both the essence of cross-cultural learning and the medium of intercultural communication.

Much of what has been said so far may be summd up in three propositions:

1. We must be secure in and positively identified with our own culture.

2. We must be aware of the degree to which we are culturally conditioned.

3. We must respect and appreciate cultural differences encountered in others.


## BRIDGING DIFFERENCES

Minority-majority relations are often complicated by difficulties in distinguishing confrontations with people who are overtly ethnocentric from encounters with those whose prejudices are more submerged or who simply follow instinctively their own cultural ways.

For instance, mainstream American culture tends to condition one to avoid entangling social obligations. This often results in denigrating one's personal role in making a gift, extending a service or doing something special for another person. This is felt to be considerate behavior because it relieves the other person of obligation. There is a tendency in Hispanic cultures to see these kinds of social obligations and exchanges as a natural and desirable part of social relationships. They are cultivated, not denied. Hispanics may feel annoyed or insulted when encountering this particular aspect of mainstream behavior, even though the intention is not to insult but to be especially considerate.

Dealing with prejudice tends to be political. You have to defuse and render powerless the prejudiced person. Behavior based on contrary cultural assumptions and values, on the other hand, is a different matter and may be approached through the communication process. Of course, no one thing nor any one person can solve the intercultural communication problems we all encounter. However, some specific guidelines and ways of approaching and responding to them do exist that can help the conscientious communicator bridge cultural differences.

Listening. It is often hard for people to believe that "listening" is a skill and that our failure to listen carefully contributes significantly to human miscommunication. The reasons for not listening are manifold. We are more concerned with what we want to say than with what is being said to us; we jump to conclusions before statements are completed; we hear "words" rather than "meanings" (often deliberately). We also make assumptions about the way other people think based on shared values and experiences, what the psychologists call "projected cognitive similarity." This is the basic unconscious belief that other people think and view the world the way we do. Within our own culture group this assumption is sufficiently accurate to offset in some degree bad listening habits. In cross-cultural situations, however, our usual listening behavior serves us poorly and more effective listening becomes critical. In the fifty or so multicultural workshops we have conducted, it has been our experience that, at the outset, all assumptions -- all assumptions -- about how the participants think and how they will behave must be discarded. It should be obvious too that speaking to someone in what is his or her second language requires particular concentration to pick up differences not only in inflection but in meaning. In intercultural communication skillful listening to the verbal and non-verbal messages without filtering them through our own system of values and expectations is an imperative.

So is perception checking. Our perceptions about the other person and about what is being said to us are imbedded in our own assumptions and values and in our expectations of the other person. Those perceptions must be checked. It is necessary to ask if what you think the other person said is accurate or if that which happens between you has the same meaning for him or her that it has for you. Our wish to control the interaction, to achieve what we want from it, may prevent us from pursuing this clarification or from seriously taking into account the different view we may discover.

Seeking feedback is equally important. If it is fair to say, and we believe it is, that some degree of misunderstanding is always present in intercultural communication then the active quest for feedback becomes critical. In short: ask if you've been understood! That may sound like an oversimplification but it is not because the feedback-giving and receiving process is itself culturally influenced. The manner in which feedback is requested may not appear to be polite; there may be inflections or even appropriate gestures or facial expressions that must accompany the request if it is to be recognized for what it is. In Japan and many other Asian countries it is impolite to say "no." A request for feedback that requires a "no" answer may be more confusing than helpful and often fails to elicit the needed information. Asking for feedback can be emotionally risky. In view of your vulnerability in cross-cultural communication it may seem easier and safer to assume that you are being understood. Seeking feedback may often be a slow and frustrating process. The wise communicator knows, however, that untangling accumulated misunderstandings or, worse yet, living with them is far more difficult than engaging in the process of requesting immediate feedback while the communication is taking place.

Resisting judgmental reactions. As stated earlier, in intercultural communication your first perceptions of meaning are very likely to be inaccurate. Premature judgments or emotional reactions are often, therefore, quite disfunctional, stimulating the other person, more often than not, to defensive responses. Judging someone on the basis of words or behaviors which may either (1) have utterly different meanings for each of you or (2) be a function of culturally conditioned habits that have little reference to the immediate situation can have serious consequences. Suspending judgment while listening, checking perceptions and seeking feedback allows us to be more open to another's thoughts, ideas and feelings and reduces defensiveness in intercultural communication.

We have already stressed the importance of cultivating self-awareness, of being conscious, at least in the initial stages of a relationship, of your own behavior patterns, communicative style, operational assumptions and values, and patterns of thinking. One, of course, cannot and should not be continuously self-conscious in relationships with other people. A periodic re-examination of one's cultural nature, however, is beneficial.

Taking risks. In order to open channels of communication with another person, we must often take emotional risks -- like asking for feedback or saying something personal which leaves us vulnerable to a hurtful response. In doing so, we have to trust the other person not to exploit our vulnerability. As usual, the significance of this factor is intensified in intercultural relations. Cross-cultural learning and intercultural communication take place best where participants have established enough trust to permit some exposure of themselves.

In dissecting the process of communication our intention is not to make it seem mechanical. Communication is a transaction between complex human beings in which each affects the other and the nature of the interaction each step of the way. Communication is a creative and highly intuitive act of discovery. It can be made more comprehensible and accessible to change, but it cannot be reduced to a set of simple axioms or prescribed behaviors.

## CONCLUSION

It is our belief that it is from within this nexus of human interaction that the clash of cultural differences reverberates through society. And it is here that teachers and teacher trainers must look for answers as to how they can most effectively meet their responsibilities as educators in a multicultural society.

Embedded in each of us is a pervasive and controlling perceptual system which is heavily conditioned by our cultural experience but which is largely unconscious. Until we become aware of that fact and its implications for our behavior, we remain at the mercy of being so conditioned. Formal education, of course, is one of the means by which we liberate ourselves. But experience shows that education alone is insufficient to the task. We must look to the more specific processes of intercultural learning to find a set of guideposts for more accurately measuring and, indeed, promoting the progress of both ourselves and our students toward multiculturalism.

Moving along the intercultural learning continium exposes us where we are most vulnerable -- in our sense of self or identity. Identity is nurtured within the context of culture and is continuously reinforced by it. When these cultural reinforcements are removed or when this cultural identity is threatened or denied, the individual may be deeply affected. Members of minority culture groups struggle to find themselves in a society in which the dominant culture disaffirms them or their group. Others may experience disorientation or culture shock in the encounter with those who are different or "foreign." As a result, the difficulties which are normal to cross-cultural relations are aggravated. The antidote is the expansion of identity through culture learning and the development of skills in intercultural communication and cross-cultural human relations.

We have sought here to provide a framework within which the theoretical dimensions of intercultural communication and cross-cultural human relations can be translated into conceptual tools useful to the teacher and teacher trainer in multicultural education. In the chapters that follow we will examine multicultural education both historically and practically and show how the conceptual tools are embodied in cross-cultural training and how they may be applied in the classroom to further the aims of multicultural education.

# REFERENCES

Banks, James A. "The Implications of Multicultural Education for Teacher Education." Pluralism and the American Teacher, Washington, D.C., American Association of Teacher Education, 1977.

Berlo, David. The Process of Communication. New York: Holt, Rinehart and Winston, Inc., 1960.

Bochner, Stephen. "The Mediating Man and Cultural Diversity." Topics in Culture Learning. Vol. 1. Honolulu, Hawaii: East-West Center, 1973.

Brein, Michael and Kenneth H. David. "Intercultural Communication and the Adjustment of the Sojourner." Readings in Intercultural Communication, Vol. IV, P. Peterson (ed.). Pittsburgh, Pa.: Intercultural Communication Network and SIETAR, 1974.

Carpenter, John and Galo Plaza. The Intercultural Imperative. New York, N.Y.: Council for Intercultural Studies and Programs, 1973.

Clark, Kenneth B. Dark Ghetto. New York: Harper and Row, 1965.

Condon, John C. and Fathi Yousef. An Introduction to Intercultural Communication. Bobbs-Merrill: New York, 1975.

Glazer, Nathan and Daniel P. Moynihan. Beyond the Melting Pot. Cambridge, Mass.: MIT Press, 1963.

Glazer, Nathan and Daniel P. Moynihan (eds.). Ethnicity: Theory and Experience. Cambridge, Mass.: Harvard University Press, 1975.

Hall, Edward T. The Hidden Dimension. Garden City, N.Y.: Doubleday, 1963.

Hall, Edward T. The Silent Language. Garden City, N.Y.: Anchor Press, 1963.

Hoopes, David S., and Gary L. Althen. "Culture and Communication in Intercultural Relations." Readings in Intercultural Communication, D. Hoopes (ed.). Pittsburgh, Pa.: Intercultural Communication Network and SIETAR, 1975.

Kluckhohn, Florence B. and Fred L. Strodtbeck. Variations in Value Orientations. New York, N.Y.: Row, Peterson, 1961.

Korn, Kenneth. "Culture Shock and the Transfer of Teachers." Bureau of School Services Bulletin, Vol. 45, No. 2, December, 1972, University of Kentucky, ERIC: ED070744 (3P005959).

Ramirez III, Manual and Alfredo Casteneda. Cultural Democracy, Bicognitive Development and Education. New York, N.Y.: Academic Press, 1974.

Rich, Andrea. <u>Interracial Communication</u>. New York, N.Y.: Harper and Row, 1974.

Samovar, Larry and Richard Porter (eds.). <u>Intercultural Communication: A Reader</u>. Belmont, CA.: Wadsworth Publishing Co., 1976. (Second Edition.)

Singer, Marshall R. "Culture: A Perceptual Approach." <u>Intercultural Communication: A Reader</u>. Larry A. Samovar and Richard E. Porter (eds.). Belmont, CA.: Wadsworth Publishing Co., Inc., 1976. (Second Edition.)

Singer, Marshall R. "Perceptions in International Affairs." <u>Overview of Intercultural Education, Training and Research, Vol. 1</u>, D. Hoopes, P. Peterson, G. Renwick (eds.). Washington, D.C.: Society for Intercultural Education, Training and Research, 1977.

Smith, Arthur L. <u>Transracial Communication</u>. Englewood Cliffs, N.J.: Prentice-Hall, Inc., 1973.

Stewart, Edward C. <u>American Cultural Patterns: A Cross-Cultural Perspective</u>. Washington, D.C.: Society for Intercultural Education, Training and Research, 1977.

Triandis, Harry and Associates. <u>The Analysis of Subjective Culture</u>. New York, N.Y.: John Wiley, 1972.

Useem, Ruth and John Useem. "Men in the Middle of the Third Culture." <u>Human Organization</u>, <u>22</u>, 1963.

Wight, Albert and Mary Anne Hammons. <u>Guidelines for Peace Corps Cross-Cultural Training</u>. Estes Park, Co.: Center for Research and Education, 1969.

CHAPTER 3

HISTORICAL DEVELOPMENT OF MULTICULTURAL EDUCATION

## CONTENTS

CHAPTER 3

HISTORICAL DEVELOPMENT OF MULTICULTURAL EDUCATION

H. Ned Seelye and Jacqueline H. Wasilewski

ACCOMMODATION OF CULTURAL PLURALISM

Underlying the controversy regarding how far public financed schools should go in recognizing cultural and linguistic pluralism within their systems is a concern for how much cultural and linguistic diversity a nation can contain and still count on enough unity to maintain its national viability. This concern is in turn based on an assumption that monoculturalism, homogeneity, uniformity is somehow a necessary condition for national viability. Glyn Lewis' (1976) exposition of the history of linguistic policy in the Western world offers some interesting insights into the historical roots of this assumption of homogeneity.

Lewis notes that the classical empires of the ancient world decided matters of linguistic policy, not according to any fixed principle, but pragmatically, empirically, and according to convenience. In the city of Dioscuris in Colchis at the eastern end of the Black Sea, an area of Greek hegemony, Pliny reports that 300 languages were in use in the settlement. The Romans required a staff of 130 interpreters to do business there. Even today there is hardly a bay in the Mediterranean world that is not "a unique complex linguistic community."

However, by the Renaissance language had begun to be regarded as an ideology synonymous with ethnic group. Whereas Roman Vidal in the late Middle Ages had written his lyric poetry in French because choice of language was determined by genre and not by the nationality of the author, Pierre Ronsard, first poet of the French Renaissance, spoke of the treachery of abandoning the language of one's country and DuBellay likened safeguarding the dignity of one's language to a natural law.

By the nineteenth century this association of human group, geopolitical space, and language was further reinforced by the absolutist aspects of romantic, idealist philosophers and their romanticization of the Volk. The rise of philology as an academic discipline also interacted in this process as well as the role of vernaculars in the rise of the European middle class.

What had happened then "between the phase of classical indifference leading to tolerance of diversity and our own sensitivity to diversity associated nevertheless with intolerance"? Latin, as the universal language of Christendom, had intervened. Latin, the sacred language, carrier of what was thought to be all man's culture, science, and faith. During the period we term the Dark Ages, Latin was the means of intellectural expression of "a beleaguered culture which found its refuge in monasteries and elitist and aristocratic schools...." (G. Lewis, 1976, 153-154).

But in the modern era, as universal Christendom was divided into nation states and kings took over temporal power from prelates by "divine right," vernaculars began to take on the absolutist aspects of Latin as the carriers of the various national cultures. Yet each particularity aspired to Latin's universality as propagator of a universal Christian culture.

Thus, the concern of nation states regarding quantity of diversity and national viability has its roots in the ecclesiastical concern of the Latin Church for unity of theory and practice, and this assumption of uniformity as a necessary condition of a nation state was exported to the rest of the world, along with the ideology of nationalism, during the period of European expansion.

Lewis argues the rationality of an alternative view:

> "No doubt the first obligation of the state is to itself and because of that it will seek to maintain untrammelled the path of communication. However, its survival is simply the means to ensure the well-being of its constituents ... the 'bene esse' of the groups of which it is composed: its integrity is justified solely by its capacity to accommodate diversity" (G. Lewis, 1976, 153).

In point of fact, most modern national states contain culturally diverse populations and they do in actuality accommodate varying amounts of diversity. To judge by current national educational policies that relate to one aspect of cultural pluralism -- language use -- different multicultural countries are comfortable with anywhere from one (Indonesia, Italy, France) or two (Belgium, Canada), to four (Switzerland, Singapore) through nine (Ghana) to fourteen (India) languages officially used in their school systems. One Indian official from the Ministry of Education in New Delhi said that if the nation could conduct its business satisfactorily in 14 languages he did not see why provinces could not manage to educate children in 40 languages. Apparently, how much language diversity a country can tolerate is partially a matter of psychology. In India, for example, there are approximately 500 languages but few Indian educators talk of the possibility of educating children through all 500. Practically all of Switzerland speaks one of four languages and education is available through all four. Besides the number of languages officially used in schools, many countries use anywhere from two to 150 other languages as a temporary bridge for linguistic minorities.

The relative openness of a country's educational system to cultural diversity is significantly influenced by how the following three questions are answered: To what extent are national institutions -- social, political, economic -- considered by the "haves" to be viable? To what extent do or can ethnically distinguishable "have nots" influence social, political, and economic institutions? To what extent is this real or imagined influence perceived by the "haves" to be disruptive? The greater the insecurity of the "haves," the less the likelihood of widespread multicultural education. Periods of intense immigration characteristically provoke anxiety among those responsible for educational policy. The result is usually increased efforts to acculturate or nationalize the immigrants. Privately funded education, often religiously motivated, offers an alternative to state policy. In these cases, the continuance of a cultural or linguistic tradition other than the officially recognized one depends largely on the prestige conferred on the particular "foreign" language and on the relative absence of societal sanctions for speakers of a non-official language.

Preindustrial societies are commonly organized along the lines of ethnic, tribal, or linguistic boundaries. Just a decade ago it was commonly thought that industrialization dealt a death blow to this subnational level of organization but there are increasing signs that ethnic identity is not so easily put aside even in countries where it has been ignored by the national institutions. France, Spain, Great Britain, to take just three Western European examples, are experiencing separatist movements by ethnic minorities. All three countries have discouraged a curriculum that accommodates ethnic and linguistic differences.

The accommodation of diversity within nation-states seems to be a problem that has re-emerged this last quarter of the 20th century. The construction of complementary diversity, the incorporation of more and more diversity into ever more complex interdependent organizational systems are problems whose resolution is being sought principally within the public education sector (Wallace, 1963; Lockland, 1973; Stewart 1978b). Metaphorically speaking, it might be that the optimum model for the organization of society is not so much the rational design of an eighteenth century classical French garden but the organically interwoven, complex multiplicity of a tropical rain forest.

G. Lewis (1976) asserts that "polyglotism is a very early characteristic of human societies, and monolingualism a cultural limitation." Africa provides hints of such models in a context where polyglotism is the norm. David Dalby, the English linguist, in a 1977 lecture at the University of London on his Linguistic Map of Africa, said that there are approximately 1,000 languages spoken on that continent, only twenty or so of which are in any danger of dying out. In some countries, like Nigeria, located in what is called the linguistic fragmentation belt which runs across the country east to west, as many as 800 languages are spoken. This level of polyglotism has remained relatively stable for the past 500 years, throughout the era of European contact. Dalby graphically states that the only way to adequately represent Africa linguistically would be to have a light on the map for every man, woman, and child on the continent, and these lights would change color every time the speakers changed languages. A common combination of African languages is to have a family language (usually that of one's ethnic group), a market language (the major language of one's region), an academic language (often the language of the former European colonial power), a religious language (such as Arabic in Muslim areas), and one or more languages of the ethnic groups nearest one's own. This latter combination is especially true if intermarriage is common among the groups (Karoma, 1977).

In this context, being multilingual is a highly prized ability. The more languages one speaks, the more languages one wants to learn, and "a polyglot has a more tolerant attitude, not only to a language he is able to speak and to its speakers but to other languages and their speakers as well" (Ansre, 1975). Language is a tool, as well as a mark of identity. One adds languages to one's repertoire rather than replacing one language with another, following a basic principle of linguistic and cultural interrelationship, that of agglomeration rather than substitution. Rarely does a new pattern completely efface an old one (G. Lewis, 1976, 198). One uses different languages in different situations for different purposes (Mackey, 1972). Superficially, monolingual communication might seem more efficient, but what are its costs in communicativeness and responsiveness?

## CONCEPTUALIZATION OF MULTICULTURALISM

The modern world must be seen as being made up of complex networks of intricately intertwined languages and cultures. There are no hard edges. Rich and Ogawa (1976) describe the effects of socio-economic variables on the different ethnic groups in America society and in so doing have described a new societal unit, the "ethclass." They question whether individuals are "more attracted to communication situations involving members of their own racial and/or ethnic group or to situations involving interaction with members of their own class and/or economic strata?" (31-32). Singer (1976, 116) considers each society as "the aggregate of the identity (cultural) groups which exist within it," and each individual in society "must inevitably be a member of a myriad of different ... groups simultaneously ..... Consciously or otherwise, he rank orders his various group identities, but because environmental and biological factors are ever changing, perceptions, attitudes and values are ever changing. Consequently,

the rank ordering of group identities is ever changing and new perceptual groups are constantly being formed, while existing groups are
constantly in a state of flux" (113). Goodenough (1976, 6) offers the
example of the little community of Romonum on Truk in Micronesia where
all four of the salaried government positions (medical assistant,
local judge, school principal, and teacher) were monopolized by the
highest ranking men in the two chiefly lineages. Even more significant, Goodenough notes, was the fact that no one but children of
chiefly rank had qualified for education beyond elementary level in
accordance with an apparently impartially administered examination
system.

Existing simultaneously with the internal differentiation within
societies is the tendency of societies to extend their range of communication beyond their borders, whether this be the Central African's
conscious incorporation of vocabulary other than that of his native
dialect into his conversations, the increasing range of Western
European languages during the colonial era, or the present increasing
range of Russian, Arabic, and Chinese. In the future, G. Lewis (1976)
speculates, these overlapping linguistic ranges will affect not only
the highly educated, but also those whose occupations bring them into
immediate contact with speakers of other languages as well, professional soldiers in multinational military organizations, oil riggers,
computer technicians, etc.

Every child when he leaves the confines of his family enters a
multicultural world.

> If by culture we have reference to the understandings about
> things and the expectations of one another that the members
> of a society seem to share, then a theory of culture
> requires us to consider the processes by which the indivi-
> dual members arrive at such sharing. In this regard, the
> differences among individuals, their misunderstandings, the
> different ways of doing family to family and village to
> village, all become noteworthy .... Culture is learned ....
> The need is to learn what the expectations are in terms of
> which others act. The understandings arrived at regarding
> the expectations of parents are tried out on other adults.
> In the absence of feedback to the contrary, one assumes
> that these others have the same expectations as one's
> parents .... In the learning process, people inevitably
> find that they cannot generalize the same expectations to
> every one ... there are different role-expectations that go
> with different social relationships and social situations.
> Each of these different expectations constitutes a differ-
> ent culture to be learned (Goodenough, 1976, 4-5).

However, what diversities we incorporate into the "us" identity
and what we leave to the "them" and the processes by which these
boundaries are actually established and maintained are still not
clearly understood (Gibson, 1976, 16). The "vastly complex skeins of
interconnectedness" (Keesing, 1974) in the midst of which we live are
only now being disentangled and examined. In the U.S., "multiculturalism as the normal human experience" (Goodenough, 1976) is complicated

by the fact that U.S. society is to a large degree ethnically stratified, that is, all ethnic groups do not have equal access to the society's influential structures. Because of this, not only is there an implicit denial of the value of the cultures of some groups, but it is only for the members of some groups that multicultural competency is a necessity for survival (D. Lewis, 1976).

The need for highly differentiated responses to the same problem is evident world wide. In Rivers State, Nigeria, a highly multilingual area, there is a project underway to develop readers for elementary school children in approximately thirty different languages (Williamson, 1976a and b). Rather than having a separate team develop materials in each language, a single team composed of a linguist, historian, and philosopher is helping community committees to develop their own materials. In its first year the project developed 1) first year readers in 15 languages, 2) teachers' notes in 14, 3) orthography booklets for 11 languages, 4) one occasional publication (in conjunction with the Rivers State Council for Arts and Culture) for further reading, and 5) three sets of alphabet charts, and all this at a cost of no more than $10,000. (Linguists generally allow about five years at $15,000 per year to develop a language (Armstrong, 1968, 234)). The points of greatest interest, however, were the decisions that local committees made about which languages in their community to develop. Language forms which to a professional linguist are so similar as to appear to be dialects of the same language the committees often earmarked for separate development, often because for historical reasons each group already had separate written traditions. Other groups, on the other hand, whose language forms appeared to the professional linguist to be completely different, would agree to develop one written set of mutually intelligible written materials, just for literacy's sake, even though their written language might turn out to be quite different from their spoken language.

In Ghana nine languages are used for initial literacy in primary education, but matching trained teachers with the proper languages to the linguistic needs of the children is a very complicated process, especially since the majority of the teachers are urban, many tribal areas lack major cities, and the majority of the children are rural (Afful, 1976).

Even where the official policy is initial literacy in the mother tongue, it is often impossible to implement in urban areas because of the heterogeneity of the student population, so by mutual consent as the fairest course under the circumstances the language of instruction is often a "neutral" European language, e.g. Kenya, Ghana, Nigeria, Zaire, etc.

There are even cases where it is thought best not even to articulate the preferred policy because it is politically volatile, and therefore, unique contextual de facto solutions are worked out informally. It is interesting to note that Nigeria, with approximately 800 languages spoken within her political boundaries, has no official language, although English, Pidgen, and Hausa are common Lingua francas, and English is the language of governmental administration and secondary and tertiary education (Bamgbose, 1976).

-45-

The United States does not have an official language for that matter either! Domestically we have some rather unique situations. For instance, in Los Angeles there is a large influx of very well-off Korean immigrants pouring into the downtown areas. The Korean parents do not want their children to attend the bilingual schools that the Chicano populace has fought so hard to establish, because they think their children will have a difficult enough time mastering English and keeping up their Korean. These children are consequently going to the predominantly Black monolingual schools in the area, and the Blacks are thus in the paradoxical position of finding themselves the diffusers of the mainstream culture (Rideout, 1977).

A further illustration of the need to tailor multicultural education to local conditions is a programmed approach (Seelye and Navarro, 1977), complete with flow charts and sample class schedules, aimed at primary and secondary school administrators and curriculum developers faced with the task of selecting a bilingual (or multilingual) program design. This publication describes nine basic models, with the selection of an appropriate design depending largely on local demographic variables such as the number and levels of the students and the languages present in the school in question.

## THE CASE OF THE UNITED STATES

The manner in which the United States became a pluralistic society spawned its ethnic stratification. It, along with Canada, Australia, New Zealand, Brazil, and Argentina, belong to a group of nations best described as immigrant nations. Forty-one million people, the largest such population transfer in the history of the world, have immigrated to the United States since the nation's founding (Gordon, 19641, 84). People came under varying conditions, both forced and voluntary. They came, at least in their own perception, to a relatively empty continent, peopled initially by tribal societies. The first ripples of this population tidal wave occurred in the 15th and 16th centuries when Europeans first began "discovering" the rest of the world.

The initial colonizers in the New World in the period 1600-1800 were Spain, France, and England; Spain motivated by its search for metals and its continuing struggle against the Reformation, France by a desire to develop a trading empire that combined military and religious ambitions (led by Jesuit priests and fur trappers, coureur des bois), and England, the most successful colonist in North America, by providing holdings in the New World that afforded a haven for religious dissidents (Brinton, Christopher, and Wolff, 1960, 575-586).

It is interesting to contrast the role of the Catholic Church in the Spanish and French expansion with that of dissident Protestant sects in the English expansion. French Protestants, the Huguenots, were not even allowed to come to the New World because of the Bourbon monarchs' preoccupation with maintaining a Catholic New France. The English dissidents were not less concerned, however, with homogeneity. Even at the inception of the country there was controversy over whether freedom meant freedom for the group or the individual and whether

-46-

different groups could harmoniously reside within a single political unit. Roger Williams' expulsion from the Massachusetts Bay Colony for refusing to conform to Puritan orthodoxy is a case in point, and his subsequent founding of Rhode Island is perhaps the first instance of the "frontier solution" to communal disagreements. Compare the Mormon experience a century later. It is also interesting to note that as the English gained hegemony in North America, the Catholic colonists on the periphery of English influence (i.e. the French Canadians and the people of the Spanish borderlands from the Matamoros haciendas on the Gulf of Mexico to the Petaluma ranchos off San Francisco Bay) were reduced to the status of second class citizens as the predominantly Anglo character of U.S. society emerged.

Simultaneous with this colonization of tribal territory by Europeans was the importation of other groups of tribal peoples from Africa as slaves. The ethnic mix in the New World was further enriched in the last half of the nineteenth century with the importation of chiefly Chinese and Japanese laborers to help build the railroads on the Western frontier. These last groups entered the country under conditions of explicit servitude. The bondage of the African slaves is obvious, but that of the Oriental laborer was less obvious. The Chinese, for instance, most often could not bring their families with them, and the famous "Gentlemen's Agreement" with Japan strictly limited the number of Japanese who could enter the country (Giles, 1977).

Furthermore, the public lands of the frontier, supposedly open to all comers, were in fact denied to Blacks, even free Blacks (Giles, 1977), and much of the land which the Land Law of 1851 opened up was in fact not "public" but part of the vast haciendas of the landholding wealthy of Spanish America (Madrid-Barela, 1976, 102). From the beginning "preferred immigrants" to populate the "empty" frontier were Northern Europeans, preferably Protestant.

Then came the great tidal wave of immigration led by the Catholic Irish fleeing both English oppression and the potato famines in Ireland. Then came Emma Lazarus' "wretched, tired, and poor," mostly illiterate peasants from Southern and Eastern Europe fleeing a chaotic situation in which the breaking up of the old European order would culminate in the First World War.

Meanwhile, the basic nature of the U.S. was changing from a decentralized agricultural society to a centralized industrial society with increased pressures toward homogeneity. The image of peasants fleeing a warring Europe seems to have become imbedded in the American consciousness giving rise to a fear that the same kind of "Balkanization" might happen in the United States if homogeneity were not maintained. Diversity thus became associated with disintegration.

These peasants were not preferred immigrants (Park, 1925). Even as enlightened a soul as Woodrow Wilson, the architect of "freedom of determination" after World War 1, publicly declared the Italians to be an inferior race! In this era, the Polish also were particularly singled out as societal problems. Newspaper accounts detailed their

"wild" behavior as they wrestled with the transition from life in a
peasant society that provided people with a complete but rigid scheme
of life controlled by the primary group largely through face to face
relationships, to life in the new American context where one's
individual characteristics rather than one's ascribed role determined
one's identity (Park and Miller, 1925, 47-48, 289).

In the decade immediately after the First World War there was
intense preoccupation with "the foreign." This is not too surprising
if one realizes that

> "... immigration in the form it has taken in America
> differs from all previous movements of population ... when
> a single country is peacefully invaded by millions of men
> from scores of other countries, when there are added to one
> American city as many Jews as there are Danes in Denmark,
> and to the same city more Italians than there are in Rome,
> we have something new in history" (Park and Miller, 1925,
> 259).

This conception of "the alien," however, was often strangely applied
to include even American communities of Indians and Mexicans that had
existed in their present locations for 300 years. The decade after
the First World War set the scene for the passage of the McClaren Act
(1928) which officially established immigration quotas for different
countries, thereby formalizing the idea of "preferred" immigrants. By
the mid 1960's just before the quotas were abolished, the differential
status of immigrant peoples from different parts of the world was
still evident. Great Britian with a population of 55,000,000 had a
quota of 65,361, while Nigeria, also with a population of 55,000,000
had a quota of 100 (Giles, 1977).

Another irony in the U.S. approach to national viability was
emergence as a world political, economic, and cultural power while its
basically monolingual monocultural world view remained unchanged.

Until the 1970's, English values had provided the predominant
model for acceptance into U.S. society. Gordon (1964) called it
Anglo-Conformity. Operating simultaneously with this model was the
ideal of the Melting Pot, but the overriding flavor of the resulting
stew was always Anglo. In fact, as Gordon (1964) revealed, even for
white Americans there were three Melting Pots -- Protestant, Catholic,
and Jewish, in descending order of status, each with its own lower,
middle, and upper classes. It is only in the present generation that
the questions posed by the Protestant Reformation have been attenuated
by the fact that religious identity is not as central to a person's
feeling of authenticity as it was earlier.

The real challenge to the Melting Pot description of American
society is the continued low status of Native Americans, Blacks, Chicanos, and Asians, each with its own history of non-acceptance in the
mainstream of society. A hierarchized mosiac structure, a salad, thus
emerges rather than a blended stew (Seelye, 1975). Those groups who
have gained most status are those which, 1) were able to most closely
approximate the Anglo model and/or 2) have been able to maintain well

organized communities in the face of non-acceptance into mainstream
society despite sometimes superior competencies in many areas, for
instance, the Jews, Japanese and Chinese (Jencks, C.S., 1972 and
Lesser, Fifer, and Clark, 1965 re superior competencies, and Giles,
1977 re community).

Those groups which have had the most trouble surviving in
America are those which entered American society in some sort of
conquered status: Native Americans, Blacks, Chicanos, and Asians.
Blauner (1972) characterizes this as the difference between the
"colonized" and "immigrant' minorities. The former are also without
exception the nation's racial minorities, those that are most "different" from the Anglo "standard."

## EDUCATION FOR A PLURAL SOCIETY IN THE UNITED STATES

It has only been in the last twenty years that the United States
has emerged as a consciously plural society and official policy only
recently is beginning to recognize and value multiplicity. This began
with the court ordered desegregation of schools in 1959 and continued
with legislation effecting bilingual education, notably the enabling
legislatron for ESEA Title VII and the Lau vs. Nichols Supreme Court
decision, and the fostering of ethnic heritage in the schools in the
1960's and 1970's. This legislation is extensively reviewed by
Teitelbaum and Hiller (1977).

Largely as a result of insights formed within the non-English-
speaking or bilingual communities, six conditions have been identified
which contribute to the hapless syndrome in which the limited-English-
speaking child in the U.S. finds himself. First, the student does not
know enough English to understand the concepts being taught in the
classroom so he fails in his classwork. Second, when enough time is
taken out of the school day to offer him intensive instruction in
English, he slips behind in the subject-matter concepts of the classes
he has missed, so he still fails when he returns to classes in mathe-
matics, science, and social studies. Third, if in the process of
learning English he is allowed to forget his first language, he
suffers alienation from his home and ethnic identity, with subsequent
loss of pride in his heritage and depletion of this country's bilingual resources. Fourth, any success that he experiences while working
exclusively with peers from the same ethnic and language background
may not transfer when he has to associate with monolingual (black and
white) Americans. Fifth, even if Anglo-American children and teachers
who have or who develop the necessary empathy to work successfully
with limited-English-speaking children are incorporated into a special
program children and especially teachers outside of the special program, with whom the bilingual children must eventually relate, often
lack the sensitivity required to deal successfully with children from
divergent ethnic backgrounds -- no matter how well these latter speak
English. And sixth, because of different priorities and past experience with incommunicant school systems, parents often place greater
value on having their children work  than on having them receive a high

school diploma. Bilingual education attempts to intervene in this discouraging syndrome to effect curriculum changes which deal in a positive fashion with the educational needs of children with limited fluency in English.

The history of education in the U.S. is, in many important ways, typical of that of scores of other culturally plural countries. The energy required to build a nation of many different bastions of vested interest led to a number of forced concessions to power groups (in the U.S. these were largely English-speaking states) coupled with an impatient anti-intellectual concern for unity against foreign powers. It is typical that the first real surge of national pride was an outgrowth of war with a foreign power (the War of 1812). The inaccurate "we licked them" led to a feeling that "we can do it." "We" was defined through the nation's major socializing agent -- the schools -- to be kind of "waspish." Differences melted. "Un-Americanism" was easily recognized in looks, dress, speech, opinion, and religion (for years it was a political maxim that a Catholic could never be president -- he might show allegiance to the Pope at the wrong time). Wisconsin missed being a German-speaking state by a slim margin in the state legislature, yet most German-Americans ceased speaking German during and following World War I in order to "prove" their loyalty. Japanese-Americans were forced into detention camps during World War II for nothing other than looking like the enemy. U.S. teachers of Russian as a foreign language, to name just one group, were regarded in one of our post World War II periods to be suspect. Regardless of the second language, with the sole exception of upper class citizens, Americans have never been defined as a bilingual people. Of multicultural roots, yes. Able to function in two societies, no.

This simplistic, stereotypic conception of "Americanism" by American educators even operated against the interests of at least half the "mainstream" people: the women. The biases in school textbooks seems endless: sex, race, religion, social class, geographic, etc. The last decade has seen more and more concern focused on these biases by those who have suffered through loss in self-esteem or job discrimination.

Textbooks are already showing the positive fruits of this concern. The need for having curricula reflect a sophisticated awareness of cultural pluralism seems evident for several compelling reasons. First, our society is composed of numerous cultural groups that think enough of their cultural origins to retain many of their own values, customs, and in many cases, even their own languages. Second, while this cultural diversity has not adversely affected our ability to do things as a nation (Hawaii's multicultural makeup and its role in World War II is but one example), the pretense of an absence of significant cultural differences (e.g., the melting pot concept) has adversely affected school achievement as viewed by drop out rates, grades, standardized test scores, college student body makeup; minorities have been disproportionately present in the deficient achievement categories and generally absent from the roles of the "gifted."

That this is not the fault of the minorities themselves is being increasingly demonstrated by social science research (see Spindler, 1974a, for classroom examples of self-fulfilling prophecies based on social class and racial traits). Third, a person produces more when he/she feels respected. Besides, respect is contageous; the more people feel respected, the more they respect others. Fourth, one learns more about the world and how to live in it when the curriculum recognizes the existence of culturally diverse groups in ways that engender understanding. This planet is not getting any bigger yet the social distances separating peoples continually contract.

The immediate popularity of Roots, and the geneological research it inspired, points to the healthy desire of people to develop a sense of continuity. Maintenance of ethnic ties helps one experience this. In U.S. education, it has become dysfunctional to continue to over-emphasize the myth of monoculturality at the expense of the educational interests of so many.

Public education in the United States began as a charitable service for the children of the poor, not so much to educate them as to control them. The emphasis was on moral training and discipline. As late as 1830 in New Jersey and Pennsylvania, and even later in Maryland, Virginia, and Georgia, public monies were used only to educate the children of the poor (Tanner and Tanner, 1975, 150). Meanwhile, during the same decade in many southern states it was actually against the law to teach Blacks to read and write. A second conviction for this "crime" brought the death penalty (Giles, 1977).

When the great migrations of the turn of the last century occurred, it fell upon public education to provide a common socialization experience for this diverse population. If we distinguish between first culture learning (enculturation), and second culture learning (acculturation), we see that formal education in homogeneous societies is but one of many mutually reinforcing elements in the enculturation of the young. In a diverse society, depending on which group's values are operative in the most prestigious forms of formal education, formal education is an acculturative experience for many of the children partipating in the system of education. That is, they are having to learn a second culture as well as the content of education, the hidden curriculum (Henry, 1960) as well as the official curriculum. This is true for diversity of social classes as well as diversity of ethnic groups (Bernstein, 1971; Rosen, 1974; Gordon, 1964; Rich and Ogawa, 1976). Little explicit attention has been paid to this double task of American education (Gordon, 1964).

In a misguided effort to provide a common socialization experience for all Americans, the school system has consistently forced children into an either/or position. Students, for instance, could not speak Spanish and English in school, they had to speak Spanish or English and were punished for speaking Spanish (or an Indian language or "Black English," etc.). An example of this process of forced acculturation carried to inane extremes can be seen in the history of the Bureau of Indian Affairs' boarding schools, where children were quite literally extracted from their first culture and dropped into an alien culture (Dumont, Jr. and M. Wax, 1976; R. Wax, 1976; Modiano, 1973). (For a similar phenomenon in a Canadian context, see Spindler, 1974b; Sindell, 1974; Wolcott, 1974.)

This process of quite literally punishing children for their first culture seems to be a standard response of formal systems of schooling when faced, particularly, with language diversity. Breton children in France had to wear a kind of yoke in class if they uttered a word in the Breton language, a Celtic tongue. The yoke was passed from child to child as each child broke "the rule," and at the end of the week each child identified the child who had passed him the yoke, and all the trespassers got a beating. This discipline was meant to promote a feeling of community in the classroom. In Bolivian classrooms, children are often punished for speaking Quechua (Vallejo, 1975, 104).

The American effort to socialize diversity to a uniform American model resulted quite by accident through the creation of a new institution in the history of the world -- universal, non-elite public education for the masses, kindergarten through university. The European models on which we had traditionally based our ideas of quality education have proved no longer functional to this system of mass education. (These European models of education are no longer functional even in Europe which is presently undergoing its own democratization process and therefore the pluralization of its own systems of education (King, Moor, and Mundy, 1974 and 1975; King, 1976).) In the course of this century, the expectations of education have changed radically. Education is now seen as the right of everyone to develop to the limit of his or her unique capacities, rather than as primarily a way by which elite talent is selected according to elite criteria. It is in the context of this larger revolution in thinking about the general purposes of education that the issue of multicultural education arises. The philosopher of mass education was John Dewey (1939; 1961). He was the first to come to grips with the needs of educating everyone for an open future, of enabling the new generation to work out a future that is not based solely on modeling the past.

## THE IMPLEMENTATION OF PLURAL EDUCATION

This brings us to the question of how a system of formal education can best respond to diversity. How can awareness of diversity in socio-economic class, culture, language and individual personality be best implemented? How is this new awareness best implemented in the every day affairs of a given school and individual classroom? Cohen and Laosa's (1976) review of twenty-eight studies of bilingual education around the world is a case in point. Each of the following largely contradictory statements is supported by from five to ten studies:

> Acquisition of literacy skills has been successful when taught ...
>
> ... in a student's first language only.

... in a student's second language only.

... in a student's first and second languages simultaneously.

Acquisition of subject matter contents has been successful when taught ...

... in a student's first language only.

... in a student's second language only.

... in a student's first and second language simultaneously.

All of these approaches have also failed in some settings. Among the reasons for these inconsistencies that Cohen and Laosa mention are differing student characteristics or educational settings, inter-actions among complex factors, and the varying research designs and methods employed.

Carlson (1976, 28) says

".... there is such diversity within sociologically defined groups that diversity is the main character-istic .... Characterizations of minority people and about majority people are filled with ethnocentric and simplistic judgments .... One cannot define multicul-tural education without regard for social interactions within the community, or by relying solely on cultur-ally meaningless statistics ...."

Phillips (1976, 30-32) observes that ethnic groups advocate

"... education programs that will both increase minor-ity access to mainstream knowledge necessary for power and contribute to the maintenance and positive devel-opment of ethnic identity and culture ... selective acculturation through which the minority groups decide what in mainstream culture will be of value to them and then transform what is borrowed so that it is meaningful in their own terms and can be successfully integrated into a distinctive way of life that con-tinues in a dynamic, not static, manner."

Troike (1978) in his review of research evidence dealing with the effectiveness of bilingual education, concludes by suggesting that "educational opportunity for subordinated minorities may rest on matters far deeper and more fundamental than the merely linguistic." Two recent reports (Seelye, et al 1979; Seelye and Wasilewski, 1979) list over 200 variables that may be necessary to understanding the circumstances that affect the extent to which vernacular-speaking students achieve in schools.

Education sponsored by a nation-state attempts to balance two goals that are often in conflict: a governable consensus among its citizenry and the development of each individual citizen's unique potential. Few U.S. educators opt for out and out brainwash; most profess that each child should be educated appropriately according to the child's own unique abilities, and that these cannot accurately be predicted by race or surname. But political success (i.e., attraction of federal, state, and local funds) may not be tantamount to achieving the objectives of multicultural education. Past experience with "special" programs limited to ethnic groups (e.g., Hebrew School, Polish School) gives little hope that they will influence public school education. Bilingual programs currently in the public schools also will miss the opportunity to influence the basic curricula if their appeal -- and political backing -- is limited to ethnic minorities.

An increasingly sticky issue is the role of bilingual education vis a vis school integration. Teitelbaum and Hiller (1977) review court precedents where bilingual programs might have been used by a school district as a substitute for desegregation. They stress the necessity that "those advocating bilingual education characterize the program as integrative, not segregative." The same authors, both attorneys, go on to discuss the question of who is to judge the validity of a given program of education and who is to decide, the courts or the school districts, whether bilingual programs for students with limited English-language fluency that result in ethnic separation constitute <u>bona fide</u> ability groupings or attempts to circumvent desegregation orders. Isaacs (1977) investigates a Boston school where a Greek bilingual program is seen by many to be precisely "an exercise in cultivated separateness." Epstein (1977) quotes A. Bruce Gaardner, former chief of the Office of Education's modern foreign language section as saying

> "What bilingual education is, more than anything else, I believe, is a jobs program ... it's fought for because it's a way of giving jobs and recognition and status to Spanish speakers, who, traditionally have been at the lowest end of the socio-economic pole ...."

The ultimate issue according to Epstein and Isaacs is the competitive arena of school finance and the federal government's responsibility to finance maintenance of ethnic languages and cultures. The introduction, under the impetus of ethnic persuasion, of multicultural education in our schools has involved two elements: the packaging into a highly visible "program," and political backing to compete for the scarce school dollar. There are, however, difficulties in this approach. Hill-Burnett (1976, 38) accurately observes that this "process of politicizing increases the emphasis on boundaries, on cultural attributions to groups. At this level, it is stereotyping, and in this form culture is used stereotypically, consequently increasing the likelihood that children will be identified and stereotyped ethnically."

There are very practical political reasons for instituting multicultural education as a basic skills program, rather than to limit it to a special group of children (Gordon, 1964). At the heart of this is the pressure exerted by ethnic "blocks" to remove barriers to upward mobility. Much of this pressure is directed toward the school which is seen as the principal agency to aid or hinder this mobility. The folklore prevalent in much of both ethnic and mainstream United States maintains that we get ahead in this country by achievement; it is hard work, not family background, that counts.

These problems and others common to the bilingual and multicultural rhetoric do not in any way invalidate the fact that we are living in a multicultural world and if we are to survive it, we will need skills designed for functioning in a multicultural world.

There are no hard edges of languages and cultures. From the middle of the fifteenth centruy to the end of World War II marked the era of European hegemony. This era ended in 1947, when India gained her independence. In 1949 Mao came to power in China, the last great man of the vanishing era, and he obviously was not a European. We are at a transition point between civilizations, between the colonial and the post-colonial world. The rest of the world is talking back. The European standard of the last five hundred years is being transformed into an unknown future configuration (Malraux, 1974).

Just as the developing world today is emerging from its colonial past, so five hundred years ago Europe was experiencing its own particularity in its emergence from the feudal world of the universal Church. In doing so, Europe "discovered" man in all his infinite variety, and the effect was mind boggling. One could almost say that eighteenth century rationalism was a reaction to the revelation of the world's multiplicity, an attempt to develop a method to order phenomena and to decide dilemmas, hence the western deification of human reason, of logic. However, logic is linear and creates linear solutions to the problem of diversity. It has hard edges. It is efficient but not flexible. Such a mode of organization has given rise to our bureaucracies, to enforced uniformity, and to artistic expression such as Mondrian's painting, whose

> "... monotonous variations of the same, exclusively geometric configurations are the final consequence of a world in which substance is superseded by forms, material by methods, essence by functions, reality by abstractions. Mondrian's world is pure, clean, rational, sterile, serene, measurable, and functional" (Zijderveld, 1974, 78).

These, among many other characteristics of the passing civilization, are being vigorously questioned, and alternatives are being considered. Some of these alternatives are blends of Eastern and Western thought that have yet to merge.

The backwater regions of U.S. teacher training institutions are to be found where one-culture professors prepare one-culture teachers to educate one-culture students. Even a cursory glance at the history of Western education raises deep questions concerning the future value of monocultural education. The cutting edge of an education aimed at improving the future -- and how can we improve the past? -- will be forged from multicultural steel.

## REFERENCES

Afful, Elizabeth. A Study of Ghanaian Language Teaching in Three Primary Schools in Acera. Paper submitted to the Language Centre, University of Ghana, in Partial Fulfillment of the Requirements for Diploma in Ghanaian Language. Legon: University of Ghana, 1976.

Ansre, Gilbert. "Madina: Three Polyglots and Some Implications for Ghana." In Sirarpi Ohannessian, Charles A. Ferguson, and Edgar C. Polomes (eds.), Language Surveys in Developing Nations. Arlington, Virginia: Center For Applied Linguistics, 1975.

Armstrong, Robert G. "Language Policies and Language Practices in West Africa." In Fishman, Ferguson, and Das Gupta (eds.), Language Problems in Developing Nations. New York: John Wiley and Sons, 1968, 227-236.

Bamgbose, Ayo. Mother Tongue Education: The West African Experience. London: Hodder and Stoughton, 1976.

Bernstein, B. Class, Codes, and Control, Vol 1. London: Routledge and Kegan Paul, 1971.

Blauner, Robert. Racial Oppression in America. New York: Harper and Row, 1972.

Brinton, Crane, John B. Christopher, and Robert L. Wolff. A History of Civilization: Vol. 1: Prehistory to 1715. Englewood Cliffs, New Jersey: Prentice Hall, 1960.

Carlson, Paul E. "Toward a Definition of Local Level Multicultural Education." Anthropology and Education Quarterly 7 (4), November, 1976: 26-30.

Cohen, Andrew, and Luis M. Laosa. "Second Language Instruction: Some Research Considerations." Curriculum Studies 8 (2), 1976: 149-165.

Dalby, David. "The Linguistic Map of Africa." Lecture delivered at the School of Oriental and African Studies, University of London, March, 1977.

Dewey, John. Freedom and Culture. New York: Capricorn Books, 1939.

Dewey, John. Democracy and Education. New York: Macmillan, 1961.

Dumont, Robert V. Sr., and Murray L. Wax. "Cherokee School Society and The Intercultural Classroom." In Joan I. Roberts and Sherrie K. Akinsanya (eds.), Schooling in the Cultural Context. New York: David McKay, 1976, 205-216.

Epstein, Noel. "The Bilingual Battle: Should Washington Finance Ethnic Identities?" The Washington Post, Sunday, June 5, 1977, CI & 4.

Gibson, Margaret Alison. "Approaches to Multicultural Education in the United States: Some Concepts and Assumptions." <u>Anthropology and Education Quarterly</u> 7 (4), Nov. 1976: 7-18.

Giles, Raymond. Lecture on "The Anglo-Saxon Bureau of Immigration," University of Southern California's Washington Education Center, August, 1977.

Goodenough, Ward H. "Multiculturalism As The Normal Human Experience." <u>Anthropology and Education Quarterly</u>, 7 (4), November, 1976: 4-6.

Gordon, Milton M. <u>Assimilation in American Life: The Role of Race, Religion, and National Origins</u>. New York: Oxford University Press, 1964

Henry, Jules. "A Cross-Cultural Outline of Education." <u>Current Anthropology</u>, 1 (4), July, 1960. Also in Joan I. Roberts and Sherrie K. Akinsanyas (eds.), <u>Educational Patterns and Cultural Configurations: The Anthropology of Education</u>. New York: David McKay, 1976, 100-170.

Hill-Burnett, Jacquetta. "Commentary: Paradoxes and Dilemmas." <u>Anthropology and Education Quarterly</u> 7 (4), November 1976: 37-38.

Isaacs, Harold R. <u>Deseg: Change Comes To A Boston School</u>. (A report of an inquiry made for The Citywide Coordinating Council - Boston.) Boston: Citywide Coordinating Council, 1977.

Jencks, C. S. <u>Inequality: A Reassessment of the Effect of Family and Schooling in America</u>. New York: Basic Books, 1972.

Karoma, Alex (Chief's son, Sierra Leone.) Personal Communication, 1977.

Keesing, R. "Theories of Culture." In Bernard Siegel (ed.), <u>Annual Review of Anthropology</u>. Palo Alto, Cal.: Annual Review, Inc., 1974.

King, E. J., C. H. Moor, and J. A. Mundy. <u>Post-Compulsory Education I: A New Analysis in Western Europe</u>. Beverly Hills, Cal.: Sage Publications, 1974.

King, E. J., C. H. Moor, and J. A. Mundy. <u>Post-Compulsory Education II: The Way Ahead</u>. Beverly Hills, Cal.: Sage Publications, 1975.

King, Edmund J. "Education for Uncertainty." Inaugural Lecture in The Faculty of Education, University of London King's College, February, 1976.

Lesser, G. S., G. Fifer and D. H. Clark. "Mental Abilities of Children From Different Social-Class and Cultural Groups." <u>Monographs of the Society for Research in Child Development</u>, 30 (4, Serial No. 102), 1965.

Lewis, Diane K. "The Multicultural Education Model and Minorities: Some Reservations." Anthropology and Education Quarterly, 7 (4), November, 1976: 32-37.

Lewis, E. Glyn. "Bilingualism and Bilingual Education: The Ancient World to the Renaissance." In Joshua A. Fishman (ed.), Bilingual Education: An International Sociological Perspective. Rowley, Mass.: Newbury House Pub., 1976.

Lockland, George T. Grow or Die: The Unifying Principle of Transformation. N.Y.: Random House, 1973.

Mackey, William F. "A Typology of Bilingual Education." In Advances in the Sociology of Language II, edited by J. A. Fishman, 413-432. The Hague: Mouton, 1972.

Madrid-Barela, Arturo. "Towards An Understanding of Chicano Experience." In Larry A. Samovar and Richard E. Porter's (eds.), Intercultural Communication: A Reader, 1976, 98-106.

Malraux, Andre. La Tete D'Obsidienne. Paris: Gallimard, 1974.

Modiano, Nancy. Indian Education in the Chiapas Highlands. N.Y.: Holt, Rinehart and Winston, 1973.

Park, Robert E., and Herbert A. Miller. Old World Traits Transplanted. Chicago: University of Chicago Press, 1925.

Philips, Susan U. "Access to Power and Maintenance of Ethnic Identity As Goals of Multicultural Education: Are They Compatible?" Anthropology and Education Quarterly 7 (4), November, 1976, 30-32.

Rich, Andrea L., and Dennis M. Ogawa. "Intercultural and Interracial Communication: An Analytical Approach." In Larry A. Samovar and Richard E. Porter's (eds.), Intercultural Communication: A Reader. Belmont, Cal.: Wadsworth Publishing Co., 1976, 24-32.

Rideout, W. Lecture on "Ethnicity." University of Southern California's Washington Education Center, July, 1977.

Roberts, J. M. Three Navajo Households. Cambridge, Mass.: 40 (3). Papers of the Peabody Museum of Archaeology and Ethnology, 1951.

Rosen, Harold. Language and Class: A Critical Look at the Theories of Basil Bernstein. Bristol, England: Falling Wall Press, 1974.

Seelye, H. Ned. "'Like Us or Like You' -- the Challenge of Continuing Bicultural Education: An Interview with H. Ned Seelye." Curriculum Review 14 (5), 1975: 271-275.

Seelye, H. Ned, and Billie N. Navarro. A Guide to the Selection of Bilingual Education Program Designs. Arlington Heights, Ill.: Bilingual Education Service Center, 1977.

Seelye, H. Ned, Martha Gonzalez Calat, Margarita Lopez Raquec, Julieta Sanchez Castillo, and Joyce A. Sween. Informe final del estudio de base sobre la educacion bilingue rural de Guatemala. Guatemala City: Ministerio de Educacion (Socio Educativo Rural), 1979.

Sindell, Peter S. "Some Discontinuities in the Enculturation of Mistassini Cree Children." In George D. Spindler (ed.), Education and Cultural Process: Toward An Anthropology of Education. N.Y.: Holt, Rinehard and Winston, 1974, 333-341.

Singer, Marshall R. "Culture: A Perceptual Approach." In Larry A. Samovar and Richard E. Porter's (eds.), Intercultural Communications: A Reader. Belmont, Cal.: Wadsworth Publishing Co., 1976, 110-119.

Spindler, George D., ed. Education and Cultural Process: Toward an Anthropology of Education. N.Y.: Holt, Rinehard and Winston, 1974a.

Spindler, George D. "Why Have Minority Groups in North America Been Disadvantaged By Their Schools?" In George D. Spindler (ed.), Education and Cultural Process: Toward An Anthropology of Education. N.Y.: Holt, Rinehart and Winston, 1974b, 69-82.

Stewart, Edward C. Lecture on "Brain Function." University of Southern California's Washington Education Center, July 1977.

Stewart, Edward C. Outline of Intercultural Communication. In press, 1978a.

Stewart, Edward C. "The Survival Stage of Intercultural Communication." International Communications Yearbook, in press, 1978b.

Tanner, Daniel and Tanner, Laurel. Curriculum Development: Theory Into Practice. N.Y.: MacMillan, 1975.

Teitelbaum, Herbert, and Richard J. Hiller. "Bilingual Education: The Legal Mandate." Harvard Educational Review 47 (2), May, 1977: 138-170.

Troike, Rudolph C. "Research Evidence for the Effectiveness of Bilingual Education." Rosslyn, Vir.: National Clearinghouse for Bilingual Education, 1978.

Vallejo, Bernardo. "La Ensenanza del Quechua Como Segunda Lengua." In Rudolph C. Troike and Nancy Modiano (eds.), Proceedings of the First Inter-American Conference on Bilingual Education. Arlington, Virginia: Center of Applied Linguistics, 1975, 96-111.

Wallace, Anthony F. C. Culture and Personality. N.Y.: Random House, 1963.

Wax, Rosalie H.   "Oglala Sioux Dropouts and Their Problems with Educators."  In  Joan  I.  Roberts  and  Sherrie  K.  Akinsanya  (eds.), Schooling  in  the  Cultural  Context.   N.Y.:  David  McKay,  1976, 216-226.

Williamson, Kay  "The Rivers Reader Project in Nigeria" in Ayo Bamgbose (ed.),  Mother  Tongue  Education:  The  West  African  Experience. London: Hodder and Stoughton, 1976a.

Williamson, Kay.   "Small Languages in  Primary Education:   The Rivers Readers  Project  As  A  Case  History."  Paper  presented  to  the International   African   Institute's   Fourteenth   International African Conference on African Languages in Education, Kinshasa, Zaire, December 13-15, 1976b.

Wolcott, Harry F.   "The Teacher As Enemy."   In George D. Spindler (ed.) Education  and  Cultural  Process:  Toward  An  Anthropology  of Education.   N.Y.: Holt, Rinehart and Winston, 1974, 411-425.

Zijderveld, Anton C.   The Abstract Society:   A Cultural Analysis of Our Time.   Middlesex, England: Pellican Books, 1974.

CHAPTER 4

CURRICULUM IN MULTICULTURAL EDUCATION

## CONTENTS

CHAPTER 4

CURRICULUM IN MULTICULTURAL EDUCATION

Jacqueline H. Wasilewski and H. Ned Seelye

We live in a multicultural world, this was the message of the
last chapter. Multicultural education and the acquisition of intercultural skills are a necessity for everyone's maximum effective
functioning, not just for the culturally "deprived" or distinct, but
for all children as cultural beings. A contemporary author expresses
this in simple language:

> "I've often thought there ought to be a manual to hand to
> little kids, telling them what kind of planet they're on,
> why they don't fall off it, how much time they've probably
> got here, how to avoid poison ivy, and so on... And one
> thing I would really like to tell them about is cultural
> relativity. I didn't learn until I was in college about
> all the other cultures, and I should have learned that in
> the first grade. A first grader should understand that his
> or her culture isn't a rational invention; that there are
> thousands of other cultures and they all work pretty well;
> that all cultures function on faith rather than truth; that
> there are lots of alternatives to our own society. Cultural
> relativity is defensible and attractive. It's also a
> source of hope. It means we don't have to continue this
> way if we don't like it" (Vonnegut, 1974, 139).

To understand cultural relativity is to recognize that different
cultures provide different behavioral options for satisfying the
universal physical and psychological needs of Homo sapiens. This
understanding lays the foundation for a kind of cultural literacy, the

-63-

acceptance of man as a cultural being. Aristotle said man was a political animal, which is much the same thing. One eminent anthropologist (Hall, 1976) says that culture is dictatorial unless understood and examined. Just as a fish never discovers water as long as it remains immersed, it is when we are called to function in another culture that our basic assumptions are revealed. Until an alternative is known, the medium of life is an unexamined given.

There are many ways teachers structure the primary and secondary curriculum so that students can examine more effectively the many ways cultural conditioning affects the quality of human thought and interactions. This chapter provides the trainer of teachers with ideas culled from many sources to increase curricular relevancy in a multicultural world.

## CURRICULA ADJUSTMENTS

The adaptation of course content already in the curriculum holds the greatest and most easily implementable possibilities for infusion of multicultural objectives. As one educator observes,

> "... every school subject, if taught truthfully and realistically requires a plural culture perspective. Science, literature, the behavioral sciences, all must be freed from the monocultural ethnocentric focus that characterizes most standard course work ... We can no longer tolerate nor afford to permit a subject area to be called generally "music," "history," "psychology," "political science," when it is really a culture specific music, history, psychology, or political science ..." (Hilliard, 1975).

Any adaptation of curriculum to more adequately reflect and articulate the multicultural world in which we live must involve the teachers responsible for "delivering" the new curriculum in the adaptation process. Teachers, as well as students, learn by doing. Teacher training experiences can often be done with elementary or secondary students. When students and teachers learn together, new instructional styles often evolve with less emphasis on exposition, dyadic interactions, and verbal teaching, and more emphasis on peer teaching, group dynamics, and role reciprocity between teachers and students. Teacher training, both preservice and inservice, can be analogous to a laboratory where emphasis is placed on exploration and experimentation, and where much learning is accomplished through demonstrations, modeling, simulations, and deduction (Gay, 1977). McLaughlin's (1976) study of the implementation of change states that "mutual adaptation is the best way to ensure that change efforts are not superficial, trivial, or transitory" (351).

Two approaches are possible in the adaptation of course content. In one, the teacher trainer helps teachers identify the instructional objectives of a given course, then helps them exploit opportunities to illustrate the existing objectives with examples that serve additionally to increase one's respect or knowledge of other cultures. An example of this approach might be a math class unit that rightly credits the Mayas with the world's first use of the zero, followed several centuries later by the Arabs.

A second approach involves training teachers to develop specific instructional objectives to enhance an appreciation of cultural pluralism, objectives that fit units into existing courses to accomplish the new objectives. Let's say, for example, that one such objective is to illustrate the interdependence of cultures. The math curriculum could cull many examples of cultural diffusion, such as why the Maya invention of the zero did not spread whereas the same invention by the Arabs (who got it from the Indians) did diffuse widely.

Whichever general approach to adapting existing courses to multicultural instructional objectives is employed, teacher training institutions can greatly facilitate the process by supervising the identification and production of relevant multicultural objectives for all courses at all levels. One should not forget the potential inherent in sports and the arts. The former provides grist for understanding the relation between competition and cooperation, while the latter affords opportunities to experience and/or express cultural symbolism.

One informative "position statement" by the National Council for the Social Studies (Banks, et al, 1976) argues that ethnic pluralism and not cultural pluralism should be the focus of curriculum reform. "Cultural pluralism suggests a type of education which deals with the cultural contributions of all groups within a society. Consequently, that concept is far too broad and inclusive to set forth effectively the boundaries of an area encompassing both the contributions of ethnic groups and the problems resulting from ethnic discrimination in American society" (6). Still, it is not yet clear that this distinction is a necessary one once we begin dealing with specific skills on an operational level. This chapter will focus on the broader concept of cutural pluralism.

A brief look at the "hard core" curricula areas will generate additional ideas and illustrations of how adjustments can be effected to exploit the multicultural content implicit in all curricular areas.

Math, Science and Technology. Math is perhaps the only world language of the present day. The Western hegemony during the last several centuries has been largely a hegemony of Western science and technology: Spanish guns in Mexico and Peru in the fifteenth century and English steam-engines three hundred years later. This latter development of industrial technology was perhaps ultimately dependent on the fact that sixteenth century Britian ran out of fire wood and turned to coal to heat the foggy isle, and this adoption of a new fuel set in motion the chain of events which culminated in the Industrial Revolution (Nef, 1977). Yet this development of the culture of technology is frought with ironies. The Western concept of zero, which resolved a mathematical problem that neither the Greeks nor the Romans were able to solve and which facilitated the mathematical description of the world, sprang from the Hindu culture which perceived the world quite differently from the Greek. The Greeks demarcated space, the dimensions of shapes and volumes were described and measured, the eye was caught by the concrete, the discrete, the some-thing. The spaces between "somethings' were seen as vacuums, as the opposite of "somethings," as "no-things." Hindu culture on the other hand saw the world as pattern on pattern, as cyclic and blending, and as kaleidoscopically transforming. Space was a manifesting field, the universe played hide and seek with itself, nothing was something, potentially anything (Dass, 1974).

The West puzzles as to why the Chinese used gun powder only for fireworks, yet it took the West 1,000 years to adopt the wheel barrow from China. And speaking of wheels, the Maya used wheels but only on toys (Casson, Claiborne, Fagan, and Karp, 1977).

Or a completely different tack might be taken to introducing "culture" to technical subjects. For instance, the principals of probability might be demonstrated through use of card games popular with different ethnic groups in the class (Gay, 1977, 54).

Social Studies. Social studies is, of course, the "natural" for multicultural content.

Simulations are particularly effective with elementary school children. Fourth grade children in California regularly turn their classrooms into the haciendas of the Spanish Colonial Era. They take Spanish names, answer roll call in Spanish, have Spanish as well as English spelling and vocabulary words, make clothes like those worn during the period, learn songs, dances, and games, tan hides, dip candles, make donkey carts, grind corn and try to prepare tortillas, read of Father Sierra, visit the local mission and dream of a differ-ent world within its cool, thick walls, then visit the local center of present day Chicano life. Students often combine everything they have learned in student created plays about the era. It can be a vivid means of evoking the flavor and the feel of another era and another way.

Older students can, if they like, be more analytic, and again, like Dimitriou's (1977) students, begin to develop sociological and anthropological skills. One superlative introduction to field research is Robert M. Coles' Children of Crisis series (1967-1978) on the children of Mexicans, Blacks, Native Americans, and Eskimos as well as those of white share croppers and plantation owners, children of both the powerless and the powerful.

A source of material for social problems courses on ethnicity is the ethnic press. Again, see Dimitriou's list of 27 Green-American publications, and see also Murphy's (1974) listing of Black, Chicano, and Native American newspapers (186 publications for Native Americans alone) and Seelye and Day (1974) and Day (1977) for student activities based on Spanish-language newspapers.

Language and Literature. Language and literature can serve as the core curriculum of a multicultural school. Language is, of course, a major transmitter of culture. Learning the culture of a language is essential for fluency. Seelye (1974) gives innumerable exercises and activities for revealing the patterns of culture while teaching a second language.

A plural society is an intercultural society, a society which optimally communicates across boundaries. A crucial skill in such a society is the ability to be expressive and articulate, whether on behalf of oneself or one's group (Friere, 1974). The most articulate form of communication is usually accomplished through language.

In mainstream U.S. society, the value placed on the ability to manipulate language in all its forms, oral and written, has a great deal to do with student achievement which, in turn, affects subsequent achievement (Massad, 1972, 49; Goodenough, 1976, 6). It is further generally felt that positive self-concept can best be nurtured in an environment which accepts a child's first culture. Inherent in this situation may be a conflict: What if a child's first culture does not value expressive, articulate children?

Teacher trainers can assist teachers develop techniques whereby each individual student learns a pattern of appropriate responses to his varying contexts, and this is likely to be quite idiosyncratic. Self-concept cannot be evaluated independently of the standard used: the mainstream culture's standard, that of the child's first culture, or a child's own idiosyncratic standard (Saville-Troike, 1973; Seelye, in press). Llabre, Ware, and Newell (1977) indicate that even the structures underlying self-concept of children across sex and ethnic groups are not the same.

In U.S. society, even a child from a cultural background which does not value articulation and expressiveness will have to be articulate and expressive enough to communicate that about his group. In fact, communication as a curriculum focus may contribute to the child's ability to cope on his own terms.

> "... to understand himself and his behavior in a social context and learn to make wise choices with which he can live ...." (Ammons, 1969, 133).

Langdon (1966) developed a language arts program in which children were encouraged to write about emotional experiences, gradually refining their style so that their composition matched their enthusiasm for orally telling their stories (Ashton-Warner, 1963; Richardson, 1964).

It is in using language to communicate that children learn a language well, whether it is their first, second, or third language (Paulston, 1974), especially if what they are communicating is "purposeful and significant" to them. One student in a bilingual program that encouraged writing about things of deep significance to the students themselves said, "This is the first time that anybody in a course like this ever asked me to tell them what I know" (Rivers, 1975, 119).

-67-

What do students know better than themselves and their friends? In what are they more interested? Every student no matter what his "level of ability," is an expert in at least one thing, his own feelings. An intriguing challenge for older students in creative writing courses could center on the concept of ethnic identity in a convergent plural world, with the end of developing in students the ability to articulate their own concerns regarding their own identities and their difficulties and opportunities of living on cultural boundaries.

The ability to enter a literary world can be seen as akin to the ability to enter another culture. In both, one suspends "usual" conventions to accept a different set. How a novelist builds his literary world, the techniques of literary analysis, how anthropologists use literature as a social science tool, all can afford topics of fruitful class discussion. A number of books offer the teacher a good background to aid student entry into literary responses to life (Hsu, 1969; Booth, 1967; Peckham, 1967; Kahler, 1967; Watts, 1969; Goonetilleke, 1977).

In operation, a classroom activity may look like this: The students prepare two products, one, an essay, drama, song, or painting, on the major themes in a recently read novel (e.g. the individual as a stranger, solitude, lack of known parentage or ancestry, types of response to "multi-" world) and two, a personal statement, prose, poetry, visual, impression or analysis on one's own background. Both products are shared with the class at large and discussed. The final class product would be a "bound" edition of the students' work, along with "reviews" of the non-print products and photographs where possible. The volume can also include transcripts of the significant class interactions while discussing the novels and class products. An appropriate title for this compendium might be "Identities in an Emergent Mode" or "The I I Know."

In Post World War II California, a girl of Chinese immigrant parents entered public elementary school in Stockton, California. Today she teaches English at the Mid-Pacific Institute in Hawaii. In 1976 her book, The Woman Warrier: Memoirs of A Girlhood Among Ghosts (1976) won the National Book Critics Award for the best book of non-fiction published that year. This book is a chronicle of Maxine Hong Kingston's own particular experiences growing up on the Chinese-American cultural boundary and of her continued attempts to find an American song that can be sung accompanied by Chinese instruments. The "ghosts" of the title are not those of ancestral memories of China but rather they are anyone who is not Chinese. You see, only the Han people are real. "You must not tell anyone." my mother said, "what I am about to tell you. ..." Activities such as that mentioned in the preceeding paragraph may help future "warriers" to understand in themselves a process that too often, when found in separate peoples, ends dialogue rather than begins it.

New Courses. Sometimes secondary schools are tempted to add a new course to the curriculum (universities practically always see this as a solution) to achieve multicultural objectives not already present in the curriculum. An example of a new course developed by classroom teachers is Dimitriou's (1977) "Suburban Ethnicity: A Case Study of the American-Greek Experience in Southern California" a teaching and resource manual for an intercultural studies curriculum developed for junior and senior high school students at Palos Verdes High School, Palos Verdes Estates, California. It was developed to reveal the Greek immigrant experience in Southern California and includes slide-tape materials to document that experience, but the general format can serve teacher trainers as a model for the development of materials about other ethnic groups or as a case study in heterogeneous classrooms. The materials can be developed in either English or the ethnic language. Activities include:

1) student preparation of three-generation family trees;

2) An inquiry into ethnic characteristics and ethnic sterotyping, both positive and negative, which begins by each student listing five positive and five negative stereotypes for his or her ethnic group (or for the student who is multiethnic, the group with which he or she most identifies);

3) an introduction to sociological and anthropological field research by having each student conduct interviews of a) an older acquaintance or relative with a strong ethnic background, b) second generation and c) third generation "ethnics";

4) church and synagogue visitations to be reported on orally or in writing by responding to an excellent set of study questions;

5) an investigation of ethnic dances as a means of exploring different worlds, i.e. what do the dance configurations tell about the values of the culture?;

6) restaurant visitations to be done singly, with one's family, or in student groups, and reported on in class by responding to another set of excellent study questions, e.g. describe the restaurant; what did you see, smell, hear, and feel;

(These last two activities allow non-verbal interaction with the culture.)

7) the preparation of an ethnic cookbook (particularly interesting in multi-ethnic classes) which can be handed out to the rest of the school and/or the dishes can be prepared by volunteers and eaten by the entire school accompanied by the songs and dances that have been learned.

-69-

The manual also includes suggested research questions, notes on religious and folk beliefs, and at the end of the book a complete compendium of Greek resources in the Los Angeles area.

Such activities create opportunities where alternative evaluation techniques to written examinations can be employed, e.g., oral testing, interviews, longitudinal audio recordings of students' performances, peer evaluations, diaries, and "demonstration" evaluations. An example of the latter, a "demonstration" evaluation, could be the student production of a play based on the Greek experience as described in Dimitriou's materials, or as Gay suggests, a multi-ethnic sociodrama of Manchild in a Promised Land, Down These Mean Streets, "I Am A Woman," "I Am Joaquin," "The American Dilemma," or "It Bees That Way." These can give evidence of ability to understand ethnic cultures and experiences, to select and organize a variety of materials, to present different ethnic perspectives on the same issues, and to use interdisciplinary knowledge, multimedia techniques, and multi-ethnic perspectives to develop an idea, issue, and/or event into a coherent, comprehensive and conceptual message (Gay, 1977, 56).

Field Experiences. The dramatic break in routine afforded by field trips can be used to advantage by teachers who avoid the common pitfalls that tend to trivialize this type of academic experience. Teacher trainers can help teachers plan carefully to insure that the potential for student learning is realized. Besides visits to things of interest, visits to people are exciting when students are prepared for the event ahead of time. Simply bringing people into contact is not enough. The history of education in U.S. overseas dependent schools is a case in point. Here are schools right in the middle of foreign cultures, yet the curricula usually barely reflect this. Almost no use is made of the fact that Germany, Japan, or Spain, etc., is just quite literally outside the door. For field experiences to be effective, there must be careful liaison work done between the schools and the communities by people comfortable working outside their ethnic and socio-economic enclaves. Teacher trainers can assist teachers plan field experiences that are integrated into each intercultural objective they develop.


## MANAGING THE CURRICULUM

Lurking in the shadows of consciousness is the "hidden curriculum," the values, assumptions, and managerial techniques used in schools to implement the formal curriculum.

More and more the task of teaching is discovering ways to elicit the behaviors we are interested in developing. Cole, Gay, Glick, and Sharps (1971), Glick (1974), and Cole and Scribner (1974) show unequivocally that cognition is not culture free, and that cognition is not a trait, but a process, "an adaptive instrument suited to the demands of an environment as seen by the subject" (Glick, 1969). Finding out which environmental demands elicit which behaviors can generate "positive statements relating behavior to occasions" (Glick, 1969, 380). An interesting approach to measuring cognition was taken by Glick. When a given test did not elicit the desired performance the test was changed until it fit the social situation in which the skills to be tested were usually elicited so that the desired test performance could be obtained. Seemingly minor variations in contextual variables sometimes affect performance, even the kinds of tasks that "all rational men" would perform reasonably.

> "... we wanted to use everyday objects as things to sort. Accordingly, we chose something that was highly familiar to our African subjects -- beer bottles of various heights and colors ... Our African subjects, though familiar with these objects and their differentiae, refused to sub-classify them -- all bottles were heaped in a single category. We had made the mistake of using empty bottles, which were clearly 'garbage' and nothing else. Prelimiary observations with filled bottles shows that these can be classified" (Glick, 1974, 379).

The difference in performance between the two groups was not in the ability to classify, "but rather in the constraints of reasonability that allow for the classification to be used" (Glick, 1969, 379).

Two theories of cognition have received extensive cross-cultural treatment, Piaget's theory of cognitive development and Witkin's theory of cognitive style. Both literatures are thoroughly reviewed in Cole and Scribner (1974). Even more extensive reviews of Plagetian research in cross-cultural areas are available in Dasen (1972) and Goodnow (1969), and of cognitive style research as it applies to cross-cultural areas in Dawson (1967) and Berry (1966, 1917). The former theory stresses universal stages of development, while the latter stresses differences in style. Both, as they have been tested cross-culturally, have become more flexible and less absolute (Cole and Scribner, 1974, 25). It is interesting to note that the entire theory of cognitive style is based on studies of visual perception, especially response to embedded figures tests, yet based on a sub-ject's functioning vis a vis visual stimuli, interferences have been made about his manner of functioning in non-visual areas. In addition, the embedded figures tests use abstract stimuli.

> "There have been no studies of responses to embedded figures using locally significant stimulus objects..." (Cole and Scribner, 1974, 96).

(It is also interesting to note that in no case have these researches been conducted by visually talented people, i.e., artists, since as "non-academics" they by definition are excluded from our research establishments.)

Cole and Scribner's (1974) <u>Culture and Thought</u> extensively reviews the research literature on the interrelationships between culture, cognition, language, perception, conceptual processes, learn-ing, memory, and problem solving. In almost every area of research reviewed

"... the nature of the operations subjects use has been shown to be sensitive to a whole host of factors connected with the particular problem situation: The specific demands of the task (giving a verbal description of a picture selecting a match, or 'modeling' it), the task material (whether it is familiar or strange, represented by objects or pictures), the semantic content of the problem (factually true or factually false syllogisms), the response mode (adjusting a rod in a frame or finding a hidden picture). Because little attention has been paid to them, we have altogether neglected motivational, attitudinal, and other factors. ..." (Cole and Scribner, 1974, 176).

Witkin et al (1977), in their recent article on the educational implications of field-dependent and field-independent cognitive styles, especially regarding educational-vocational interests caution "against using the relations now found to exist between cognitive style and ... performance to perpetuate a self-fulfilling prophecy."

As Ramirez and Castaneda (1974) point out, just because a child has an Hispanic name does not mean that his preferred cognitive style is field-sensitive. There is great diversity in the Hispanic community as to whether the child's early environment is traditional, dualistic, or a-traditional.

Research in cross-cultural contexts generates even more questions about just how to respond to differences in cognitive style. Our school system is supposed to favor field-independent cognitive modes, yet most hunting-gathering peoples have been among the worst academic performers in the learning environments we provide.

Preferred cognitive style, is also supposed to be related to which hemisphere of the brain is dominant in mental operations, the left hemisphere for field-independence, the right hemisphere for field-dependence. According to this theory, verbal-analytical processes are carried out in the left hemisphere, and non-verbal, spatial skills are right-brained phenomena. Cross-cultural research on brain-damaged individuals has revealed some interesting wrinkles in this sharply dichotomous picture. Frenchmen suffering from aphasia lose their written language if damage occurs to the left hemisphere, their spoken language if the damage is more to the right. Japense aphasics, however, lose their spoken language if damage is more to the left, their written language if the damage is more to the right (Stewart, 1977). It is also interesting to note that dyslectic Japense children are unusually dyslectic in the Katakana alphabet (the phonetic alphabet), and almost never in Kanji (the ideographic alphabet) (Samples, 1977, 690). What does this all mean in terms of our conventional dichotomies about the verbal and the non-verbal, about alphabets and art?

Recent research also indicates that humans have extraordinary powers of recovery and that even "the mind may have some of the qualities of an elastic surface, easily deformed by shearing forces, but able to rebound when those forces are removed" (Kagan, 1978). So many

aspects of human personality that used to be considered as fairly
stable "traits," now appear to be learned behaviors. For instance,
altruism, generosity, personal consideration, and sharing are all
prosocial behaviors that are learned (Mussen and Eisenberg-Berg,
1977). Different cultures and different child-rearing practices help
or hinder to varying degrees the development of these behaviors.
However, because prosocial behavior is learned, it can also be modified. And more and more we are seeing how different environments
elicit different behaviors. Even ethnocentrism is context bound
(Brewer, 1977).

The fruitfulness of this concept of cognition as an adaptive
instrument responsive to context and of concentrating on what people
can do rather than what they cannot do is powerfully demonstrated in
Frailberg's recently published book (1977), Insights From the Blind:
Comparative Studies of Sighted and Blind Infants. Fraiberg noted the
absence of communicative expression in the faces of blind children,
yet blind children do convey the same expressions -- in their hands.
"The hands give meaning to emotional experience," Fraiberg says of
blind children. Sighted children, on the other hand, get so locked
into reading faces that they miss the expressiveness of the blind.
When Fraibert showed film clips to Piaget of blind Robbie adaptively
pursuing a sound-making toy to the place where it was "lost" thereby
demonstrating that he had reached the level of "object permanence"
Piaget threw up his beret in the air and cheered.

This necessity of discovering ways of enabling children to grow
is also exemplified in the work of Maria Montesorri. She especially
provides a model for those instances where "a genuine cultural difference can interfer with academic process ...." (Carlson, 1976). Her
system of education, developed for Roman slum children at the turn of
the century, assumes no previous knowledge, even of basic concepts.
Everything is taught from scratch in its most concrete form, from what
is round to how you hang up your coat. This formal learning occurs in
a highly structured environment where the hidden curriculum also reinforces the cognitive patterns (problem solving, independence of
action, responsibility) being developed in the formal part of the
curriculum. Originally, parents were encouraged to participate in the
classroom and learn with their children, and interesting to note in
view of our present great difficulty in teaching people to read,
Montesorri believed in teaching children to write before they learned
to read. Expressive functions first.

Lest the importance of assuming nothing is underestimated,
another finding in Cole and Scribner (1974) regarding a test of simple
inference in which an apparatus consisting of a key, a locked box with
three compartments, and a piece of candy (the goal) presented all
sorts of difficulties for the subjects. In different permutations of
this experiment it became apparent that

> "the difficulty that young children and tribal Liberians
> experience with our simple inference task is that they do
> not know how to begin. For some reason, the process invol-
> ved in obtaining a key from the side panel of the original

apparatus interfers with later phases of the response sequence. Cultural differences seem in this case to reside in the kinds of initial situations that promote a good beginning for problem solution, not in the ability to link separately learned elements in order to solve the problem" (Cole and Scribner, 1974, 159).

The multicultural child begins life less able than the mono-cultural child to indulge in "thinking as usual" because already he or she is the inheritor of a cultural pattern which provides alternative "recipes" for "typical solutions for typical problems available for typical actors" (Schutz, 1964, 95-102). Nothing is given. Everything must be negotiated. "A common domain of activity" and "shared congru-ent objectives" (Stewart, in press) must be established. In the multi-cultural context a child is always learning new responses to old stimuli, old responses to new stimuli, and totally new stimulus-response patterns. The child is always engaged in trying to figure out when to generalize a response across situations and when to con-textualize responses, i.e., how to behave appropriately in different contexts.

The optimum environment for doing all this effectively is one which is characterized by a high tolerance for flexibility, ambiguity, and paradox. Most cultural environments are not so constituted, since one of the main functions of culture thus far in human history has been to resolve dissonance and to provide those nice comfortable "recipes" for action in recurring situations (see the later section on multicultural environments).

Once again, the situation specific variables cannot be emphas-ized enough.

"The familiar nursery school activity of having children mix flour and water to make paste ... fails completely when Native American children refuse to make the paste because flour is food and one does not play with food" (Rivlin, 1977, 109).

In addition, a teacher unfamiliar with this prohibition would have great difficulty "extracting" this piece of cultural information from students, especially early in the year, because of the additional social custom of keeping silent initially with unfamiliar people in unfamiliar situations (Saville-Troike, 1973, 42).

Perhaps one reason for the emphasis on decision-making and choice in American society is the tension arising in a culturally diverse society with a dominant cultural tradition which features an assumption that, at least once all the information is in and all the data processed, one is able to decide, to choose the one right answer. However, India, another culturally diverse society, presents us with a contrasting dominant pattern, one with an opposite assumption of the necessity of not making choices. "The Westerner's choice is to make choices; the Hindu's is to lose his choosing self ..." (Gilliat, 1972). And to do that the Indian has developed a "habit" of ignoring the obvious (of) making a detour to preserve his calm" (Theroux, 1975, 97).

-74-

So, in the words of Maxine Hong Kingston, we are left with the problem of how one can learn "to make (one's) mind large, as the universe is large, so that there is room for paradoxes ..." (Kingston, 1976, 35). When is choice in its turn simply a strategem for avoiding difference (Stewart, in press)? Adler (1976, 375) says that a multi-cultural style is able to evolve when an individual is capable of negotiating the conflicts and tensions inherent in cross-cultural contacts. This ability to negotiate is greatly facilitated in plural societies with their many "alternative and equivalent ways of reaching the top" (King, 1975, 343).

Children who are multicultural can realize that theirs for a large part is a situation without precedent. They are heirs to a fledgling tradition which has the possibility of seeing the world whole. They will perhaps have the chance to architect a future which allows for more complex kinds of wholeness. At present the people who are engaged in this task are an invisible community of poets, writers, dancers, scientists, teachers, lawyers, scholars, philosophers, students, and citizens for whom the old boundaries are irrelevant (Taylor, 1969; Gordon, 1964).

Ackerman (1976) believes that perhaps the challenge of our time is "helping man to relate to unknown man" (304). Intercultural skill is thus the ability to function as a stranger and to interact with strangers (Bochner, 1973; Schutz, 1964).

The cultural pattern of the approached group is regarded by multicultural people as "not a shelter but a field of adventure, not an instrument for disentangling problematic situations, but a proble-matic situation itself." This pattern is not a shelter but a laby-rinth in which one has lost all one's bearings (Schutz, 1964, 104-105).

In this encounter with strangeness, the stranger

1) tries to define the new fact

2) tries to catch its meaning

3) then begins to transform it little by little so that the strange fact is compatible and consistent with all his other facts.

Experience has been enlarged and adjusted (Schutz, 1964, 104-105).

We know very little about this "relating with unknown man." There are tribes today in the Amazon basin who kill strangers on sight because the concept of a stranger who is also a human being is lack-ing. There has been little research into conditions needed for creat-ing trust among strangers. Or into cultural perception, that is, how people differentiate the important from the unimportant patterns in a strange culture. For instance, in U.S. society use of the left hand is purely idiosyncratic, an individual just happens to be left handed. In Muslim culture however, what one does with which hand is a matter of formal culture with severe effects if one transgresses the rules. How does one learn what is a "rule" and what is not and in which cases to apply the rule? Or in a given social situation, an American might act as an individual where a Japanese might act in terms of his role. How are these confusions noticed and effectively dealt with (Stewart, in press; Seelye and Wasilewski, 1977)?

Connected with multiculturalism but different from it is inter-cultural skill. One may grow up multicultural in the sense that if one's parents belonged to two different cultural groups one may have learned to function in both. However, unless one has generalized those processes which enable one to participate effectively in two cultures to learning how to interact with cultures as yet unknown, one could conceivably tolerate the dissonances which are "all in the family," so-to-speak, but not be so tolerant of those that appear when interacting with "strange" cultures.

## ALTERNATE PEDAGOGIES

In an integration of Piagetian cognitive developmental and Witkenian cognitive style theories, Samples (1977) characterizes men-tality as consisting of four metaphoric modes: the symbolic which takes two forms, the abstract and the visual, the synergetic compara-tive, the integrative, and the inventive. There is a natural capacity to perform in all the modes throughout all the Piagetian stages of development (sensory-motor, pre-operational, concrete operational, and formal operational), but formal schooling consistently rewards only the symbolic-abstract mode. Text materials, curriculum emphasis, and pressure on teachers and administrators for skill in the 3-R's exclude all other modes. Yet it is ironic that as one observes the most profound development in learning, children are learning holisti-cally, particularly during Piaget's pre-operational stage when children are acquiring language simultaneously with learning to walk upright. Jonas Salk defines wisdom "as the use of both sides of the mind, the analytic and the analogic" (Samples, 1977, 692). What are some strategies for exercising the whole mind?

Soon Bob Samples, Cheryl Charles, and Dick Barnhart will publish The Whole School Book: Teaching and Learning Late in the Twentieth Century, the result of a decade and a half's search for interdiscip-linary, inter-grade-level, intercultural curricular materials. The project was made possible by heavy funding from the National Science Foundation. The method to develop the materials was one of descrip-tion rather than prescription of culling structures from experience rather than imposing structures upon experience (Samples, 1977, 689-690). A simple example of such strategies (we will have to await publication of the book to be informed of others) is that of allowing symbolic-visual expression if a student falters with symbolic-abstract expression, of allowing a student to paint, draw, or sculpt his response. Later the student would be encouraged to tell or write the idea (Samples, 1977, 690). (The opposite journey from symbolic-abstract to symbolic visual would be equally as interesting for those with an analytic preference.)

-76-

Pedagogies that are truly alternatives to the "symbolic-abstract-mode" that Samples among others finds prevalent in most formal school systems are currently being discovered or, in many cases, re-discovered. Books like The Centering Book: Awareness Activities for Children, Parents and Teachers (Hendricks and Wills, 1975) suggest activites from outside the Western, logical, linear cognitive tradition, which present an introduction to yoga, Zen, the dream work of the Senoi people of the Central Malay Peninsula, and to the Muslim Sufi tradition. This almost programmed text with chapters on basic centering, relaxing the mind, expanding perception, relaxing the body, working with dreams, imagery, stretching the body, movement and dance, and story telling is essentially an elementary text for what has come to be called "transpersonal education." It seeks a synthesis in education of intellect and intuition, mind and body, fact and feeling.

Houston and Master's book Mind Games (1973) presents specific alternative methods of teaching and learning. For instance, teaching math rhythmically, i.e., as patterns of sound and movement rather than as symbolic abstract patterns, clapping, tah-teh-tah-teh-tah, tah-teh-tah-teh-tah, instead of saying, "Five and five are ten." This "method" recognizes that mathematical and musical skill often coincide, but opts to approach this linked universe through the music rather than through the geometry of the spheres.

The best description in the literature of a truly alternative pedagogy in a modern setting are Rohlen's papers (1974, 1978) or Seishin Kyoiku or "spiritual education," which forms part of the corporate training programs for many medium and large Japanese companies. In the course of this training young executives run marathons, mediate, and do unpaid labor.

Multicultural Environments. What are the characteristics of those settings which elicit multicultural behavior? How are they created?

These environments value many behaviors and provide an atmosphere where children can expand their repertoire of behaviors. No child is forced into an either/or position, e.g., where he must give up speaking Pidgin in order to speak English. He is rather encouraged to use all behaviors appropriately. It is an environment which values uniqueness, idiosyncracy, incomparability in individuals and facilitates that individual's interaction with the world at large. The micro-environment of the school must be attuned to the community in which it exists.

What does good teaching in a multicultural context look like? Two highly idiosyncratic New Zealand teachers provide possibilities, Sylvia Aston-Warner who taught in Maori schools for twenty-four years and Elwyn Richardson who took a job as school master in a mixed Maori/European school in an isolated rural school when he could not find a job as a marine biologist. Neither had funding, just necessities and time.

Sylvia Ashton-Warner (1963) developed an approach to reading and writing based on the simple notion that children learn to read and write more readily from materials affectively important to themselves, preferably from materials they have written themselves. In Ashton-Warner's school it all began in kindergarten. When each child arrived in class they would tell the teacher which word he or she would like to learn. The word was written on two cards, one to keep at school and one to carry around all day, take home, and learn. Next morning the words kept at school were dumped onto the floor. Everyone scrambled for their word. Then the children paired off and taught each other their words. Eventually, the words became sentences and the sentences stories, and the children learned to read by reading their own and each other's stories.

Meanwhile, in Oruaiti School, a square wooden room built in 1889, roofed with red-painted corrugated iron, gable-ended, weather-boarded, and with three windows, Elwyn Richardson was creating a community of artists and scientists out of rural Maori and European school children, children whose only "academic" resource at home was the Bible. They set about learning by collecting specimens -- words, seashells, different spellings, new thoughts, -- gradually sorting out observations, discarding stock responses, testing generalizations, and evaluating their inventions over long periods.

> "The primary demand on the child was that he should think through exactly what he observed, felt, or believed ... a great deal of careful training went into eliminating the merely stock response and the expected answer. But combined with this demand for ... a personal view, and of course necessary to it, was the filling acceptance of idiosyncracy and the affectionate acceptance of the strengths and limitations of each member of the group ..." (Richardson, 1964).

There are, in addition, at least two American and one German school described in the literature that seem to be providing promising environments for diversity. Frances Sussna's multicultural school in San Francisco uses "bi-cultural teachers to assist in the teaching of specialized knowledge and skills in a context where both one's own group accomplishments and inter-group interaction are stressed." The program thus fosters individual self-confidence and situations of meaningful inter-group contact. In the mornings the students interact in mixed groups to learn basic skills, and in the afternoon they meet in their ethnic groups for history and language. When each group has a holiday, the others are invited to help celebrate it. Stress is on pride in one's own heritage and respect for the heritage of other groups. The aim is to stimulate interaction among groups who feel themselves to be equal (D. Lewis, 1976).

There is a public school in Urbana, Illinois, in which half the students speak one of 21 different languages (Bouton, 1975). The whole school is acquiring a second or third language. An important point about this school is that every person on the staff, from the principal to the janitor, is culturally "literate." They all have intercultural skills. With such sensitivity the janitor was able to adequately take care of an Indian boy who in his first week in school had an attack of diarrhea on the playground and sensitively handled the boy's embarrassment despite a language barrier. In another case, aids were able to help a new Japanese student understand that the boy who had hit her had done so accidentally. She thought she had been attacked.

Another interesting school in a rapidly changing, heterogeneous community is in Schonhausen in the Remstal in West Germany (Spindler, 1974 ). Since WWII Schonhausen's population has increased almost 100%. What was a homogeneous, agricultural folk community is now a heterogeneous, only partly agricultural, largely suburban community. Some Catholics have come into the formerly totally Protestant area, many do not speak the local dialect of German and have dialects of their own. Yet Schonhausen has assimilated this diverse influx while maintaining low incidence of crime, suicide, and juvenile delinquency.

If there is an overriding theme to all of the examples of successful implementation of multicultural education contained in this chapter it is that in each case the reality of where the children are at that particular time is being responded to. It is no good wishing they were someplace else. It falls to the teacher trainer to inspire the development and implementation by classroom teachers of creative curricula that fit the multicultural world in which we live.

# REFERENCES

Ackermann, Jean Marie. "Skill Training for Foreign Assignment: The Reluctant U.S. Case." In Larry A. Samovar and Richard E. Porter (eds.). Intercultural Communication: A Reader. Belmont, Cal.: Wadsworth Publishing Co., 1976, 298-306.

Adler, Peter S. "Beyond Cultural Identity: Reflections on Cultural and Multicultural Man." In Larry A. Samovar and Richard E. Porter (eds.). Intercultural Communication: A Reader. Belmont, Cal.: Wadsworth Publishing Co., Inc., 1976, 362-380.

Ammons, Margaret. "Communication: A Curriculum Focus." In Alexander Frazier (ed.). A Curriculum for Children. Washington, D.C.: National Education Association, Association for Supervision and Curriculum Development, 1969.

Ashton-Warner, Sylvia. Teacher. N.Y.: Bantum, 1963.

Banks, James A., Carlos E. Cortes, Geneva Gay, Ricardo L. Garcia, and Anna S. Ochoa. Curriculum Guidelines for the Social Studies. Arlington, Vir.: National Council for the Social Studies, (1515 Wilson Blvd.), 1976.

Berry, J. W. "Temme and Eskimo Perceptual Skills." International Journal of Psychology 1 (3), 1966: 207-229.

Berry, J. W. "Ecological and Cultural Factors in Spatial Perceptual Development." Canadian Journal of Behavioral Science 3 (4), 1971: 324-336.

Bochner, S. "The Mediating Man and Cultural Diversity." Topics In Culture Learning, Vol. 1, 1973: 23-27.

Booth, Wayne C. The Rhetoric of Fiction. Chicago: University of Chicago Press, 1967.

Bouton, Lawrence F. "Meeting the Needs of Children with Diverse Linguistic and Ethnic Backgrounds." Foreign Language Annals 8 (4), Dec. 1975: 306-316.

Brewer, Marilynn B. "Perceptual Processes in Cross-Cultural Interaction." In Overview of Intercultural Education, Training and Research: Volume I, Theory. Edited by D. S. Hoopes, P. B. Pederson, and G. W. Renwick. Washington, D.C.: Georgetown University, SIETAR, 1977, 22-31.

Carlson, Paul E. "Toward a Definition of Local Level Multicultural Education." Anthropology and Education Quarterly 7 (4), Nov. 1976: 26-30.

Casson, Lionel, Robert Claiborne, Brian M. Fagan, and Walter Karp. Mysteries of the Past. Marion, Ohio: American Heritage Books, 1977.

Cole, Michael, John Gay, Joseph A. Glick, and Ronald W. Sharp. The Cultural Context of Learning and Thinking: An Exploration in Experimental Anthropology. Basic Books, 1971.

Cole, Michael and Sylvia Scribner. Culture and Thought: A Psychological Introduction. N.Y.: Wiley, 1974.

Dasen, P. R. "Cross-Cultural Piagetian Research: A Summary." Journal of Cross-Cultural Psychology, 3, 1972: 23-29.

Dass, Ram. The Only Dance There Is. Garden City, N.Y.: Anchor Books, 1974.

Dawson, J. L. M. "Cultural and Physiological Influences Upon Spatial-Perceptual Processes in West Africa, Part 1." International Journal of Psychology, 2, 1967: 115-128.

Day, J. Laurence. The Sports Page: Based on Selection from Major Newspapers from the Spanish-Speaking World. Skokie, Ill.: National Textbook Co., 1977.

Dimitriou, James F. Suburban Ethnicity: A Case Study of the American-Greek Experience in Southern California. A Teacher's Manual and Curriculum Guide for Activities and Resources. Palos Verdes Estates, Ca.: Palos Verdes High School, 1977.

Fraiberg, Selma. Insights From the Blind: Comparative Studies of Blind and Sighted Infants. N.Y.: Basic Books, 1977.

Friere, Paulo. Pedagogy of the Oppressed. N.Y.: Seabury Press, 1974.

Gay, Geneva. "Curriculum For Multicultural Teacher Education." In Frank H. Klassen and Donna M. Gollnick (eds.). Pluralism and the American Teacher: Issues and Case Studies. Washington, D.C.: American Association of Colleges for Teacher Education, 1977, 31-62.

Gilliat, Penelope. "The Current Cinema: Self-Colloquy. About a Subcontinent." (Review of Malle's Phantom India.) The New Yorker, July 8, 1972.

Glick, Joseph. "Culture and Cognition: Some Theoretical and Methodological Concerns." In George D. Spindler (ed.). Education and Cultural Process: Toward An Anthropology of Education. N.Y.: Holt, Rinehart and Winston, 1974, 373-381.

Goodenough, Ward H. "Multiculturalism As the Normal Human Experience." Anthropology and Education Quarterly, 7(4), November, 1976: 4-6.

Goodnow, J. J. "Research On Culture and Thought." In D. Elkind and O. H. Flavell (eds.). Studies In Development. N.Y.: Oxford University Press, 1969.

Goonetilleke, D.C.R.A. Developing Countries in British Fiction. N.Y.: MacMillan, 1977.

Gordon, Milton M.  <u>Assimilation in American Life: The Role of Race,</u> <u>Religion, and National Origins</u>. N.Y.: Oxford Univ. Press, 1964.

Hall, Edward T. <u>Beyond Culture</u>. Garden City, N.Y.: Anchor, 1976.

Hendricks, Gay and Russel Wills. <u>The Centering Book: Awareness Activ-</u> <u>ities for Children, Parents and Teachers</u>. Englewood Cliffs, N.J.: Prentice-Hall (Spectrum), 1975.

Hilliard, A. "Cultural Pluralism: The Domestic International Connec- tion." Paper presented at the American Association of Colleges For Teacher Education Conference, Fort Lauderdale, Florida, 1975.

Houston, Jean and Robert E. L. Masters. <u>Mind Games</u>. N.Y.: Dell, 1973.

Hsu, Francis L. K.  <u>The Study of Literate Civilizations</u>. N.Y.: Holt, Rinehart and Winston, 1969.

Kagan, Jerome. "The Baby's Elastic Mind." <u>Human Nature</u> 1 (1), January 1978: 66-73.

Kahler, Erich.  <u>Out of the Labyrinth: Essays in Clarification</u>. N.Y.: Brazillier, 1967.

King, Edmund J.  <u>Other Schools and Ours: Comparative Studies for To-</u> <u>day</u>, N.Y.: Holt, Rinehart and Winston, 1975.

Kingston, Maxine Hong  <u>The Woman Warrier: Memoirs of a Girlhood Among</u> <u>Ghosts</u>. N.Y.: Knopf, 1976.

Langdon, Margaret.  <u>Let the Children Write</u>. London: Longmans, Green, and Co., 1966.

Lewis, Diane K.  "The Multicultural Education Model and Minorities: Some Reservations". <u>Anthropology and Education Quarterly</u> 7 (4), Nov. 1976: 32-37.

Llabre, Maria M., William B. Ware, and John M. Newell. "A Factor Anal- ytic Study of Children's Self-Concept in Three Ethnic Groups." Paper presented at the Annual Meeting of the National Council on Measurement in Education, April, 1977.

Massad, Carolyn Emrick. "The Developing Self: World of Communication." In K. Yamamoto (ed.). <u>The Child and His Image</u>. N.Y.: Houghton and Mifflin, 1972, 26-53.

McLaughlin, Milbrey Wallin.  "Implementation as Mutual Adaptation: Change in Classroom Organization." <u>Teachers College Record</u> 77 (3), February 1976:  339-351.

Murphy, Sharon. <u>Other Voices: Black, Chicano, and American Indian</u> <u>Press</u>. Dayton, Ohio: Pflaum/Standard, 1974.

Mussen, Paul and Nancy Eisenberg-Berg.  <u>The Roots of Caring, Sharing,</u> <u>and Helping: The Development of Prosocial Behavior in Children</u>. San Francisco:  W.H. Freeman and Co., 1977.

Nef, John U. "An Early Energy Crisis and Its Consequences." Scientific American 237 (5), November 1977: 140-142, 146-151.

Paulston, Christina Bratt. Implications of Language Learning Theory for Language Planning: Concerns in Bilingual Education. Arlington, Va.: Center for Applied Linguistics, 1974.

Peckham, Morse. Beyond The Tragic Vision: The Quest for Identity In The 19th Century. N.Y.: Brazillier, 1967.

Ramirez, III, Manuel, and Alfredo Castaneda. Cultural Democracy, Bicognitive Development and Education. N.Y.: Academic Press, 1974.

Richardson, Elwyn S. In The Early World. N.Y.: Pantheon, 1964.

Rivers, Wilga M. "Motivation in Bilingual Programs." In Rudolph C. Troike and Nancy Modiano (eds.). Proceedings of The First Inter-American Conference on Bilingual Education. Arlington, Va.: Center For Applied Linguistics, October 1975, 114-122.

Rivlin, Harry N. "Research and Development in Multicultural Education." In Frank H. Klassen and Donna M. Gollnick (eds.). Pluralism and the American Teacher: Issues and Case Studies. Washington, D.C.: American Association of Colleges for Teacher Education, 1977, 81-113.

Rohlen, Thomas P. "Seishin Kyoiku in a Japanese Bank: A Description of Methods and Consideration of Some Underlying Concepts." In George D. Spindler (ed.). Education and Cultural Process: Toward an Anthropology of Education. N.Y.: Holt, Rinehart and Winston, 1974, 219-229.

Samples, Bob. "Mind Cycles and Learning." Phi Delta Kappan, May 1977: 688-692.

Samples, Bob, Cheryl Charles, Dick Barnhart. The Whole School Book: Teaching and Learning in The Twentieth Century, in press.

Saville-Troike, Murielle. Bilingual Children: A Resource Document. Arlington, Va.: Center For Applied Linguistics, 1973.

Schutz, Alfred. Collected Papers, Vol. II: Studies in Social Theory. The Hague: Martinus Nijhoff, 1964, 91-105.

Seelye, H. Ned. Teaching Culture: Strategies for Foreign Language Educators. Skokie, Illinois: National Textbook Company, 1974.

Seelye, H. Ned. "Self Identity in the Bicultural Classroom." In H. LaFontaine, B. Persley, and L. Golubchick (eds.). Bilingual Education. Wayne, N.J.: Avery Pub. Group, 1978, 290-298.

Seelye, H. Ned, and J. Laurence Day. The Spanish Newspaper. Skokie, Ill.: National Textbook Co., 1974.

Seelye, H. Ned, and Jacqueline H. Wasilewski. "Toward a Taxonomy of Coping Strategies Used in Multicultural Settings." Proceedings of the Rutgers University Graduate School of Education of Education Conference on Intercultural Communication, in press.

Spindler, George D. "Schooling in Schonhausen: A Study of Cultural Transmission and Instrumental Adaptation in An Urbanizing German Village." In George D. Spindler (ed.). Education and Cultural Process: Toward An Anthropology of Education. N.Y.: Holt, Rinehart and Winston, 1974, 230-271.

Stewart, Edward C. Lecture on "Brain Function." Univ. of Southern Calif., Washington Education Center, July 1977.

Stewart, Edward C. Outline of Intercultural Communication. In press.

Taylor, H. "Toward A World University." Saturday Review, 1969: 24-52.

Theroux, Paul. The Great Railway Bazaar: By Train Through Asia. N.Y.: Houghton Mifflin, 1975.

Vonnegut, Kurt, Jr. "Afterword." In Francine Klagsbrun (ed.). Free To Be ... You and Me. N.Y.: McGraw-Hill, 1974.

Watts, Alan W. Psychotherapy East and West. N.Y.: Ballantine, 1969.

Witkin, H. A., C. A. Moore, D. R. Goodenough, and P. W. Cox. "Field-Dependent and Field-Independent Cognitive Styles and Their Educational Implications." Review of Educational Research 47 (1), Winter 1977, 1-64.

CHAPTER 5

TRAINING FOR MULTICULTURAL EDUCATION
COMPETENCIES

## CONTENTS

CHAPTER 5


TRAINING FOR MULTICULTURAL EDUCATION
COMPETENCIES


Margaret D. Pusch, H. Ned Seelye,
and Jacqueline H. Wasilewski


As we have seen, the curriculum offers a variety of opportunities not only to deal directly with our cultural diversity, but to
infuse the perspectives of multiculturalism into different parts of
the student's educational experience.  No curriculum, however, is
worth much more than the teachers who preside over it.  What are the
skills or competencies, then, which teachers need to be effective in
teaching multiculturalism?  Do these competencies differ significantly from other skills needed by professional teachers?  How best
can they be taught?  What kind of training is needed?  These are
questions which will be addressed in this chapter.

Embedded in many if not most people in this society is a naive
but tenacious belief that all one has to do to overcome cultural
differences among people is to bring them together and, rational
animals that they are, they will more or less automatically acquiesce
in if not strive for harmony.  Despite vast evidence to the contrary,
this belief persisted until Amir (1969) and other researchers began to
demonstrate not only that it wasn't true, but that in fact, by itself,
cross-cultural contact is likely to create disharmony.

As a result, it became clear that if we are going to overcome
the barriers raised by cultural differences, we must do so through
conscious effort.  Cross-cultural training was the method developed to
enable people to better manage, consciously and deliberately, the
contact and interaction of culturally different groups and individuals.  It assumes (1) that culturally diverse people are more vulnerable to mutual misunderstanding, mistrust and conflict than those who

are homogeneous, (2) that the reasons why this happens may be defined and comprehended, and (3) that specific methods of education and training can be developed which will better enable people to manage intercultural relationships, thus reducing the misunderstanding, mistrust and conflict. It is further believed that such training provides the individual (1) with skills needed to manage the personal stresses involved in cross-cultural experience, (2) with an expanded self-awareness, and (3) with the kind of knowledge about human existence which is the hallmark of the educated person.

What was needed was something that could get at deeply buried values and culturally conditioned attitudes and beliefs, something that could reach people at both intellectual and emotional levels so as to have direct affect not only on attitudes but on behaviors as well.

As noted earlier, the origins of cross-cultural training lay in the effort to prepare people for immediate entry into other cultures. It was found that new educational approaches were required which offered to the trainees practical concepts and personal skills which could be applied in the face-to-face cross-cultural encounters they would soon be experiencing.

The traditional approach to things cross-cultural has been to study about them, to learn about other countries, other peoples or other groups within one's own society. Even when the imperative became social justice, one learned about empathy, prejudice, discrimination and ethnocentrism, but they remained abstractions. Little was done to relate them to the real attitudes, behaviors and experiences of the students (or teachers) themselves.

Multicultural programs, like most educational activity, are strongly oriented toward knowledge-gathering. Perhaps because learning about something is more manageable, less threatening, and easier to evaluate than actual skill building and performance, teacher training programs in general tend to emphasize the former more than the latter. Searching curriculum materials for negative stereotypes to eliminate and identifying readings that increase knowledge about a given culture are both easy things to do. As multicultural training programs grow in confidence, however, bridges will be built from a knowledge base to a base in experience. Let us take as example the reduction of ethnocentrism.

Social scientists themselves do not fully agree on the correlates of ethnocentrism but there have been a number of theories advanced to explain the differential treatment accorded "ingroup" members and others perceived to be "outgroup." An ambitious review of the postulates concerning this phenomenon is available (LeVine and Campbell, 1972), as is a detailed analysis of ethnocentrism in one specific cultural area, East Africa (Brewer and Campbell, 1976). Counterpart studies exist for many other cultural areas. For example, the ethnocentrism and acculturation of Americans in Guatemala has been studied by Seelye (1969) and Seelye and Brewer (1970). So, after extensive reading in the social science literature, augmented by readings in fiction, autobiography, and poetry (Marquardt, 1969), the prospective multicultural teacher gains a sophisticated awareness of the dynamics of ethnocentrism. Then what? Here is where the bridge to experience needs to be constructed.

One avenue is suggested by Brewer (1977). She observes that the characteristics that classify one as a member of the "outgroup" are not immutable, but that their salience fluctuates. For example, when a group of men are talking together and then are joined by a woman colleague, the fact that the colleague is a woman may affect the subsequent behavior of the men. If, on the other hand, a woman joins a mixed group there probably will be no behavioral effect occurring in the group. In the first instance, sex was considered to be a salient characteristic of outgroup members, while in the second instance it was not. Brewer says that the quality of intercultural exchanges can be improved by reducing the saliency of ingroup-outgroup distinctions in contact situations. "Perhaps the best mechanism for accomplishing this will be to provide individuals with new bases for defining group boundaries that overlap existing group identities" (Brewer, 1977, 28). Brewer goes on to note that the recent hope for easing tensions in Northern Ireland have arisen "not along Catholic-Protestant lines but through an organization formed by mothers from both groups who recognize themselves as a new common interest group."

Teacher training institutions can tackle the problem of how to develop strategies that will reduce ethnocentrism to use in schools. This will require a knowledge of the dynamics of ethnocentrism and a creative invention of activities or strategies that will reduce the relevancy of ethnic background to outgroup membership.

It is in the development of these kinds of experiential strategies that cross-cultural training excells. The question then becomes: how do we draw on cross-cultural training as a resource in aiding prospective (or inservice) teachers in developing needed competencies in multicultural education? Let's look first at the role of the teacher, especially as it is affected by ethnic or cultural background, since it may legitimately be asked: "Is ethnicity itself a competency?"

## ETHNICITY AND THE ROLE OF THE TEACHER

Implementing change, particularly in settings where hostility has characterized teacher-student relations, may not be feasible through either the idealized teacher-student relationships suitable for the monolithic transmission of culture or through many of the human relations techniques recently in vogue. It may be more functional, according to Wolcott (1974), for the teacher in such a situation of "antagonistic acculturation" to regard him- or herself as an enemy and the students as prisoners of war, because of the students' need to "survive and to maintain their own identity in the face of overwhelming odds" (118). The student does not want to "sell out."

One last dimension of the enemy perspective is that few
demands are made of enemy prisoners. Demands are made
explicitly; they are not based on assumptions of shared
values about fair play, individual rights, ultimate purposes, or dignity of office. In a sense behavior between
enemies gives more overt evidence of respecting the other
person's cultural ways than does that between friendly
groups ... (Wolcott, 1974, 420-424.)

And from the bottom of the world comes this Aboriginal voice:

There are those who are very sincere in wanting to help and
teach but remain sincerely wrong. (There is an old saying,
'Sincerity often blinds one's eyes to reality.') Many of
these educators are themselves suffering from culture con-
version, berating their own life style. ... A teacher
should maintain the values of his own culture. ... Many
educators come out of a sense of pity and debt. What
Aboriginal people do not need today is pity from anybody,
but an acceptance of the fact that we are a people equal to
any in the world. I remember in my high school days there
was a teacher who really wanted to help me. He was a bigger hindrance to me than those who did not want to simply
because he pitied me to boredom and almost to death ....
(Brown, 1975, 118).

Can this discouraging situation be ameliorated by recruiting
teachers of the same ethnic culture as the students they teach? A
report to the U.S. Commission of Civil Rights (Cosca, Jackson, et al,
1973) documented in three Southwestern states that teachers as a whole
gave Mexican-American children less favorable attention than they did
Anglo children, but there was no difference between the way Mexican-
American teachers and Anglo teachers treated Mexican-American
students. Laosa's (1974) review of research indicates that "mere
membership in a particular cultural-linguistic group does not insure
superior teaching ability." In some situations, however, teachers who
are culturally similar to the students may be more effective, especially if their knowledge of subject matter, general teaching skills,
etc. are more or less equal (see Modiano, 1973).

In a review of research and development in multicultural education, Rivlin (1977) concludes that

There is no research evidence I have found to justify the
assumption that all members of any ethnic group are sympathetic and understanding in their relationship with children of that group. An upwardly mobile minority teacher may
even resent pupil behavior that reminds him of his own
early background. With the notorious zeal of the convert
he may be more intolerant ... than other ... teachers might
be. ... In a sense, assigning teachers in terms of matching
their ethnic background with that of their children exalts
racial stereotypes to a degree of rigidity only extreme
bigots accept. ... What do we do, moreover, in an urban

school in which almost every class has children from many ethnic groups and some from a mixture of ethnic backgrounds? (106-107).

Parents, when given the choice, almost always opt for the teacher judged to be the more professionally competent, irrespective of ethnic background. But again, what is competence? No one method of teaching has yet been identified to be superior to other methods. In fact, after fifty years of research, there are no educationally significant relationships which are demonstrable between specific teacher skills and student achievement (Heath and Nielson, 1974). An exception to this may well be the linguistic variable of whether the teacher can communicate concepts in a language the student understands (Engle, 1975).

In spite of the lack of correlation between student achievement and teacher enthnicity, there are several compelling reasons to insure that teachers from many ethnic backgrounds are included/recruited. Since there are many different kinds of students, there is a need for teachers of diverse bents and backgrounds to be available as models students can emulate. Exclusion of any ethnic background from visibility in the school is a strong negative statement. Then, too, one fears for the content of multicultural education in the absence of a wide range of cultural backgrounds among the instructional staff.

Teachers display their own cultural assumptions and values in their behavior. They cannot be expected to leave them at the schoolhouse door. A multicultural staff can demonstrate their recognition and acceptance of each other's differences and the importance of those differences as a resource to learning. Teachers can then function as change agents, illuminating values, expressing respect for differences among cultures and mediating between various culture groups. In short, they model behavior that clearly indicates there are ways to expand each person's space to include and learn from diversity.

## COMPETENCIES FOR TEACHERS IN MULTICULTURAL EDUCATION

There is no single list or statement of teacher competencies in this area. Though much has been written about the subject -- the most comprehensive to date are Hunter (1974) and Klassen and Gollnick (1977) -- there is no general agreement as to what the competencies should be. Yet before training institutions can prepare professionals to employ intercultural or multicultural approaches to learning, the trainers must know what skills are needed. It will therefore be useful to draw out of the writings available the most suggestive ideas on the subject.

One can identify five different approaches which have been taken in discussing the criteria for teacher competencies in multicultural education. These are in terms of: (1) personality, (2) affective skills, (3) pedagogical skills, (4) the target student population, and (5) desired student competencies.

1.  Personality. The focus here is on the kind of person who
is socially and psychologically adaptive in a variety of cultural
environments, what Adler (1974) calls the "multicultural man" (meaning
"person"). This person is one who:

     a.   is psychoculturally adaptive; that is, he is situa-
          tional in his relationship to others and his connec-
          tions to culture;

     b.   is ever undergoing personal transitions. He is always
          becoming something different or giving up what he has
          been; yet he is mindful of the grounding he has in his
          own cultural identity;

     c.   maintains indefinite boundaries of the self; the para-
          meters of his identity are neither fixed nor predict-
          able. They are instead responsible to temporary form
          and are open to change.

     Bochner (1973) suggests there is a "mediating" personality, one
which believes in "the common unity of mankind and cultural relativism
of values; and has cognitive flexibility, membership in international
and trans-national social networks, and supra-national reference
groups."

     But these concepts are rather grand and abstract and need to be
made more concrete for the purposes of dealing with something so
practical as teaching competencies. A number of authors have done
this, translating the abstractions into specific skills.

2.  Affective Skills. These are primarily modes of response to
other people and to new and different experiences. Gudykunst (1977)
identifies them as a "third culture perspective" -- the perspective of
someone able to play the mediating role Bochner describes. This
perspective consists of:

     a.   open-mindedness toward new ideas and experiences;

     b.   empathy toward people from other cultures;

     c.   accuracy in perceiving differences and similarities
          between the host culture and one's own;

     d.   nonjudgmentalness, a willingness to describe behavior
          rather than evaluate it;

     e.   astute noncritical observation of one's own and
          other's behavior;

     f.   relationship-building skills;

     g.   freedom from ethnocentricity.

Ruben (1976), somewhat more explicitly, suggests seven behaviors as indicators of intercultural competency, such behaviors as the ability to:

a. express respect and positive regard for another person through eye contact, body posture, voice tone and pitch, and general displays of interest;

b. respond to others in a descriptive, nonevaluating, and nonjudgmental way;

c. recognize the extent to which knowledge is personal in nature (i.e., that one's perceptions of an object have more to do with individual view than with the object itself);

d. put oneself in someone else's place;

e. function in a variety of appropriate roles within group settings, especially those involving both task and relational roles, and the capacity to avoid highly individualistic behaviors which are authoritarian and/or manipulative;

f. govern one's contributions to an interactive situation so that the needs and desires of others play a critical role in defining how the exchange will proceed;

g. react to new and ambiguous situations with little visible discomfort.

3. <u>Pedagogical Skills</u>. Reyes Mazon (1977) deals with the question more in terms of "educational tasks" than competencies. Among the tasks teachers should be expected to perform are: (1) to diagnose and evaluate individual language learning needs and utilize effective testing methods and procedures in a bilingual/bidialectical situation and (2) to utilize paraprofessionals, community members and community resources in the diversification of classroom strategies, the facilitation of individualized and group instruction and peer teaching.

H. Prentice Baptiste, in his article on multicultural education at the University of Houston (1977), identified 18 more specifically pedagogical competencies, of which the following is a sample.

The teacher for multicultural education should indicate the ability to:

a. demonstrate a basic knowledge of the contribution of minority groups in America to all mankind;

b. acquire, evaluate, adapt, and develop materials appropriate to the multicultural classroom;

    c.    recognize and accept both the language spoken in the home and the standard language as valid systems of communication, each with its own legitimate functions;

    d.    assist students to maintain and extend identification with and pride in the mother culture.

Gay (1977) categorizes the curricular-related competencies in this manner: knowledge (contents, philosophy, classroom dynamics, ethnic resource materials); attitudes (toward cultural diversity, self awareness, sense of security about teaching cultural diversity); and skill components (cross-cultural interaction, multicultural curriculum development, multi-ethnic instructional strategies). Gay's article is replete with rich detail illustrating the kind of content designed to increase teacher sensitivities.

Joyce and Weil (1972) provide a useful overview of 16 cognitive models (inductive, jurisprudential, concept attainment, group investigation, non-directive, operant conditioning, etc.) along with a succinct statement of the pedagogic goal each model lends itself to. For example, William Gordon's synectics model is seen as relevant to "personal development of creativity and creative problem-solving."

While the bilingual education literature highlights language fluency as a highly critical teacher competency, few writers in multicultural education pay much attention to it. One notable exception is Condon and Yousef (1975). At the conclusion of their excellent book, they discuss a number of questions frequently asked about intercultural communication. It is significant that the first four deal with variations of the issue of how much knowledge of the other person's (or culture's) language must one know for effective communication. While the authors hedge somewhat in their reply, they do recognize the importance of language as a tool in penetrating another culture.

    4.    <u>Target Student Populations</u>. Saville-Troike (1973) offers competencies and training procedures for people involved in early childhood bilingual programs. She says, for example, that personnel working in an early childhood program with limited English-speaking children should:

    a.    understand and make provisions for culturally determined and differing concepts of (a) what order is, (b) acceptable dimensions of action and noise, and (c) perspectives on time and space;

    b.    understand how information is transmitted formally and informally in the community; and

    c.    recognize the potential biases for linguistic and culturally diverse children in existing tests for intelligence, language and concept development.

5. <u>Desired Student Competencies</u>. Turning to what teachers should teach their students, Seeyle (1970, 1974) identifies seven areas of intercultural learning in which he believes students should be able to demonstrate competency.

     a. The functionality, of culturally conditioned behavior. The student should demonstrate an understanding that people generally act the way they do because they are using options the society allows for satisfying basic physical and psychological needs.

     b. Interaction of language and social variables. The student should demonstrate an understanding that social variables such as age, sex, social class, and place of residence affect the way people speak and behave.

     c. Conventional behavior in common situations. The student should be able to demonstrate how people conventionally act in the most common mundane and crisis situations in the target culture.

     d. Cultural connotations of words and phrases. The student should indicate an awareness of the culturally conditioned images associated with the most common target words and phrases.

     e. Evaluating statements about a culture. The student should demonstrate the ability to make, evaluate, and refine generalities concerning the target culture.

     f. Researching another culture. The student should show that he has developed the skills needed to locate and to organize information about the target culture from library holdings, the mass media, people, and personal observation.

     g. Attitudes toward other societies. The student should demonstrate intellectual curiosity about the target culture, and empathy toward its people.

The question here is: should the teacher be able to demonstrate the same skills as the students to which they are being taught. If the answer is yes -- as it seems obvious it should be -- then Seelye's list can be extremely valuable.

All of these discussions of multicultural competency are useful in identifying those most applicable to a particular environment or situation. Most preservice or inservice training must be adjusted to meet the needs of particular locales. One recent study of teacher training programs for bilingual education (Migdail, 1976) found that the perceived inservice needs of teachers varied considerably region to region. It is clear that training institutions will profit from dialogue with their client schools. So much of effective teaching stems from experience, from knowledge gained from the active practice of teaching. This is why the Banks Street College of Education in New York City has designed its entire teacher training curriculum around "interning" with master teachers. A new teacher training program in the Chiapas (Mexico) Highlands is also experimenting with the master-apprentice relationship as a training vehicle which builds upon the propensity of highland Indians to prefer an observational rather than a verbal mode of learning (Modiano, 1975). Many kinds of complicated behavior are learned best by emulation, by copying a model, or at least by active participation in an appropriate simulation.

Where does this leave us? A final, undisputed compilation of competencies has yet to emerge from the fields of intercultural communication or multicultural education. Clearly, however, we must look to both affective and teaching (pedagogic) skills, though the teaching competencies are those which best develop in the student the affective skills and attitudes of mind needed for effective functioning in a multicultural environment. While there is marked variation in approach and content among the commentators who are cited, common strains do exist. Being able to suspend judgment, observe and interpret culturally determined behaviors, tolerate ambiguity, and perceive the differences and similarities that exist between cultures are skills which appear repeatedly in the literature in one form or another. Accepting the relativity of culture, building cultural self-awareness, and developing respect for other cultures are equally prevalent. Developing these abilities and attitudes and incorporating them into a communicative style that transcends cultural barriers is a principal aim of cross-cultural training.

## THE NATURE OF CROSS-CULTURAL TRAINING

The overall goal of cross-cultural training is to provide a framework within which people can develop skills and acquire the knowledge that increases their ability to function effectively in a bi- or multicultural environment and to derive satisfaction from the intercultural experience. It fosters sensitivity to, appreciation of and respect for all cultures. It is an affirming experience and this affirmation works to reinforce the role and position of minority groups in a pluralistic society. It functions to reduce tensions and build bridges among people of different cultural backgrounds. It also places heavy stress on the learning potential available in intercultural encounters, ways of taking advantage of those opportunities and the acceptance of cultural diversity as a human resource rather than merely as an impediment to communication (Stewart, 1973).

It must not be forgotten, of course, that the individual exists within one or more larger culture groups and that these groups (or communities or nations) have complex relationships between and among themselves. The individual, however, is the unit one trains. That individual is, therefore, the focus of cross-cultural training.

More specifically, the goals of cross-cultural training as they emerge from our analysis of intercultural communication and multicultural education may be summarized as follows (for a discussion of goals specific to international cross-cultural training programs, see Adler and Warren, 1977):

1. <u>To expand cultural awareness</u>, to provide the student or trainee with an understanding of his or her own culture and of the degree to which he or she is conditioned by it.

2. <u>To increase tolerance and acceptance of different values, attitudes and behaviors</u>.

3. <u>To foster the affirmation of all cultures</u>, especially those which because of minority status have received a disproportionate amount of negative reinforcement from the society as a whole.

4. <u>To develop intercultural communication skills</u>, cultural and, as called for, linguistic.

5. <u>To integrate cognitive and affective (or experiential) learning</u> so that our intellectual understanding of cultural differences and acceptance of another culture's validity is congruent with our emotional response and behavior in the actual cross-cultural contact.

6. <u>To prepare for effective personal adjustment</u> to the stresses of intercultural experience such as disorientation, weakened self-esteem, culture shock, frustration, anger, etc.

7. <u>To open avenues of learning and growth</u> which inter- or multicultural experience makes accessible.

8. <u>To develop the ability to seek information</u> about the economic, political and social stresses and the aspirations of various culture or ethnic groups within a society and in the international arena.

There are two orientations, though not mutually exclusive, to the process of cross-cultural training. One stresses learning the language and acquiring information about a specific culture -- the values, the behavior patterns and the prevalent attitudes -- all of which can be used upon entering that culture. The second emphasizes learning the basic <u>processes</u> of intercultural communication, the understanding of which may then be used in any intercultural encounter. The first is usually referred to as "culture-specific training;" the second as "culture-general training." The merits of these two approaches have been argued in the profession for a number of years. Should one study the culture of India or Brazil or Chicanos if that culture group is the one with whom one plans to interact? Or should one study the basic principles and learn the basic skills of intercultural communication and cross-cultural human relations which may then be applied to <u>any</u> cross-cultural interaction?

It has been our experience that attention to the basic principles and skills (culture general) is fundamental to all cross-cultural training. By becoming familiar with the basic concepts, issues and skills that have general application, a framework is provided for the trainee into which culture-specific information can be integrated. One can, therefore, become aware of one's own cultural conditioning and discover ways to learn about other cultures while acquiring skills useful in the intercultural experience.

Within the two broad orientations to training mentioned above, several models are available. Adler (1977) lists four, the "practical-functional approach," "the cognitive-didactic approach," "the affective-personal approach," and "the experiential approach." The limitations of the cognitive-didactic approach have already been discussed although we note that some innovative training techniques have been developed by those who employ this traditional model. "Cultural Assimilators," one example of such techniques, are described in the strategy section of this manual.

The practical-functional model is analogous to criterion refer-enced instruction (CRI) used to train Peace Corps volunteers (Peace Corps, 1973). Sometimes called "training by objectives," CRI focuses on the preparation of trainees to perform specific, practical tasks in a second culture but deals extensively with the relationship of cul-ture to task performance and the problems of personal adjustment.

The theoretical basis of the affective-personal approach comes largely from the human relations movement in the United States and many of its techniques are drawn from sensitivity, encounter and T-group methodologies. Experimentation with this method occurred early in the development of cross-cultural training and is used less today. Our reservations with this approach are detailed in the intro-duction to the strategies.

We favor the experiential approach which stresses the importance of both cognitive and affective techniques for learning and views both as important. In this method of cross-cultural training there is an emphasis on learning both information and skills as well as on the creative integration of the two. Hereafter, our use of the term cross-cultural training presupposes that it is experiential, with a culture-general orientation, yet with information about specific cultures often included.

Cross-cultural training tends to be relatively directive and structured. Definite objectives and goals are established, concrete information is provided that can be discussed in small groups and experiential learning techniques are used to illuminate cognitive materials and produce new insights. More detailed consideration of those techniques may be found in the "Strategies" section of this manual. Emphasis is placed on interaction and communication among participants (often in small groups) and with training staff. The learning model is informal and affective since the learning is expect-ed to come from the interaction between participants rather than from studying about other cultures. For this reason, it is desirable that the participant group be multicultural in composition.

It is also important that the participants have a cognitive framework within which to classify and organize their experiences. During relatively brief training programs (from several days to two weeks), short lectures, exercises, simulations, case studies, group discussion and other techniques are sequenced in a manner that allows participants to explore cultural issues themselves and allows the instructor to establish theoretical foundations and forge linkages between theory and experience. During a longer program, library research, assigned readings, and other more extended strategies can be employed. (One of the better models for intercultural education is outlined in <u>Cross-Cultural Learning and Self Growth</u> by Mildred Sikkema and Agnes Niyekawa Howard. The authors describe a two-term academic program for social workers which combines solid theoretical preparation with an unstructured immersion experience in the culture of the Pacific island of Guam.)

In either situation, using the participants' experience as a learning resource, practicing skills that are useful to intercultural communication and helping participants develop the ability to extract learning from any intercultural situation should be underscored. No course or program can anticipate and provide everything that participants may need to know. Information or "facts" rapidly become outdated in a changing society and a changing world. The best that these programs can do is to prepare participants to find out what they need to know for themselves.

Teacher trainers should be familiar with the spectrum of training methodologies and be comfortable and creative in their use. They should have a firm grasp of basic theoretical concepts in communication, perception, culture, cross-cultural adjustment and intercultural learning. In addition, they should know their own culture and how it influences their attitudes and behavior. Finally, they should be as familiar as possible with the cultural backgrounds of their trainees.

The purpose of this chapter has been to introduce the process and goals of cross-cultural training and the competencies necessary to effectiveness in multicultural settings. Heightened sensitivity to the manifestations of culture in all aspects of human endeavor is an important factor in being able to adequately analyze and effectively respond to the dynamics that are present in cross-cultural relations. It does not always insure that one will "know" what is occurring in a particular situation but being able to recognize when the cultural dynamics are not understood is nearly as important as being able to analyze them correctly. It is a step toward discovering what is present and how to change one's approach to similar situations in the future. Another issue that arises in cross-cultural training is, having learned what is expected in another culture, whether an individual actually wants to adjust his or her behavior to meet those expectations. It is often necessary to search for ways to respond that are acceptable but personally comfortable, ways that do not require changes people are unable or unwilling to make in themselves.

Training has been dealt with as if it occurs in a separate and discreet program, additional to other training or educational programs that may be provided for the trainee/student. Many of the people who will be using this manual, however, will most likely incorporate the strategies and concepts into courses that are already available. It is not possible to make specific recommendations for how this may be done. The concepts and techniques that have been discussed can be used in many courses that are currently being offered with thought as to how they relate to each subject and can be coherently integrated into the course structure. It is the job of the individual instructor to determine how this can be accomplished.

# REFERENCES

Amir, Yehuda. "Contact Hypothesis in Ethnic Relations." Psychological Bulletin. Vol. 71, No. 8; May, 1969.

Adler, Peter and David Warren. "An Experiential Approach to Instruction in Intercultural Communication." Communication Education, Volume 26, March, 1977.

Adler, P.S. "Beyond Cultural Identity: Reflections Upon Cultural and Multicultural Man." Topics in Culture Learning, 2, 1974.

Barna, LaRay. "Stumbling Blocks To Intercultural Communication." Readings in Intercultural Communication, Volume 1, D. Hoopes (ed.) Pittsburgh, Pa.: The Intercultural Communication Network, 1975.

Batchelder, Donald. "Preparation For Cross-Cultural Experience." Beyond Experience, D. Batchelder and E. Warner (eds.). Brattlesboro, Vt.: Experiment in International Living, 1977.

Baptiste, H. Prentice, Jr. "Multicultural Education Evolvement At The University of Houston: A Case Study. In Frank H. Klassen and Donna M. Gollnick (eds.). Pluralism and the American Teacher: Issues and Case Studies. Washington, D.C.: American Association of Colleges for Teacher Education, 1977.

Blubaugh, Jon A. and Dorthy L. Pennington. Crossing Difference ... Interracial Communication. Columbus, OH.: Charles E. Merrill Publishing Co., 1976.

Bochner, S. "The Mediating Man and Cultural Diversity." Topics in Culture Learning, Vol. 1, 1973: 23-27.

Brewer, Marilynn B., and Donald T. Campbell. Ethnocentrism and Intergroup Attitudes: East African Evidence. N.Y.: Wiley, 1976.

Brewer, Marilynn B. "Perceptual Processes in Cross-Cultural Interaction." In Overview of Intercultural Education, Training and Research: Volume 1, Theory. Edited by D.S. Hoopes, P.B. Pederson, and G.W. Renwick. LaGrange Park, IL.: Intercultural Network, 1977, 22-31.

Brown, Robert. "Education: A New Start in a Different Direction." In Education in Melanesia: The Eighth Waigani Seminar, Canberra, Australia: The Research School of Pacific Studies, The Australian National University, (and the University of Papua New Guinea, Port Moresby), 1975, 117-120.

Condon, John C. and Fathi Yousef. An Introduction to Intercultural Communication. Indianapolis, IN.: Bobbs-Merrill, 1975.

Cosca, Cecilia E., Greg B. Jackson, et al. Teachers and Students: Differences in Teacher Interaction with Mexican American and Anglo Students. Report V: Mexican American Education Study. Washington, D.C.: U.S. Government Printing Office, 1973.

Engle, Patricia Lee. The Use of Vernacular Languages in Education: Language Medium in Early School Years for Minority Language Groups. Arlington, Va.: Center For Applied Linguistics, 1975.

Gay, Geneva. "Curriculum For Multicultural Teacher Education." In Frank H. Klassen and Donna M. Gollnick (eds.). Pluralism and the American Teacher: Issues and Case Studies. Washington, D.C.: American Association of Colleges for Teacher Education, 1977, 31-62.

Gudykunst, W. B., R. L. Wiseman and M. Hammer. "Determinants of the Sojourner's Attitudinal Satisfaction." Communication Yearbook 1, B. Ruben (ed.). New Brunswick, N.J.: Transaction-International Communication Association, 1977.

Hanvey, Robert G. An Attainable Global Perspective. New York, N.Y.: Center for Global Perspectives, nd.

Heath, R. W. and M. A.. Nielson. "The Research Basis For Performance-Based Teacher Ed." Review of Educational Research 44, 1974: 463-484.

Hunter, William A., (ed.). Multicultural Education Through Competency-Based Teacher Education. Washington, D.C.: American Association of Colleges for Teacher Education, 1974.

Jaramillo, Mari-Luci Ulibarri. In-Service Teacher Education in a Tri-Ethnic Community: A Participant-Observer Study. Ph.D. dissertation, University of New Mexico, 1970.

Jaramillo, Mari-Luci Ulibarri. "Public School Education in a Pluralistic Society: Problems of Program Implementation." Paper Presented at the Cubberly Conference in Cultural Pluralism held at Stanford University, October, 1973.

Joyce, B. and M. Weil. Models of Teaching. Englewood Cliffs, N.J.: Prentice Hall, 1972.

Kagan, Jerome. "The Baby's Elastic Mind." Human Nature 1 (1), January 1978: 66-73.

Kahler, Erich. Out of the Labyrinth: Essays in Clarification. N.Y.: Brazillier, 1967.

Klassen, Frank H. and Donna M. Gollnick (eds.). Pluralism and the American Teacher: Issues and Case Studies. Washington, D.C.: American Association of Colleges for Teacher Education, 1977.

Laosa, Luis M.  "Toward a Research Model  of Multicultural Competency-Based Teacher Education."  In Multicultural Education Through Competency-Based  Teacher  Education.  W.A.  Hunter  (ed.). Washington, D.C.:  American Association of Colleges for Teacher Education, 1974.

LeVine, Robert A.  and Donald T. Campbell.  Ethnocentrism: Theories of Conflict, Ethnic Attitudes and Group Behavior.  N.Y.:  Wiley, 1972.

Marquardt, William F.  "Creating Empathy through Literature between the Members of the Mainstream Culture and the Disadvantaged Learners of the Minority Culture."  Florida FL Reporter 7 (1), 1969.

Modiano, Nancy.  Indian Education In The  Chiapas Highlands.  N.Y.: Holt, Rinehart and Winston, 1973.

Modiano,  Nancy.  "Using  Native  Instructional  Patterns  for Teacher Training: A Chiapas Experiment."  In Rudolph C. Troike and Nancy Modiano  (eds.),  Proceedings  of  the  First  Inter-American Conference on Bilingual Education.  Arlington, Va.:  Center For Applied Linguistics, 1975, 347-355.

Morris, Van Cleve  and Young Pai.  Philosophy and the American School: An Introduction to the Philosophy of Education.  Boston, Ma.: Houghton Mifflin, 1976.

Peace Corps Program  and Training Manual, Vol. 1,  No. 6.  Washington, D.C.:  Planning  Group,  International  Relations,  ACTION,  June, 1973.

Reyes Mazon, M.  "Community,  Home,  Cultural  Awareness  and Language Training:  A  Design  For  Teacher  Training  in  Multicultural Education."  In Frank H. Klassen and Donna M. Gollnick (eds.). Pluralism  and  the  American  Teacher:  Issues  and  Case  Studies. Washington, D.C.:  American Association of Colleges for Teacher Education, 1977, 81-113.

Rivlin, Harry N. "Research and Development in Multicultural Education." In Frank H. Klassen and Donna M. Gollnick (eds.).  Pluralism and the  American  Teacher:  Issues  and  Case  Studies.  Washington, D.C.: American Association of Colleges for Teacher Education, 1977, 81-113.

Ruben, Brent D.   "Assessing Communication Competency for Intercultural Adaptation."  Group and Organization Studies.  September, 1976.

Ruben,  Brent D.,  Lawrence R. Askling  and  Daniel J. Kealey.  "Cross-Cultural Effectiveness." in Overview of Intercutural Education, Training and Research, Vol. I: Theory, D. Hoopes, P. Peterson & G. Renwick (eds.).  Washington, D.C.:  SIETAR, 1977.

Saville-Troike,  Murielle.  Bilingual  Children:  A Resource Document. Arlington, Va.: Center For Applied Linguistics, 1973.

Seelye, H. Ned.   "An Objective Measure of Biculturation:  Americans in
Guatemala, A Case Study."  The Modern Language Journal 53 (7),
Nov. 1969:  503-514.

Seelye, H. Ned.   "Performance Objectives for Teaching Cultural
Concepts."  Foreign Language Annals 3 (4), May 1970: 566-578.

Seelye, H. Ned.   Teaching Culture:  Strategies for Foreign Language
Educators.  Skokie, Illinois: National Textbook Company, 1974.

Seelye, H. Ned, and Marilynn B. Brewer.   "Ethnocentrism and Acculturation of North Americans in Guatemala."  Journal of Social
Psychology 80, April 1970: 147-155.

Singer, Marshall R.  "Culture:  A Perceptual Approach."  In Readings in
Intercultural Communication Vol. 1, D. Hoopes (ed.).  Pittsburgh,
Pa.:  Intercultural Communications Network, 1975.

Smith, M. Brewster.   "Attitudes and Adjustments in Cross-Cultural
Contact."  The Journal of Social Issues, XII, No. 1, 1956.

Stewart, Edward C.   American Cultural Patterns:  A Cross-Cultural
Perspective. Washington, D.C.:  SIETAR, 1971.

Stewart, Edward C.   "Dimensions in Cross Cultural Instruction."
Presentation at International Communication Convention, April,
1973.

Wolcott, Harry F.   "The Teacher As Enemy."  In George D. Spindler,
(ed.).  Education and Cultural Process:  Toward an Anthropology
of Education.  N.Y.:  Holt, Rinehart and Winston, 1974, 411-425.

CHAPTER 6

TEACHING STRATEGIES:  THE METHODS AND TECHNIQUES OF
CROSS-CULTURAL TRAINING

CONTENTS

CHAPTER 6


TEACHING STRATEGIES:  THE METHODS
AND TECHNIQUES OF CROSS-CULTURAL TRAINING


David S. Hoopes and Margaret D. Pusch


This chapter is concerned with specific educational methods and
techniques through which students in teacher training may be prepared
to function more effectively as teachers in a multicultural
educational system and as persons in a plural society.

The function of training exercises and of the techniques we have
collected here is to introduce an element of experience into the
learning process.  This is particularly important in cross-cultural
training and education for two reasons:

(1)  The concepts, terms and, for many people, the experience of
intercultural communication and interpersonal relations across
cultures  are so unfamiliar that they must be made as vivid as
possible during a training or educational program.

(2)  It is at the affective level that the learning must take
place if it is to have an impact on behavior -- the ultimate aim
of the educational experience.

There are other advantages in using experiential learning
techniques.  They provide for an immediate application of theory or,
conversely, they provide an experience on which to base a discussion
of theoretical questions.  Simply stated, they offer an immediate test
of cognitive learning rather than waiting for life, probably some
years hence, to offer a confirming experience.  Another advantage is
that experiential learning engages more of the person in the
educational process.

While there are a number of objections still raised to experience-based learning, it is becoming increasingly accepted. Ruben and Budd (1975) in the introduction to their excellent Human Communication Handbook provide a thorough examination of the issues which cluster around the use of affective learning exercises. It is our experience that these methods are very effective in both monocultural and multicultural groups when sensitively used for the purpose of intercultural learning.

There is a difference, however, in the learning process that occurs in groups composed of members from a single culture and in those that are multicultural. In the former there is a greater need to simulate cultural differences around which to build the learning. In multicultural groups the differences are immediately and sometimes explosively present in the group. The challenge is to find ways to use the interaction of people from different cultures as the learning base. This requires, of course, different approaches and adjustments in the application of these methods. The simpler exercises which provoke mild feelings and responses are often quite sufficient as stimuli to learnings in a multicultural classroom.

One of the special qualities of cross-cultural training and multicultural education is that you are engaged with the essentials of human difference and diversity and there is a necessary tentativeness about everything you do or say. Culture is too complex; oversimplification is a constant danger. So is the tendency to stereotype, ironic when displayed by a cross-cultural teacher or trainer. There is an inclination (if you're good) to feel you must always start at square one, ridding yourself of all your assumptions and preconceptions. This is particularly true when the group is multicultural. Nothing is given. The givens have to be drawn out in the learning process -- indeed, a strength of education and training in a multicultural group lies in the fact that this 'drawing out' is part of the learning itself.

The instructor needs, perhaps above all else, to be flexible. No matter how much time is devoted to preparation, there will be surprises. This is especially true in a multicultural group. Some cross-cultural trainers argue against making specific program plans at all, depending instead on a general concept and an arsenal of techniques. This is not feasible -- and probably quite undesirable -- in a formal educational environment. In any event, alternative plans should be readily available. Further, specific exercises may not always produce the intended learning. Though unexpected, the learning or learning potential that emerges is likely to be no less valuable. It is up to the instructor to roll with the punches and be able to capitalize on whatever happens. The participants and their learning should not be sacrificed to an exercise or to a program expectation.

Talk is crucial in cross-cultural education, particularly in multicultural classes. Acquiring new knowledge during these programs is largely dependent on the participants' abilities to articulate their thoughts and feelings. This may be a problem for people from less verbal cultures. Some people feel that cross-cultural training is, in fact, culturally biased in favor of those who are more articulate. This means that the role of the instructor as communication facilitator is especially important -- the participants are resources to each other and their interaction must be facilitated. There are those who like neither the term nor the role. "Facilitator" is often associated with sensitivity training and encounter groups and carries the stigma which has been attached to these programs in some circles. We do not use the term here in the encounter group sense. By facilitator we mean "one who assists, sustains and advances the communication and learning of the participants."

How then should the exercises in this section be used? First, they should not be strung together in a series of disconnected experiences. They should be used in contexts which give them meaning and impact. Second, they should be imbedded in discussion. Third, excessive use of exercises should be avoided. Time is better spent in the selection and extensive processing of a few particularly effective activities or in using other learning methods.

Cross-cultural training and education can take place in virtually any setting, from sophisticated learning centers with elaborate equipment to the average garden variety classroom. One thing important, particularly in multicultural groups, is that every effort should be made to identify the site as neutral territory. Any multicultural event will take on the characteristics of the dominant culture (any culture that is dominant in number for that occasion) unless it is deliberately programmed to be multi- or cross-cultural. Maintaining a sense of cultural equality for purposes of learning is critical to multicultural education. Establishing the neutrality of the setting is an important step toward achieving true multiculturalism within the training program. Achieving this neutrality may be difficult in the average classroom where the atmosphere is determined by other factors, but it is worth a try.

# PERCEPTION

One of the most enjoyable phases of cross-cultural training is that which focuses on perception. Demonstrating how deceptive the perception process can be is both easy and fun. There are many visual aids (Ruben and Budd, 1975). One of the best is the "Ambiguous Lady," used here. It is so good, in fact, and is so widely used that it is in danger of being over exposed. It is one of the most effective ways to translate perceptual theory into practical learning at the feeling level. After a brief introduction to the theory, the "Ambiguous Lady" brings the group into the presentation with laughter and learning.

"Predicting Attitudes" can be enjoyable too, this time as people recognize their tendency to project their own attitudes and expectations onto others.

The literature on perception is replete with other devices that engage peoples' emotions as well as their intellect in comprehending the implications of perceptual theory. The individual instructor can adapt these to his or her needs.

# AMBIGUOUS LADY

## OBJECTIVE

To illustrate that we "select" what we see and do not understand or shift easily to a different point of view.

## PARTICIPANTS

Almost any size group.

## MATERIALS

"Ambiguous Lady" or another perception picture. It is very effective to screen the picture from an overhead projector, though having a copy to give to each student also has advantages.

## SETTING

No special requirements except that everyone should be able to see the picture with little difficulty.

## TIME

Varies with the group. The facilitator should move this exercise at a pace that keeps participants interested but insures that everyone sees both pictures and is able to express his or her reactions. Approximately 30 minutes.

## PROCEDURE

1. Show the picture to a group for a brief period (about 10 seconds) and ask everyone to write down what they saw.

2. Have group members tell each other what they saw. Usually people see one or the other women (young or old) although occasionally someone will see both, perhaps because they have seen the picture before. It is useful to ask if anyone has seen this picture and suggest they wait until others have discussed the picture before sharing their earlier experience.

3. Have people who saw the "old woman" describe her to the others as they look at the picture again. Check to determine if everyone is beginning to see the old woman. Use the same procedure for the young woman.

4. Ask how they feel or felt when they cannot see the "other" woman. If feelings of being "dumb" or "stupid" are expressed, point out the similarity between this response in a rather simple exercise and the discomfort that is experienced when a person enters an unfamiliar cultural environment where others perceive things he or she doesn't. Also point out that studies have shown that young people tend to see the young lady and older people, the old lady.

5.  The discussion during and following
center around how we select out of our perceptu~
want to see and that it is sometimes difficu~
are obviously there.  Discuss ideas from perce~
we select our perceptions, what the influence o~
is, what results in terms of sterotyping and o~
responses, and what can be done about it.  By using t~
exercise, differences in perception and the feelings tha~
when those differences are not understood can be
experienced, explored and generalized to other situations.
provides a common experience within the group that sets the st~
discussing individual experiences.  These experiences should rela~
an inability to recognize or to comprehend how different people ~
groups of people select data, evaluate it and respond to a given
situation or set of conditions.

Source:  Based on an exercise used in Intercultural Communication
Workshops by the Intercultural Network, Inc.

# PREDICTION AND PERCEPTION

To explore the manner in which misperception about a person and what that person will do results from making judgments and predictions based on insufficient information.

## PARTICIPANTS

Group of 10 or fewer persons.

## MATERIALS

Chalkboard or sheets of newsprint.

## SETTING

Classroom or other meeting room.

## TIME

Forty-five minutes to one hour.

## PROCEDURE

1. Ask for volunteer "subject" from the group. Instructor may use him- or herself if not too well known personally to the group.

2. Group may ask five questions of the subject (only five questions from the total group are permitted, not five questions from each participant).

3. Group members are then asked to write down their individual judgments as to:

    a. aspects of the subject's personal background (three to five items) such as place of birth (city or country), economic status of the family, profession of father and/or mother, where the person attended school, family size, etc.

    b. predictions as to the person's cultural or recreation preferences (music, art, sports, etc.), opinions about significant social issues (desegregation, restriction of Mexican immigration, rights of homemakers, etc.), and actions the person would take in certain circumstances (being fired arbitrarily from a job, hearing a woman scream "rape," watching a fight between groups of students in a school, etc.).

The instructor can provide specific examples of issues on which to make predictions or allow group members to select their own.

4. Ask some of the participants to read their judgments and predictions to the group and discuss why they made them.

5. Ask the subject to tell the group about his or her personal background and attitudes and, as much as possible, estimate what he or she would do under the circumstances that were presented. This should be dealt with cautiously. There may be some ambivalence about how the subject feels he or she might act or even in how strongly opinions or attitudes are held. Being sensitive to this is important and also provides an opportunity for discussing the problems involved in making accurate or "final" judgments and predictions about people.

6. The discussion that concludes this exercise focuses on these questions:

How accurate were the predictions and perceptions?

How did they reflect the attitudes of the predictors?

What information or cues were used by the participants to form judgments or make predictions?

Did any stereotyping occur?

How frequently in real life do we make judgments and predictions on the basis of insufficient information?

<u>Source:</u> Adapted from "Prediction and Interpersonal Perception," <u>Readings</u> in Intercultural Communication, Volume V, David S. Hoopes, editor.

## CULTURAL SELF-AWARENESS

How do you know when you have reached a state of cultural self-awareness? It is basically an internal, personal experience (though it can be identified ultimately in behaviors). Therefore, the exercises included here are directed inward, designed to help individuals assess themselves. It enhances the learning if responses are shared, but it is important to make it clear that sharing is not required. "Dialogue Within Ourselves" has been constructed to include group discussion but can easily be used privately, by individuals. The main purpose of all of these exercises is to start a thought process within the students.

Actually, a large percentage of any cross-cultural education is directed at stimulating cultural self-awareness. This is particularly true of the exercises grouped under "Values." You will find, in fact, that the expansion of cultural self-awareness is intended to be a side-effect of almost every strategy chosen for inclusion here.

# INTERCULTURAL LEARNING CONTINUUM

OBJECTIVE

To help students become more aware of the intercultural learning process and how they have moved along it. (See page 18.)

PARTICIPANTS

Any number.

MATERIALS

Pencil, continuum chart.

SETTING

No special requirements.

TIME

30-45 minutes.

PROCEDURE

1. Ask each person to write three culture or ethnic groups in spaces provided at the top of the chart (could be limited to those represented in the class or group if there are enough).

2. Then instruct participants to place themselves on the continuum according to where they feel they are relative to each of the culture or ethnic groups.

3. Ask participants to look back and see if they can remember any events or points in time at which they moved from one stage to the next relative to each culture.

Looking ahead where would they ultimately like to get to with each culture -- and why.

4. Divide into subgroups for discussion of the charts, then have general discussion in large group.

## DISCUSSION

Focus on illuminating the intercultural learning process and how it helps the students understand better where they are personally in relation to other cultures and how they can analyze the learning process others (their future students for example) are experiencing. Lively and illuminating discussion can be developed out of reactions to the last five items. The intercultural learning process may also be fruitfully compared and contrasted with James Bank's "Stages of Ethnicity" which are: (1) Ethnic Psychological Captivity; (2) Ethnic Encapsulation; (3) Biethnicity; (4) Multiethnicity or Pan-Humanism. (See page 21).

Source: Developed by trainers of the Intercultural Network, Inc.

## INTERCULTURAL LEARNING CONTINUUM

| CULTURE/ETHNIC GROUPS | | | |
|---|---|---|---|
| Ethnocentrism | | | |
| Awareness | | | |
| Understanding | | | |
| Acceptance/respect | | | |
| Appreciation/valuing | | | |
| Selective Adoption | | | |
| Assimilation | | | |
| Adaptation | | | |
| Biculturalism | | | |
| Multiculturalism | | | |

# SELF-ASSESSMENT OF MULTICULTURAL EDUCATION SKILLS

## OBJECTIVE

To assess the level of competence in skills relevant to working in multicultural education prior to a cross-cultural education program (or a program including cross-cultural training techniques) and to evaluate changes in those skills at the close of the program.

## PARTICIPANTS

Used by individuals in the group. May or may not be shared with others.

## MATERIALS

Assessment instrument and gummed tabs with words or phrases typed on.

## SETTING

No special requirements.

## TIME

Twenty minutes. Discussion time if desired by any of the participants.

## PROCEDURE

At the outset of a course, students are asked to place on a continuum adhesive tabs upon which are printed skills or attitudes which it is important for the student to have when working in the field of multicultural education. When given the tabs, participants are asked to place each on the continuum according to their personal assessment of their skills. Words which they do not recognize or understand should be placed on the lines under "I have no knowledge or understanding of the following."

Participants may wish to discuss their profiles with others in the group for feedback purposes. If so, time should be allotted for this discussion.

At the conclusion of the course, each student is asked to repeat the self-assessment exercise, using a second profile sheet. This provides a check on the degree to which the student feels he or she has progressed during the course.

One word or phrase is placed on each tab. The terms that are used may be selected from the list that follows or may include others that have been chosen to meet the defined objectives of a program or course. Students may want to preceed (mentally) each term with phrases such as "I can ..." or "I am skilled in ..." or "I possess ..." (whichever is appropriate) for clarity. Terms that may be used include:

| | |
|---|---|
| self awareness | openness |
| respect for other cultures | adaptability |
| withholding judgment | tolerance |
| perception checking | cross-cultural analysis |
| overcoming prejudice | comfortable with difference |
| non-verbal communication | awareness of stereotyping |
| bicultural | feeling of self-worth |
| acceptance of diversity | acceptance of cultural pluralism |
| affirmation of own culture | self-knowledge |

non-evaluative feedback

Tabs are placed on the self-assessment instrument according to the person's degree of strength or weakness in each area. This is a personal assessment and need not be discussed or revealed to anyone if the individual prefers to keep it private. The important thing is that the individual be honest with him- or herself.

In some cases, increased understanding of a particular set of concepts in intercultural communication or the experiences in an educational program can result in an individual "lowering" his or her assessment at the close of the course. This should not be viewed with dismay. It may be an indication of new insights and awareness. Those terms that appeared under "I have no knowledge or understanding of the following" should, however, be clarified during the course of the program.

Source: Adapted from a "Self assessment of Leadership Skills" instrument developed by Lowell Ingram, University of Washington.

# SELF ASSESSMENT

## of

## Multicultural Education Skills and Attitudes

```
------------------- Range of Competence -------------------
STRONG                        AVERAGE                       WEAK
   |                             |                            |
   |                             |                            |
   |                             |                            |
   |                             |                            |
```

I have no knowledge or understanding of the following:

1._____

2._____

3._____

4._____

5._____

PROFILE OF ATTITUDES AND FEELINGS

## OBJECTIVE

To provide students in a training program with a profile of their attitudes and feelings about various cultures, persons and concepts.

## PARTICIPANTS

Used by individuals in a group. May or may not be shared with others.

## MATERIALS

Profile Sheet(s) and gummed tabs.

## SETTING

No special requirements.

## TIME

Approximately twenty minutes. Discussion time if desired by the participants.

## PROCEDURE

At the outset of a course, a profile sheet is given to each student. They are told that they will be given a series of words which have been printed on adhesive tabs. They are to place each tab on the instrument in the place which best describes their initial emotional response at the time it is read; it should be placed as much as possible according to free-association or first emotional response without reflection on specific individuals or events.

The various areas on the instrument are then carefully described:

a.  AREA OF IGNORANCE (no contact)
    Have had no contact with the term or group whatsoever and therefore are completely ignorant of it. Exposure through mass media, etc. would preclude placing a tab in this zone.

b.  POSITIVE/COMFORT ZONE
    The word on the tab evokes close, warm and the most positive of feelings.

c.  NEGATIVE ZONE
    The word evokes negative feelings. If a tab is placed at the point of "most negative," it would indicate a total rejection of the word or group.

d.  LINE OF AMBIVALENCE
    If a tab is placed on this line, it means a response of indifference, no opinion one way or the other, neither negative or positive.

-121-

Tabs may be placed at any point along the continuum from most positive to most negative. However, the inner circle or "Comfort Zone" represents feelings that indicate an acceptance into one's own "life space" and of course, if placed at the tip of the arrow at "most negative," represents total and unqualified non-acceptance.

The students are instructed that the exercise is completely private and they will not be required at any time to share the completed profile publicly. It is suggested, however, that they fill it out honestly and discuss with someone any disturbing aspects of the profile. If an individual chooses to share the profile in a group discussion, this is acceptable.

Some terms that may be used for the tabs:

| | | |
|---|---|---|
| foreigners | Japanese | Greeks |
| my family | French-Canadians | Latin Americans |
| God | Blacks | Africans |
| Arabs | Native Americans | Irish-Americans |
| Italians | Puerto Ricans | Anglos |
| Jews | Orientals | poor whites |
| my classmates | Haitians | my neighbors |
| Chicanos | Eskimos | Japanese |
| Chinese | pluralism | freedom |
| equality | honesty | authority |
| nationalism | whites | |

A profile may be made prior to a seminar or workshop and another completed at the end of the program to determine whether or not attitudinal change has taken place on any subject.

Note:  The instructor may want to restrict the terms to culture groups and people. Interesting results can be obtained from including persons identified by profession, i.e. taxi drivers, waitresses, businesspeople (of either gender), doctors, pilots, dentists, construction workers, social workers, teachers, school administrators, etc. The list is endless and should be selective according to the makeup of the group and the particular aims of the exercise.

Source:  Adapted from a Self-Assessment Instrument of Attitudes and Feelings developed by Lowell Ingram, University of Washington.

PROFILE SHEET

AREA OF IGNORANCE (no contact)

LINE OF AMBIVALENCE

most negative

range of attitudes / feelings

most positive

COMFORT ZONE

L. Ingram 3/75

-123-

# DIALOGUE WITHIN OURSELVES

## OBJECTIVE

To gain practice in listening to and making cultural interpretations based on an "internal dialogue" about a cross-cultural issue or experience that has generated ambivalent thoughts and feelings.

## PARTICIPANTS

Small group.

## MATERIALS

Pencil and paper.

## SETTING

A private, quiet place with a writing surface. Class or meeting room.

## TIME

Thirty minutes for writing. Approximately one hour for discussion.

## PROCEDURE

Ask students to do the following:

1. Select a cross-cultural subject or experience which produces ambivalent thoughts and feelings within them. For example, dislike for a person of another culture that the student feels may involve prejudice; an unpleasant experience at another culture group's social event which caused feelings of self-doubt; the advisability of having multicultural education programs; U.S. policy toward the country from which the participant or his/her forebears originally came, etc.

2. Listen to your ambivalent thoughts and feelings, and listen to the two sides of your internal dialogue.

3. Do one of the following:

   a. Describe in writing the two sides of the issue and your feelings of ambivalence about them, or

   b. write down as a script of a play or conversation the dialogue between your internal voices, attempting to identify the emergence of cultural bias.

4. Return to the group.

Instructor can ask for one or two volunteers to read what they have written and discuss this with the class. The discussion should center around the reasons for the ambivalence rather than trying to judge what was "right" or "wrong" in the situation. In fact, any attempt to make judgments should be strongly discouraged.

This exercise can be used individually as well as in a group setting. The number of "dialogues" processed depends upon time available.

Source: Adapted from "Dialogue Within Ourselves," A Manual of Structured Experiences for Cross-Cultural Learning, Weeks, William H., Paul B. Peterson and Richard W. Brislin, Editors, East-West Center Culture Learning Institute, Honolulu, Hawaii.

## HIERARCHY OF NEEDS
## EXERCISE

OBJECTIVE

     To identify personal needs and interests, their level of importance to each individual, how those choices are determined by cultural background and how they relate to social and professional roles.

PARTICIPANTS

     Any size group.

MATERIALS

     Paper and pencil.

SETTING

     No special requirements.

TIME

     Approximately one hour.

PROCEDURE

     Participants are asked to list ten activities they enjoy doing most -- just a word written close to the left edge of the paper so there is plenty of room for what follows.

     The the following instructions are given:

1.    Next to these activities place an "A" if you would usually engage in the activity alone or "P" if with people.

2.    Place an "I" if an inside activity, or an "O" if outside.

3.    Place a "$" if it costs more than $4.00 to do it.

4.    Write "V" if it is primarily verbal or "NV" if non-verbal.

5.    Write "W" if it relates primarily to work or study, and "L" if it is primarily a leisure activity.

6.    Write "HSD" if it demands a high degree of self-disclosure and "LSD" (no pun intended) if low degree of self-disclosure.

7.    Place an "*" if this would not have been on your list two years ago.

8.    Write down the last time you engaged in each.

9.  Write a summary description of yourself from what your responses tell you.

When this procedure has been completed, students are paired and asked to "discuss what you learned about who you are according to your lists and determine a hierarchy of needs for yourself, based on how important you feel each of the items is to you personally."

The pairs return to the large groups after fifteen minutes and a discussion ensues focusing on how students' personal hierarchies have been influenced by their cultural backgrounds and how they relate to professional and/or social roles of each (i.e. teachers, parents, administrators, trainers, etc.)

Source:  Adapted from Values Clarification, Sidney Simon by Dan K. Smith, University of California.

# VALUES

While "perception" is the core idea in intercultural communication, values are the bed rock of culture. Values, value issues, learnings about values inhere in virtually every training exercise. The more we become conscious of the assumptions and values that govern our behavior, the better we are able to deal with the values we encounter in others.

There is no intent in cross-cultural education to have people discard their own values. Indeed, greater understanding of their own value system is an important goal in training programs. The more students and trainees understand about their own value systems, the greater will be their ability to affirm and tolerate themselves. Affirmation of self is a long and necessary step toward acceptance and tolerance of others.

In cross-cultural training, discussions that get directly at the values of the participants in a non-conflictual way are among the most enjoyable and the most deeply moving experiences. The role of the instructor is critical here since he or she must continually demonstrate an attitude of respect for the values of others. The instructor is thus providing a model for the respectful behavior that is expected of the students.

# ASSUMPTIONS AND VALUES CHECKLIST

## OBJECTIVE

To bring different value systems to awareness by comparing the value systems of different cultures and identifying the conscious and unconscious assumptions about man and his world on which their values are based.

## PARTICIPANTS

Any size group.

## MATERIALS

Copies of the Assumptions and Values List, pencils.

## SETTING

No special requirements.

## TIME

Variable, usually about an hour.

## PROCEDURE

The outline provided identifies some of the basic areas in which human beings make the assumptions on which they base their values. It then contrasts two cultures, Mainstream North America and the Philippines, in each of the categories. (The comments on Philippine culture were prepared by a sociologist from the Philippines.)

This analysis is by necessity composed of generalizations. It is recognized that any society or culture-group is composed of personality types of great variety, indeed, probably every variety. What we are concerned with here are those beliefs and patterns of behavior which are most prominent or most widespread and which give a culture its special character.

Participants are provided with copies of the outline and asked to fill in what they feel dominant values are for their own culture-group in each categroy. After the outline has been completed, the information provided by each participant is discussed with emphasis on the differences that have emerged in basic assumptions and the values they produce. Similarities are also considered and why participants think they occur. Mainstream Americans and Filipinos in the class may either critique the classification of their own culture, project themselves into another, or both.

Bringing the differences in value systems to awareness can help participants know themselves and come to better understand some of the cultural differences which confuse them (often unconsciously) when they are encountered in people of other nationalities or culture-groups.

Source: Adapted from Gary L. Althen and Josephine Jaime. "Assumptions and Values in Philippine, American and other cultures," in Readings in Intercultural Communication, Vol. I, David S. Hoopes, editor.

ASSUMPTIONS AND VALUES IN
PHILIPPINE, AMERICAN AND OTHER CULTURES

1. Perception of the Self and the Individual

| | North American | Filipino | Other Culture |
|---|---|---|---|
| A. General perception of self | human being of a particular self | self perceived in context of family | |
| B. Self as point of reference | autonomy encouraged; solve own problems, develop own opinions | dependence encouraged; point of reference is authority, older members of family | |
| C. Nature of man | evil but perfectible; notion of progress: man can change and improve self and it is his responsibility to do so | evil, but there is not too much that can be done "ganyan talaga ang buhay" (such is life) | |
| D. Cultural variation of self-concept | self is identified with in-dividual; behavior aimed at individual goals | point of reference is network of obligations among members of a group summarized in concept of "face"; behavior aimed at preserving group affiliations and maintaining smooth inter-personal relationships | |
| E. Self-reliance | old self-reliance value still upheld (though American often now functions best as member of organization) | dependence not deplored be-cause it strengthens relation-ships among people | |

| | | North American | Filipino | Other Culture |
|---|---|---|---|---|
| II. | Perception of the World | | | |
| A. | Man's relation to nature | man is separate from nature | | man is separate from nature |
| B. | Materialism and Property | clear distinction between public and private property; materialism is important value | public property divertible to private hands with little guilt; spiritual, religious things are more important than material things | |
| C. | Progress related to concept of time | time moves fast, from past, to present, to future; one must keep up with it, use it to change and master environment | time moves slowly; man must integrate himself with the environment, and adapt to it rather than change it | |
| D. | Progress & Optimism in Contrast to Limited Good | optimism exists that there is enough for everybody; economics is final arbiter | peasants only: there exists a finite amount of good that can be divided and redivided but not augmented; therefore phenomenon of sociostat: if one member of a community increases in wealth, he is seen as a threat because of the concomitant loss to other members, tendency for community to pull him down to old level by temporary ostracism | |
| E. | Quantification | stress on measurement and concreteness | stress on qualitative feeling | |
| F. | Comparative Judgments | what is not American is bad | what is not Filipino is different or American; moral judgments not so easily made | |

| | North American | Filipino | Other Culture |
|---|---|---|---|
| **III. Motivation** | | | |
| A. Achievement as Self-motivation | fulfillment in personal achievement; status is achieved | fulfillment in smooth interpersonal relationships; status is ascribed | |
| B. Fragmentation and Totality of Personality | personalities can be fragmented; totality of other person does not need to be accepted in order to be able to work with him | personalities reacted to in their entirety; tendency to accept or reject person completely | |
| C. Competition and Affiliation | competition is primary method of motivation | communal feeling towards one another excludes the incentive to excell others | |
| D. The Limits of Achievement: The Individual | expansive view of achievement: "Where there's a will, there's a way" | achievement is a matter of fate | |
| **IV. Form of Relations to Others** | | | |
| A. Characteristics of Personal Relation | friendships are numerous but not deep or permanent; social obligations avoided | social obligation network: "utang na loob" | |
| B. Equality | equality is mode of interaction | continual shift from high to low status depending on other person | |
| C. Confrontation | face-to-face confrontation | confrontation through an intermediary to avoid "losing face" | |
| D. Informality and Formality | informal and direct | more formal; social interactions more structured | |
| E. Specialization of Roles | specialized roles distributed among members of group | all functions vested in leader | |

| Form of Activity | North American | Filipino | Other Culture |
|---|---|---|---|
| V. | | | |
| A. Doing | "doing" and being active are highly valued | "doing" not emphasized as much, especially in rural areas; it is just as important to "take it easy" | |
| B. Decision-making | decisions made by individual; every member feels responsible for group decisions | decisions made by authority or group; group decisions are usually product of key group members even if they are apparently made by all | |
| C. Work and play | dichotomy of work and play | work and social life are not separated | |
| D. Temporal orientation | stress on future | stress on present and past; life is lived from day to day | |

Reference:

Steward, Edward C. American Cultural Patterns: A Cross-Cultural Perspective. Washington, D.C.: Society for Intercultural Education, Training and Research, 1971. (Available from Intercultural Press, Inc.)

# RANK ORDERING VALUES

## OBJECTIVES

To explore cross-cultural perceptions of one's own values and the values of other culture groups.

## PARTICIPANTS

Any number.

## MATERIALS

Rank ordering chart, chalkboard or newsprint

## SETTING

No special requirements.

## TIME

One hour.

## PROCEDURE

Using the "Value Rank Ordering Chart," ask each student to rank order the values as follows:

List the three most important and the three least important values for:

a.   Your own culture,

b.   Mainstream American culture (if different),

c.   One other culture represented in the group.

Divide into subgroups that are either culturally homogeneous, culturally heterogeneous or organized according to other criteria such as job status, sex, etc.

Instruct the groups to rank order the values for the entire group and produce a list which they can agree reflects those values that are most important and least important for the total group. It may not be possible for them to arrive at a consensus.

Bring the full group together to discuss the results.

Discussion:

Were the groups able to arrive at a consensus? If not, why not?

How were the values rank ordered by individuals and/or by the groups? (Record these responses on the board so everyone can see them.)

Was there agreement among participants who are from the same culture groups?

What other factors influenced their value selection, i.e., personal interests, working conditions, sex, etc.

While discussing the reasons for participants' selections, look for biases (cultural or other) that are being subtly expressed and gently point them out within the context of the discussion.

Source: Intercultural Communication Workshop Program of the Intercultural Network, Inc.

# VALUE RANK ORDERING CHART

| | SELF | OTHER | OTHER |
|---|---|---|---|
| A COMFORTABLE LIFE<br>a prosperous life | | | |
| AN EXCITING LIFE<br>a stimulating, active life | | | |
| A SENSE OF ACCOMPLISHMENT<br>a lasting contribution | | | |
| A WORLD AT PEACE<br>free of war and conflict | | | |
| A WORLD OF BEAUTY<br>beauty of nature for all | | | |
| EQUALITY<br>brotherhood, equal<br>opportunity for all | | | |
| FAMILY UNITY AND SECURITY<br>maintaining kinship bonds and<br>taking care of loved ones | | | |
| FREEDOM<br>independence, free choice | | | |
| HAPPINESS<br>contentedness | | | |
| INNER HARMONY<br>freedom from inner conflict | | | |
| MATURE LOVE<br>sexual and spiritual intimacy | | | |
| NATIONAL SECURITY<br>protection from attack | | | |
| PLEASURE<br>an enjoyable, leisurely life | | | |
| RELIGIOUS HARMONY<br>living in harmony with<br>religious principles | | | |
| SELF-RESPECT<br>self-esteem | | | |
| SOCIAL RECOGNITION<br>respect, admiration | | | |
| TRUE FRIENDSHIP<br>close companionship | | | |
| WISDOM<br>a mature understanding of life | | | |
| MORALITY<br>living according to believed<br>moral principles | | | |

# THE PARABLE

## An Introduction to Cultural Values

OBJECTIVES

    This is a useful exercise for

1. helping participants get acquainted with each other
2. demonstrating, through the discoveries they will make themselves, how their decisions are determined by cultural values
3. acquainting participants with specific cultural differences and similarities among other members of the group
4. stimulating awareness of problems in transmitting one's own ideas and listening to others'.

    This sort of novel beginning also tends to provide a congenial atmosphere which often leads to some laughter, informal conversation, as well as cultural understanding. Participants are likely to pursue their conversations after the session.

PARTICIPANTS

    The size of the group is unimportant -- from 10 to as many as 100 people.

MATERIALS

    1. Chalkboard and chalk. 2. Paper and pencils. 3. Comfortable seating arrangements, in which chairs can be moved into small groups.

TIME

    About 25 minutes for the exercise itself.

PROCEDURE

    The leader tells a simple yet somewhat ambiguous parable, in this case one involving 5 characters. He may draw stick figures on the board as "illustrations" of the story. The behavior of each of the characters is intended to suggest a number of different values. After the telling each participant is asked to select, in order of rank, the characters whose behavior he or she most approves; then the large group is divided into groups of four or five to discuss individual choices with the assigment to arrive, if possible, at unanimity of rank ordering. An open discussion follows, in which participants are asked to share on a voluntary basis what they have learned during the small group sessions.

<u>Steps to Follow:</u>  1.  The leader tells the following parable to the group, illustrating with rough drawings if he chooses:

"Rosemary is a girl of about 21 years of age.  For several months she has been engaged to a young man named -- let's call him Geoffrey.  The problem she faces is that between her and her betrothed there lies a river.  No ordinary river mind you, but a deep, wide river infested with hungry crocodiles.

"Rosemary ponders how she can cross the river.  She thinks of a man she knows, who has a boat.  We'll call him Sinbad.  So she approaches Sinbad, asking him to take her across.  He replies, 'Yes, I'll take you across if you'll spend the night with me.'  Shocked at this offer, she turns to another acquaintance, a certain Frederick, and tells him her story.  Frederick responds by saying, 'Yes, Rosemary, I understand your problem -- but -- it's your problem, not mine.'  Rosemary decides to return to Sinbad, and spend the night with him.  In the morning he takes her across the river.

"Her reunion with Geoffrey is warm.  But on the evening before they are to be married, Rosemary feels compelled to tell Geoffrey how she succeeded in getting across the river.  Geoffrey responds by saying, 'I wouldn't marry you if you were the last woman on earth.'

"Finally, at her wits' end, Rosemary turns to the last character, Dennis.  Dennis listens to her story and says, 'Well, Rosemary, I don't love you . . . but I will marry you.'  And that's all we know of the story."

2.  The leader now asks the students to write down on a piece of paper, the five characters, listing them in a descending order from the person who's behavior is most approved to the person who's behavior is least approved.

3.  Next, students are split into groups of four or five and asked to discuss the choices they made.  Not more than 10 - 15 minutes should be allowed for this discussion; its main purpose is to sharpen the issues, not exhaust them.

4.  Calling them back to the larger group, the instructor asks what results of their discussions have been.  Some open discussion is allowed to get a full expression of value perspectives on the story.

5.  The instructor may then ask the group; "Can anyone point to some place, some source within your own past where you learned the values that caused you to take the position that you did?"  Students may have some difficulty with this question; no matter.  It is intended to be a difficult question.

6.  Next the leader says, "Now I would like you to ask yourselves -- I don't want an answer on this one, just want you to consider -- how many of you feel you could faithfully re-state, to the satisfaction of someone else in your small group, the point of view, the <u>value</u> being expressed by that person?  Again, I don't want you to answer, just think about the question."

7.   The leader may then summarize the session briefly, making the following points, preferably on chalkboard or newsprint:

> a.   Values come out of one's cultural background. They are difficult to track down to a particular source and are often part of a person's unconscious behavior.

> b.   Within any particular culture a person's values are usually very logical. They make sense in that culture.

> c.   For these reasons people should be very cautious about making moral judgment about other people's values.

> d.   If one really wants to understand someone else, one has to listen extremely well and try to "get inside" the other person. This is the reason for the question, "How accurately do you think you could re-state someone else's opinion?" Those of you who would have to answer "not very" have some work to do.

> e.   What are some other areas in life where people's values differ?

8.   If the students keep a journal (which can be a useful aid to learning), they should be asked to record what they have learned during the session.

9.   The leader should conclude the session almost as if it were the beginning, rather than the end, of a learning experience. One way to do this is simply to say that this is the end of the formal session and then join one of the small groups for conversation, rather than leave the room.

Source:  Developed by Sidney Simon, Professor of Education, University of Massachusetts. First published in A Manual of Teaching Techniques for Intercultural Education, (UNESCO), Henry Holmes and Stephen Guild, editors, October, 1971.

# WE AND YOU

## OBJECTIVE

To identify inter-group, culture-based perceptions and stereotypes.

## PARTICIPANTS

A group of eight to fifteen persons over twelve years of age and of mixed cultural backgrounds is recommended.

## MATERIALS

Questionnaire (prepared by facilitator along suggested lines), pencils.

## SETTING

No special requirements.

## TIME

At least sixty minutes.

## PROCEDURE

1.  Two cultures are selected to be the focus of attention. The facilitator prepares a questionnaire to focus on issues to which there are contrasting reactions in the two cultures. The group may participate in selection of the issues. The following are examples.

Attitudes toward - man's basic nature; control of one's environment; women and work; change, life, authority; material objectives, science, technology; time, death; achievement; value of experience; old people; strangers; relationships between sexes; dating; under-dogs; homosexuals; meeting commitments; government bureaucracy; classroom discipline; children being brought up to be independent.

Three questions are asked relating to each issue: How each student

a.  Thinks most people from the "other" culture feel about the issue in question.

b.  Thinks most people from his own culture feel.

c.  How he himself feels about it.

Each question is answered on a scale from 1-9 representing opposite extremes, and the individual must answer for the two target cultures and his own by selecting a number on the scale for each. A typical attitude statement might be:

| Most<br>Hispanic<br>Americans | Most<br>Mainstream<br>Americans | Myself | 1. Believe that man's basic<br>nature is |
|:---:|:---:|:---:|:---|
| 6 | 3 | 4 | Basically Good/Basically Evil<br>1 2 3 4 5 6 7 8 9 |

2.    Each participant is given a copy of the finished questionnaire. Working alone for fifteen to twenty minutes participants answer all questions.

3.    Participants form into small groups and try to reach a consensus (one number) upon their conceptions of each culture. This focuses the group's attention on real differences. The exercise ends when each group has reached consensus on all items, or when an arbitrary time limit is reached. (Individuals are not asked to reach consensus on their own perceptions.)

4.    A thorough discussion of the experience both in terms of their reactions to the substantive issues and the process of interaction which occurred during the exercise can follow. A great deal should have been revealed about the way people respond to cultural questions.

Adapted from "We and You" in A Manual of Teaching Techniques for Intercultural Education (UNESCO). Henry Holmes and Stephen Guild, eds. October, 1971.

# SHOULD THE CHILD BE TAUGHT

## OBJECTIVE

Explore contrasting culturally-based values through a consideration of what value orientations should be taught to students.

## PARTICIPANTS

Any number.

## MATERIALS

Pencil, paper and questions from "Should the child" list.

## SETTING

One that enables students to talk in pairs or small groups.

## TIME

Half-hour to 45 minutes.

## PROCEDURE

Break students into pairs, threes or foursomes. Assign each pair or group one of the "Should the child" questions to discuss. Allow them approximately 10 minutes to come to agreement as to how to answer the question. Reassemble and ask each pair or group to describe their answer and the thinking behind it.

Discussion will focus on the fact that in most cases one or more American cultures can be found on each side of each question. When this does emerge the instructor should point it out. There is not only no right and wrong, it is easy to identify embodiments of these values and argue the desirability of them in the context of the different cultures. Discussion should lead students to a greater awareness of the relativity of culture and of the fact that positive value can be found in opposite behaviors when viewed from different cultural perspectives.


## SHOULD-THE-CHILD LIST

1. Should the child be taught to respect and accept obligations to parents or to become an independent person? (Each sentence begins with Should the Child be Taught -- this introductory phrase will not be re-written for each question.)

2. ... to control or use the natural environment or to value and derive spiritual sustenance from it?

3. ... that we are progressing toward better and better life or that we should appreciate what we have?

-143-

4. ... to be motivated by the challenge of competition or by the benefits of cooperation?

5. ... to judge people according to separate or specific actions or as a whole person?

6. ... to relate to many people and have many friends or to have only a few deep friendships?

7. ... to confront problems and interpersonal relations directly or to be sensitive and avoid embarrassing confrontations with people?

8. ... to think that what they do or achieve is more important than who they are, the quality of their being?

9. ... to believe that work and play should be separated or woven together so that play or personal enjoyment occurs during their work?

10. ... to feel that everyone is equal or that there are levels of status relative to age, family role, profession, education, etc.

Source:  David S. Hoopes, Intercultural Network, Inc.

# PROVERBS: CULTURE AND VALUES

## OBJECTIVE

To explore cultural assumptions and values by examining proverbs - which usually express values and attitudes broadly accepted and understood within a culture group.

## PARTICIPANTS

Any group.

## MATERIALS

Paper, pencil and list of Proverbs

## SETTING

No special requirements.

## TIME

Variable.

## PROCEDURE

Although we all know a proverb when we hear one, it is difficult to define the term precisely. The introduction of a specific culture can include a study of its proverbs: what they are and what purpose they serve in communication of attitudes, values, and beliefs. Proverbs can be defined as "short, pithy epigrammatic statements which set forth a general well-known truth." When viewed as part of a communicative act, they are vehicles for sending messages about opinions, feelings, manners or customs of a people. They serve as witnesses to the social, political, ethical and religious patterns of thinking and behaving of a culture group.

Proverbs are characterized by a touch of the fanciful in their unique turn of a phrase, the unusual use of a word, or perhaps a specific rhythm. Many are paradoxical, or antithetical, while others are strongly metaphorical. Here in an educational setting, we are concerned with how to use proverbs to get at underlying cultural assumptions. We can examine proverbs for their exaggeration of attitudes commonly held by a cultural group. Hyperbole, personification, and alliteration are common attributes of the proverb which give us an unforgettable phrase or kernel of thought. Each proverbial statement has a quality of permanence in the culture and recurs in its folk lore.

Give participants a sheet of paper containing the following proverbs:

1.   "You got eyes to see and wisdom not to see."

2.   "Muddy roads call the mile post a liar."

3.    "Every bell ain't a dinner bell."

4.    "A mule can tote so much goodness in his face that he don't have none left for his hind legs."

5.    "The graveyard is the cheapest boarding house."

For each of the above proverbs, choose a phrase in your own language or dialect which approximates the meaning of the proverb. Use familiar language, and symbols, for example: "Kumquats are both sweet and sour," if you aren't familiar or comfortable with "kumquats," substitute "oranges."

What does the original proverb mean?  What is its message?

What does the proverb indicate to you about the culture?  Can you generalize about it, whether it is traditional, rural, submissive, dominant, happy-go-lucky, cautions, etc.?

What are the dominant values of the culture represented in the proverb?

Think of some parallel proverbs from your own culture.  Convey a similar message if you can.  If you cannot, why not?  For example, "For the turtle to make progress, it must stick its neck out," is similar to "To learn to swim, you must first get your toes wet."  The message is similar, the symbols are slightly different.

Try to identify the culture from which all five examples are drawn.  What type of culture do you think it is, and some reasons why you characterize it that way ... elaborate.

At the end of the exercise, the trainer reveals that the culture we are looking at is Afro-American Slave - these are real examples of proverbs taken from the folk literature.

The first example, "You got eyes to see and wisdom not to see," is pointing to the slave culture's accurate perception of what goes on around the people, but the sense not to "see" or acknowledge the reality.  Emphasis is placed on not knowing something which would upset you or get you into trouble if you acknowledged being aware of it.

In the next example, the muddy roads are relatively impassable, therefore the person traveling them cannot count on the mile posts to gauge how long his journey will take.  We can tell this is a rural culture, and that its people are used to translating signals into their own particular knowledge about dealing with nature.

Number three indicates frequent conflicts between the dinner bell, a safe cue, and the bell calling slaves in from the fields, sometimes a warning of imminent danger.  Again, the rural culture is reflected in the image of the bell.

The mule often looks like he will be a kind of helpful farm animal, but his legs still can kick you or refuse to budge - so don't be deceived by appearances. Again, an agricultural culture is reflected in the imagery, and a realism born of knowing the environment and what you can expect.

The graveyard, in the last example, is escape from the troubles of a hard life - so don't worry about death - death is a kind of freedom for the slave, rest from all the hard times.

Source:  Sandra Tjitendero, University of Massachusetts.


A variation on this exercise is to ask a group to simply list the proverbs and axioms of mainstream American culture. A few examples can be supplied to get the group started, such as:

A woman's place is in the home.

Little children should be seen and not heard.

Then the group is asked to determine what value is being taught by the axiom.

| Examples | Values |
|---|---|
| Cleanliness is next to godliness | Cleanliness |
| Time is money | Value of time thriftiness |
| A penny saved is a penny earned | Thriftiness |
| Birds of a feather flock together | Guilt through association |
| Don't cry over spilt milk | Practicality |
| Waste not; want not | Frugality |
| Early to bed, early to rise ... | Diligence |
| God helps those who help themselves | Initiative |
| It's not whether you win or lose, but... | Good sportsmanship |
| A man's home is his castle | Privacy; property |
| No rest for the wicked | Guilt; work ethic |
| You've made your bed, now sleep in it | Responsibility |

Many of these proverbs were brought from the more traditional societies of Europe. Discuss which no longer apply to mainstream society and why. List proverbs of other culture groups represented in the class and identify cultural meaning and values conveyed by them.

Source:  Robert Kohls, International Communication Agency.

# SOCIAL STATUS

## OBJECTIVE

To demonstrate the proposition that "social status" is not an abstract concept, that it is made evident by day-to-day behavior, and that these behaviors are culturally based.

## PARTICIPANTS

Approximately seven persons in a group.

## MATERIALS

Instructions; equipment for taping if desired for playback and analysis.

## SETTING

Classroom or lounge with moveable chairs.

## TIME

Variable. Can be conducted within a regular class period.

## PROCEDURE

Have individual participants role-play the following encounters:

1. facing a judge in traffic court for having run a red light;

2. asking a professor for an extension on a term paper;

3. ordering a hamburger in a small restaurant;

4. ordering a complete dinner with wine in a large restaurant;

5. meeting the Governor at an official function;

6. making an appointment with a busy doctor or lawyer;

7. discussing, briefly, with the principal of the school a disciplinary problem that has occurred in your classroom.

These role-plays should be done rather completely. Participants should be asked what preparatory steps would be taken for the encounter, i.e., clothes, grooming, etc. The trainer should be prepared to supply details of background and setting, i.e., if the other person is of the same or a different cultural background, etc., if requested. Each role-play should be discussed and analyzed in terms of what behavioral changes the participant displayed and how cultural origin influences behavior in situations of this nature. Each participant should do at least two of the encounters if there is time.

Variations can be introduced which draw out cultural contrasts. Especially useful is having people of different cultural backgrounds role play the same scene or switch roles in the same scene. If the group represents only one culture, have them role play another culture, desirably with someone from that culture present.

# MARITAL ROLES SCALE

## OBJECTIVE

Clarification of one's preferred marital roles as they pertain to his/her cultural identifications.

## PARTICIPANTS

One or more persons. Group members should represent various cultural viewpoints if possible.

## MATERIALS

Pencils. Scales for each participant

## SETTING

No special requirements.

## TIME

At least ten minutes.

## PROCEDURE

1.  Each student is given a copy of the scale and a pencil.

2.  Students fill in one response before each of the statements to indicate what they believe is right as a matter of principle. The responses are to be marked as follows:

    SA -- Strongly Agree;  A -- Agree;  U -- Undecided;
    D -- Disagree;  SD -- Strongly Disagree.

3.  If done as a group exercise, compare and discuss responses in regard to different cultural beliefs.

4.  This exercise also provides an opportunity to discuss sex roles in different cultures and the changes that are occurring in them.

_____  1.  The husband should help with the housework.

_____  2.  The wife should take a job if she wants to.

_____  3.  The husband should help wash dishes.

_____  4.  If a husband runs around, so can his wife.

_____  5.  Wives are too independent these years.

_____  6.  If the husband wants children, the wife should agree.

_____  7.  The husband should decide who is to spend the extra money.

_____ 8.   Husbands should be more strict with their wives.

_____ 9.   What a husband does in his spare time is his own business.

_____ 10.  The husband should decide where to live.

_____ 11.  The wife should fit her life to her husband's.

_____ 12.  The husband's wishes should come first in most things.

_____ 13.  Marriage is the best career for the woman.

_____ 14.  The husband should wear the "pants" in the family.

_____ 15.  If the husband is running around with another women, his wife should put up with it until he comes to his senses.

_____ 16.  It's okay for the wife to earn as much as her husband.

_____ 17.  A wife should let her husband decide most things.

_____ 18.  Almost all money matters should be decided by the husband.


Discussion of this excercise may become quite heated so the instructor should be ready to limit non-productive conflict.

# CULTURAL VALUE SYSTEMS WITH CONFLICTING POINTS OF VIEW

## OBJECTIVE

To demonstrate the contrasting and conflicting aspects of interaction between persons who do not share the same basic assumptions and to provide participants with the experience of defending a different cultural perspective.

## PARTICIPANTS

Two or more persons representing different cultures.

## MATERIALS

None

## SETTING

No special requirements.

## PROCEDURE

1.   Define the major dimensions of the value systems of the culture groups represented among the participants in the group.  (Don't worry if a little stereotyping occurs.)

2.   Pose an issue or problem which, during discussion, will bring the values represented into conflict.  (Example:   What kind of teaching style or personality should a teacher exhibit in the classroom?)

3.   Students are then asked to discuss the issue arguing from the perspective of one of the value systems different from their own. This may be done in two ways:

   a.   the discussion could take place before the whole group, perhaps in the form of a panel, with one person representing each culture; or

   b.   the issue could be discussed in small groups so that more people could have the experience of defending someone else's culture.

4.   Close the discussion when either a solution to the issue has been reached or the discussion has continued long enough to demonstrate the cultural issues involved.

5.    Suggested questions for processing:

    a.    How did discussants feel about defending another value system?

    b.    Was the issue resolved? If so, how? If not, why not?

    c.    Was there more or less disagreement during the exercise than might have occurred in a "real" situation? Why?

    d.    Did participants reach an understanding of the different viewpoints?

Prior to conducting this exercise, each student can be assigned a particular culture group and asked to research how people from that group would respond to the issue chosen for discussion. The assigned culture groups need not be represented in the class ... but students are expected to be able to defend their position with empirical data (could include interviews with individual(s) of the culture group). It should be pointed out that the attitudes represented may not be absolute for all people of a particular culture. Stereotyping should be avoided here.

Source:  Developed by trainers of the Intercultural Network, Inc.

# COMMUNICATION

There is an abundant supply of communication exercises available in various publications (see reference list). The eight included in this volume were originally constructed or have been adapted by the authors expressly to demonstrate how communication is influenced by culture. They also focus on practicing specific skills (giving feedback, listening, etc.) and exploring the process of communication that is simply illustrated by this model:

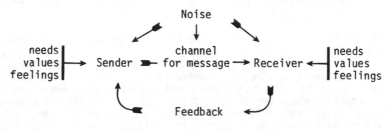

Need: empathetic listening

(Noise refers to any distraction or disturbance which distorts or interferes with the transmission of the message.)


DEFINITION: Communication is an exchange of meaning of information and ideas. The basic aim in communication is to transmit a message from a sender to a receiver with the least possible loss of meaning.

Basic communication theory suggests that the identification of similarities is the basis of communication or, expressed differently, that similarities constitute the matrix in which communication takes place. Differences are seen as barriers. In intercultural communication this is turned around and differences are not only <u>not</u> seen as barriers to communication but they themselves constitute the matrix in which communication occurs. Cultural differences are thus both a necessary medium of intercultural communication and a context for cross-cultural learning. They are also the pathway to the ultimate identification of similarities.

It is often difficult to get across the significance of the communication process. It seems so simple. It is so automatic. In fact, its seeming simplicity comes from the fact that it is such an unconscious behavior. It is, of course, one of the more complex of human functions and may need more attention than seems appropriate to clarify it to students.

# ONE WAY - TWO WAY COMMUNICATION

## OBJECTIVE

To illustrate that one-way communication, while more efficient, is less accurate than two-way communication; also underscores the imprecision of language and the difficulty in describing one's experiences to others in a manner that leads to identical understanding by them.

## PARTICIPANTS

Groups of up to forty people.

## MATERIALS

Task sheets for the speaker and scoring sheets for students.

## SETTING

No special requirements.

## TIME

About forty-five minutes.

## PROCEDURE

A pictogram is given to one student selected by the instructor. The student is asked to describe the picture while standing behind a screen (or being out of visual contact with the group) and the group is to try and draw the pictogram on the basis of the instructions given. People in the group are not permitted to ask questions or give any verbal cues to the speaker. When the speaker feels he/she has conveyed the drawing, the group is asked for an accuracy estimate (how many figures each person thinks he/she drew correctly) and this is recorded on the board. The elapsed time for the exercise is also recorded. The pictogram is then shown to the audience and the actual number of drawings drawn correctly recorded.

The second phase of the exercise calls for the same speaker to describe a different drawing while standing in front of the group. The group may ask any questions necessary for them to understand what the speaker is trying to communicate. When the speaker and group members are satisfied with the instructions given and they've drawn pictures, another accuracy estimate is taken and the elapsed time recorded. Again the pictogram is shown and an actual score is recorded.

The discussion and processing begins with a review of the accuracy rate and elapsed time. The usual result is that one-way communication takes less time but two-way communication is more effective. The person who described the pictogram is asked his/her feelings in both situations, what importance visual and verbal cues had in the communication process? The group is asked to discuss feelings of frustration or ease in understanding the instructions. An observer may also be used to record observations during the exercise and report them to the group.

Source: Readings in Intercultural Communication, Volume V, David S. Hoopes, editor.

## SAMPLE SCORING SHEET

### One-Way Communication

Elapsed Time _____

| | Estimate | Actual |
|---|---|---|
| 3 figures correct | _____ | _____ |
| 2 figures correct | _____ | _____ |
| 1 figure correct | _____ | _____ |
| 0 figures correct | _____ | _____ |
| correct configuration | _____ | _____ |

************************************************************************

### Two-Way Communication

Elapsed Time _____

| | Estimate | Actual |
|---|---|---|
| 3 figures correct | _____ | _____ |
| 2 figures correct | _____ | _____ |
| 1 figure correct | _____ | _____ |
| 0 figures correct | _____ | _____ |
| correct configuration | _____ | _____ |

## One-Way Communication

Your task is to communicate <u>orally</u> everything the other participants
need to know in order to reproduce the pictogram illustrated below.
Those drawing the figures are not allowed to ask you any questions,
nor are they to see the diagram.

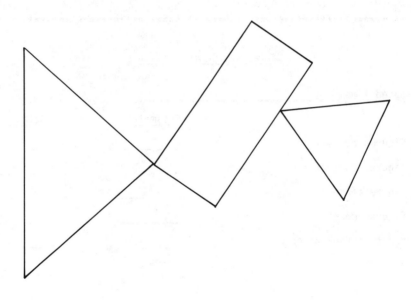

## Two-Way Communication

Your task is to communicate <u>orally</u> everything the other participant
need to know in order to reproduce the pictogram illustrated below
You are not allowed to use any gestures, but the participants may as
you any questions they wish in order to clarify your instructions t
them.

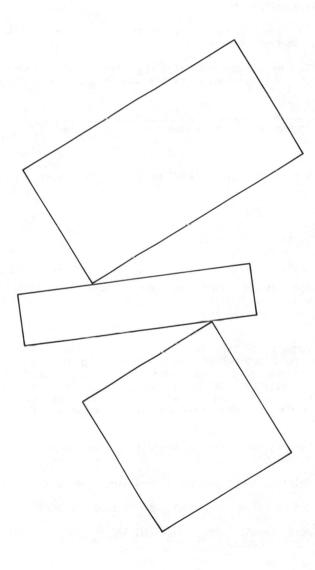

# SELF-DISCLOSURE WHEEL

## OBJECTIVE

1.  To be able to demonstrate the degree to which individuals are willing to disclose themselves verbally to others.

2.  To be able to identify the differences in self-disclosure patterns among people in one's own culture group and with those who are culturally different.

3.  To recognize what is "cultural" in the self-disclosure patterns and what is "personal."

4.  To be able to identify those areas where useful communication can occur between people who are culturally different.

## PARTICIPANTS

Small groups of not more than ten, if possible.

## MATERIALS

Enough copies of the "wheel" to supply each participant with two or three.

## SETTING

No special requirements.

## TIME

Variable but at least one hour should be allotted to this exercise.

## PROCEDURE

The purpose of this exercise is first, to discover how much information about themselves people are willing to disclose in five conversational areas: opinions, interests and tastes, work or studies, finances, personality and one's body. Secondly, to discuss how participants' cultural and personal backgrounds determine what they consider private and what they consider appropriate for discussion with others.

1.  Explain that the six broad topics on the wheel are defined as including the following:

    a.  Opinions about political, religious and social issues;

    b.  Interests in food, music, television and books;

    c.  Work goals and difficulties, special talents and limitations;

d.   Financial status, including income, savings, debts and budgets;

e.   Personality, specific assets and handicaps, sources of pride or shame;

f.   Physical attributes including feelings about one's face and body, illness, sexual adequacy.

2.   Ask participants to shade in the disclosure wheels for a same sex friend and an opposite sex friend (they may mentally identify a real person in each category). When the wheels are completed, draw a darker line to connect the boundaries in each area.

3.   Allow comparisions and discuss the reasons for the differences in personal disclosure patterns for each sex friend:

Some useful questions:

a.   In what areas are you least willing to share information?

b.   Why do you feel reluctant to talk about _____ (salary, sex, etc.) with _____ (same or other sex friend)?

For example: experiences as a child, how we learn what is acceptable to talk about, etc.).

c.   When, in the course of getting to know someone, do you begin to talk about more personal matters?

d.   Do you think/feel it is important to be able to talk about . . . (finances, appearance, etc.) with others or should certain areas remain private?

e.   What areas of yourself would you never discuss with another person? Outside your family?

f.   What areas would you discuss and would want others to discuss? What are you most interested in finding out about other people?

Other concerns and ideas will, of course, emerge in the discussion. It is helpful to explore how people feel when someone asks about areas that they are not willing to discuss or when another person attempts to discuss an area in greater depth than they find acceptable or comfortable.

4.   If participants in the group are culturally similar, it may be interesting to shade a group wheel and try to arrive at a composite that the group can agree indicates the boundaries of self disclosure that generally exists in their culture. During this process, those differences in self disclosure patterns which are personally unique should emerge and can be discussed.

5. Further discussion can explore how much people are willing to reveal about themselves in discussions with fellow workers, classmates, a stranger, a supervisor or principal.

6. Discuss the question: when talking with someone from a different culture or who has a personal preference about what is appropriate for discussion, how would you be willing to adjust your disclosure pattern and what would you expect of them?

PROCESSING

The degree to which people articulate their feelings and thoughts verbally often depends on how their culture rewards or punishes verbal expression. In the U.S., those who are able to talk easily and are willing to contribute their ideas and views in a conversation are often considered to be valuable members of a group. In another culture, verbal initiative may be viewed as detrimental to the preservation of group harmony or, in fact, to the individual's esteem in that society. The person who is attempting to be "open and honest" could, therefore, be erecting barriers to realistic communication with someone who finds such self-exposure embarrassing or even foolish.

The problem lies in finding a way to determine when you are treading on dangerous conversational ground. How, for instance, you recognize and interpret non-verbal indicators that sensitive areas are being verbally invaded? This exercise is aimed at discussing what topics are considered to be private or public, how people signal others that they are uncomfortable with the content of a conversation and how people learn to avoid some topics and discuss others. It is not intended to elicit specific information about any of the topics nor in any way to invade the student's privacy.

Adapted from The Self-Disclosure Wheel devised by Dr. Dean Barnlund as a variation on the Self Disclosure scale perfected by Sidney Jourard and Paul Lasakow. Dr. Barnlund has used the scale for his research on the comparison of verbal self-disclosure patterns between people of different culture groups and introduced the wheel as an exercise for workshops on intercultural communication. Dr. Barnlund's research is reported in: Barnlund, Dean C. Public and Private Self in Japan and the United States. Tokyo, Japan: The Simul Press, Inc., 1975.

# SAME SEX FRIEND

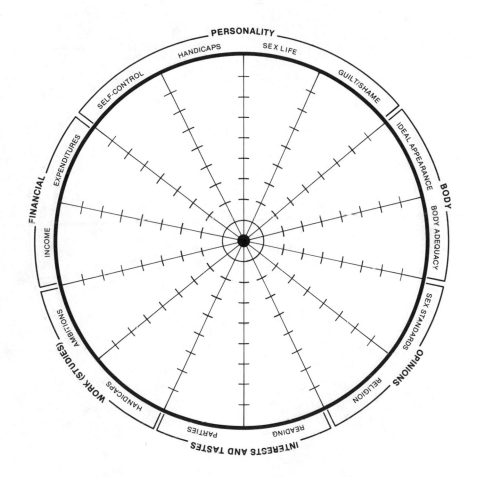

**SHADE IN EACH TRIANGLE FROM THE OUTSIDE TOWARD THE CENTER
ACCORDING TO HOW MUCH YOU WOULD SHARE IN EACH TOPIC.**

-163-

# OPPOSITE SEX FRIEND

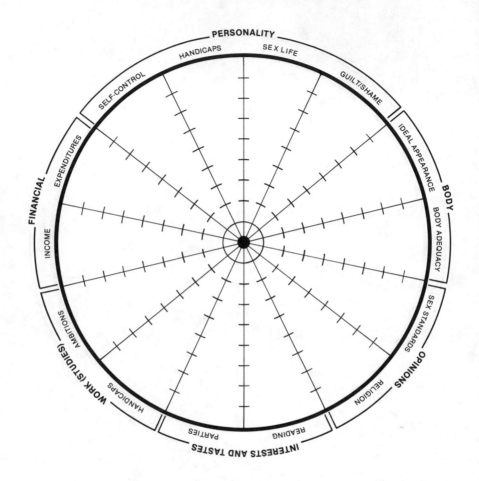

**SHADE IN EACH TRIANGLE FROM THE OUTSIDE TOWARD THE CENTER ACCORDING TO HOW MUCH YOU WOULD SHARE IN EACH TOPIC.**

# LISTENING

## OBJECTIVE

To practice listening to verbal and non-verbal messages, summarizing what was "heard" and checking the accuracy of the message received with the speaker.

## PARTICIPANTS

Normal class size.

## MATERIALS

None.

## SETTING

Room where the class can be separated into small groups.

## TIME

Variable.

## PROCEDURE

The class is broken into groups of from 3 to 9 people.

Two members of each group volunteer to engage in a conversation; the rest of the group observes. One of the volunteers picks a subject he or she feels is very important (possibly some aspect of religion, politics, male-female relations, career goals, etc.) and begins to discuss it. After approximately 2 minutes the second volunteer or listener summarizes what the speaker has said. The speaker confirms and/or corrects the listener's summary. The listener rephrases until able to state accurately what the speaker said. The other members of the group then comment on the communication process they observed. There is no attempt by anyone to answer or argue the points made by the speaker.

Then two other members of the group do the exercise until all have had a chance to participate.

Afterward the whole class discusses the exercise with the instructor, who draws out the difficulties people have in accurately hearing what is being communicated to them. Students may be asked if they identified any differences in culture or perception between the speaker and the listener, but these are usually difficult to find in a short exercise of this kind.

PERCEPTION CHECKING

## OBJECTIVE

To help students develop their skills in accurately hearing and understanding what someone else is saying by focusing on or distinguishing between the "message" and the "meaning" of a statement.

## PARTICIPANTS

Usually done in groups of ten or less. Can be done in a larger group if introduced into regular discussion periods.

## MATERIALS

List of questions.

## SETTING

Any comfortable room that is large enough for pairs to talk without disturbing others in the class.

## TIME

Approximately one hour although it may take longer. Time must be allowed for people to move into pairs and return to group.

## PROCEDURE

1.    This can be introduced in the course of a regular discussion or structured into a small group focusing on communication issues.

2.    When introduced into a discussion of an issue, the instructor role models by intervening and commenting on what someone has said to illustrate how a meaning has been expressed that goes deeper or beyond the apparent meaning of the statement. For example, "Your statement was, 'Teachers who oppose bilingual education must be shortsighted.'" "What I think you mean" (sometimes phrased "what I hear you saying") "is that you're upset with these teachers because they don't realize the damage that's being done to some students in the usual educational setting." The discussion can continue until what the person "means" is clear to the group and the instructor.

3.    As a structured exercise the teacher instructs the students in how to distinguish between what is <u>said</u> and what is <u>meant</u>. He or she then selects issues which are apt to bring out subtle cultural differences in attitudes and values and raises them for discussion.

The intent is to enable the students to become better listeners by helping them learn to check their perceptions of what a person is saying. By getting at the meanings which are not obvious, the listener avoids inserting his or her own meanings and feelings into what someone else has said.

-166-

Once the students have learned to check their perception of what they are hearing, the communication becomes clearer and more accurate.

The focus in this exercise is on interpersonal communication skills but individual communicative style is strongly influenced by cultural background. Some cultures are not as open as others to directness and feedback. In multicultural groups, it is necessary to proceed with great tact and patience and to avoid insisting on a high degree of 'exposure'.

Source:   Paul Pedersen, University of Hawaii.

## OBJECTIVE

To assess how perceived racial and cultural differences influence the level at which people communicate or fail to communicate with each other.

## PARTICIPANTS

Any number.

## MATERIALS

Pen and paper although it may be desirable to construct the grids and provide them for the group.

## SETTING

No special requirements.

## TIME

Variable.

## PROCEDURE

Supply students with copies of the attached chart and read over the instructions for using it.

After they have filled in the grid, have participants discuss it with at least one other person, preferably from a racial or cultural background different from their own, or a small group. Instruct them to describe what they felt while filling out the grid. Discussing these feelings will help get through inhibitions about inter-ethnic relations to establish a more accurate picture of the levels of communication.

Source: Blubaugh, Jon A. and Dorothy L. Pennington. Crossing Difference . . . Interracial Communication. Columbus, Oh.: Charles E. Merrill Publishing Company, 1976. Used with permission of the authors, all rights reserved.

LEVELS OF COMMUNICATION

| Culture-Groups | Intimate Communication | Respectful Communication | Social Communication | Casual Communication | Rejection of Communication |
|---|---|---|---|---|---|
| Blacks | | | | | |
| Native Americans | | | | | |
| Mainstream Americans | | | | | |
| Chicanos | | | | | |
| Oriental Americans | | | | | |
| (fill in other groups if desired) | | | | | |
| | | | | | |
| | | | | | |

1.  Make an X under the categories for each racial group with whom you would attempt each type of communication. Be honest.

2.  Now go back and circle the Xs for each type of communication you have actually engaged in with a member of each group. Be honest again.

# SPEAKING WITHOUT SPEAKING

## OBJECTIVE

To examine the meanings and feelings communicated by non-verbal behaviors (1) some of which are common among cultures, and (2) some of which differ across cultures.

## PARTICIPANTS

Two _equal_ sized groups of three or more persons each.

## MATERIALS

None required.

## SETTING

A room large enough to allow for some separation between the two groups.

## TIME

Approximately one hour.

## PROCEDURE

1.    The instructor may announce to participants that this session will deal with culture or even with communication; but he does not mention its focus on non-verbal behavior, lest the impact of the exercise be reduced. He then asks the students to split into two groups of equal size, A's and B's, who then assemble at opposite ends of the room.

2.    The teacher first goes over to the A group. He tells them in a confidential voice that they are to choose a partner from the B group and engage in conversation. The subject of the conversation is not too important; it may be differences the partners may have noticed in the treatment of women in different cultures, different attitudes toward work and professional life, or some of the problems that interfere with good communication. It is essential however, that during the conversation each "A" will sit or stand about 4 inches closer to B than he normally would. All other behavior should be normal -- even the voice should be at the normal pitch.

(Other non-verbal behaviors can be used in this exercise. The instructor should select a non-verbal behavior which will contrast sharply with the behaviors of most of the participants, however. Some possibilities are:  no eye contact or intense eye contact, touching on the arm continuously throughout the conversation, smiling constantly, showing no facial expression, looking over the other person's left shoulder while talking, winking fairly regularly, snapping fingers, holding hand to head, gently ·pushing with hand against shoulder of other, twisting body often, etc.)

3.   The instructor now joins the B group, telling them in a confidential voice that they are to discuss the chosen subject with one of the A group and that the As will come over to select them shortly.

4.   Next the partners are asked to meet and go to separate parts of the room, relax, and exchange views on the chosen subject. They should not go out of sight of the teacher.

5.   After about five to ten minutes the facilitator apologizes for breaking into the conversation and asks the A's and B's to return to their respective groups. He joins the B group this time and asks in a low voice, "Without looking back at your partner, each of you tell the others in this group, as best you can, what your partner "A" looked like. For example, did he wear glasses or not? Moustache? Complexion? What kind of clothes? Neat or sloppy? Long or short hair?" Each is asked to share with his group whatever details he can recall.

6.   Meanwhile the instructor returns to the "A" group. He asks them the same question about what they can recall about their partner's appearance. He gives a few minutes for them to begin to share recollections but then apologizes and breaks in.

7.   He tells the "A" group that he next wants them to engage in a second conversation with their partners. Another subject is assigned to them to discuss. This time the "A's" are told to avoid looking directly into their partners' faces; look any where that seems natural except their faces. All other behaviors should be normal.

8.   The instructor now asks the participants to rejoin their partners and reiterates the subject they are to discuss. After five to ten minutes he again interrupts and asks them to gather, this time as a single group. He then asks for volunteers to describe how they felt during the exchange, especially: "Did you feel strange?" A brief discussion, about ten minutes, should be encouraged. Finally, the teacher tells everyone the instructions that had been given to the "A" group and offers a short lecture concerning the significance of non-verbal communication.

9.   Lastly, participants are asked to demonstrate examples of specific differences in non-verbal behavior which they have noticed among themselves and other cultural groups.

Suggested by Melvin L. Schnapper to Henry Holmes and Stephen Guild, eds., A Manual of Teaching Techniques for Intercultural Education (UNESCO), October, 1971.

# ROLE PLAYING EMOTIONS

## OBJECTIVE

To explore how emotions are expressed differently (or similarly) in different culture groups.

## PARTICIPANTS

Any number of persons who are familiar enough with one another to interact in a relaxed manner -- desirably representing a variety of cultures.

## MATERIALS

None.

## SETTING

Enough open space to allow students to engage in pantomime activity.

## TIME

Variable; depending on group size, length of pantomimes, and processing phase.

## PROCEDURE

1.   The facilitator will ask for volunteers to pantomime an emotion.

2.   Each volunteer will then select an emotion; embarrassment, anger, fear, hate, compassion, disapproval, envy, etc. and pantomime it to the group.

3.   Group members will be asked to guess what emotion is being acted.

4.   Discussion follows in regard to how emotions are expressed and interpreted similarly or differently across cultures.

Source:  Developed by Paul Pedersen, University of Hawaii.

# METHODOLOGIES

There are some training methods that cannot be classified under the preceeding topical headings.  They include or generate data that is equally relevant to all or most of them.  Those methods are the content of this section.

# SIMULATIONS

The simulation is probably one of the most powerful experiential learning tools used in classrooms and training programs. It can raise a wide variety of issues; it can translate those issues from abstractions to a situation of surprisingly accurate simulated reality; it can involve learners intensely; and it can produce feelings and thoughts that constitute a rich resource for discussion and learning. Simulations tend to be long, especially since ample time must be left for discussing and "processing" the experience, but the scheduling adjustments which may be necessary are worth it.

One simulation, "Albatross," is not included in this manual but should be mentioned. It was developed at the Experiment in International Living and can be found in Batchelder and Warner, 1977. It is an effective device for intercultural learning, but it often raises strong emotions and should be used only by skilled trainers and teachers.

Scheduling a simulation in a course or training program depends on the function it is expected to serve. Placed at the beginning, it tends to create group cohesion, but is less effective as a learning tool. It does serve as a point of reference for later learning, however. Scheduled later, when the participants have more experience and knowledge in the subject, it tends to add depth to the learning.

It is best for the instructor to experience the simulation before attempting to run it. In most simulations there is so much happening that it is easy for the inexperienced leader to stumble. Just reading the directions is insufficient preparation, though someone experienced in simulations may be able to learn a new one by running through it with a small test group.

Changing the rules of a complex simulation is not advised. Simulations have been carefully constructed and the repercussions of even minor adjustments can so alter the experience that it does not produce the desired results -- or it may simply fall apart.

Finally, simulations are, in our opinion, among the most enjoyable ways to learn.

# BAFA BAFA

Simulation Game written by Gary Shirts
Published by
Simile II
P.O. Box 910
Del Mar, CA  92014

## OBJECTIVES

1.  To increase awareness of our own cultural identity; to increase intercultural communication skills; to increase understanding of "culture" and its function in interpersonal relations; to understand the problems of adapting in a new environment; to become better interpreters of nonverbal communcation; and to stimulate thoughtful discussion about differences in values, attitudes, and communication styles across cultures.

2.  To have an enjoyable educational experience with other people; to practice new roles in a non-threatening environment; to become aware of the effects of social interaction and the dynamics of groups.

## MATERIALS

A set of materials can be ordered from Simile II at a cost of over $30.00.  Instructions for making a set is available at less cost.  The ease of using the ready-made game, however, is worth the price.

## PARTICIPANTS

A minimum of twelve and a maximum of forty participants.

## SETTING

Two connecting or adjacent rooms which can be closed off from each other; moveable chairs.

## TIME

Two to three hours, an hour to an hour and a half is needed to explain and play the game; a minimum of one hour should be set aside to discuss issues and deal with participants' feelings.

## PROCEDURE

Participants are divided into two groups, Alpha culture and Beta culture.  Each group is taught a new (and different) set of cultural values, behaviors and communication styles.  Then by sending visitors back and forth each group attempts to learn or figure out the culture of the other.  The participants are urged to join in the game uninhibitedly, to exaggerate, and to have fun acting out the designated roles for the duration of the game.  Participants usually

-175-

experience the major pitfalls of cross-cultural interaction:
stereotyping, misperception, culture-shock, in-group/out-group
feelings, etc.

Strengths -- Its ability to draw people into the game emotionally, so
    that the learning comes through experience rather than abstract
    concepts. It also sharpens intercultural communication skills.

Weaknesses -- Long opening explanations may drag and/or make partici-
    pants take the game too seriously. The simplicity or rigidity
    of the new cultures may bother some participants. It must be
    made clear that the focus is on the intercultural relations
    process, not the content of the cultures.

Leadership -- BaFa can produce strong feelings which need to be aired
    and resolved at the end. It is one of the functions of the
    leaders to accomplish that resolution. Two trainers are needed,
    one for each group. They should be experienced and able to deal
    with the variety of reactions which occur. They should also be
    imbued with enthusiasm, persistence and stamina.

Processing -- Participants should be assisted in getting a clear under-
    standing of what happened and exploring with each other their
    reactions. It is the role of the leader to highlight the issues
    and draw out the learning. A list of discussion questions is
    included in the trainers' manual.

    Themes or topics that can be the focus for discussion:

    Male-female relationships (cross-culturally or in one culture)
    Family life - norms, beliefs, communication
    Work and play
    Adaptation to new environments (as it affects self-esteem,
    perhaps)
    Interrelationship of language and culture
    Materialism, competition, alienation
    Friendship, hospitality, intimacy
    Task orientation vs. relationship orientation

Source: Adapted from a description of BAFA BAFA written by Ann
Gillespie for Handbook for Leaders in Cross-Cultural Exchange
Programs, Barbara Ostrander and Peggy Pusch, editors, unpublished.

# STAR POWER

Simulation Game written by Gary Shirts
Published by
Simile II
P.O. Box 910
Del Mar, CA 92014

## OBJECTIVES

To examine the nature of bargaining and negotiation between groups; to explore intra- and inter-group dynamics; to develop a better understanding of how individuals and groups relate to and communicate with each other when power and economic status are important; to identify the cultural dimensions of these behaviors.

## PARTICIPANTS

Minimum of 18 participants, maximum of 35.

## MATERIALS

Star Power Kit (a set of materials or directions for assembling your own can be purchased from Simile II), trainer's manual and blackboard.

## SETTING

A large room with chairs that can be arranged in three circles (each as far away from the other as possible) and space for people to walk around.

## TIME

Variable, about 1-1/2 hours to play the game and at least 45 minutes for processing. The processing will probably take longer, however.

## PROCEDURE

This is a trading game in which poker chips are used to represent owned or acquired goods and serve as instruments for trading and bargaining. Players try to gain as many points as they can as they trade and bargain for chips. After the first trading session, participants are arranged into three groups according to the 'scores' acquired during the round. Those with the highest scores are labeled "Squares," the middle range become "Circles," and those with the lowest scores are called "Triangles." They are provided with appropriate emblems to wear and are seated together. At this point, the game director "stacks" the game in favor of the Squares so that in each subsequent round they become wealthier and wealthier. While there is a little mobility between groups, the game has essentially created a three-tiered society with the Squares dominant. Conflict, competition and resentment among the groups arise.

Next, the Squares are permitted to revise the rules of the game -- and almost invariably construct rules that enhance or secure their power position. Anything can happen after the new rules have been announced. The disadvantaged groups may attempt to manipulate the system, form liaisons in an effort to force changes within it or revolt when the rules are blatantly unfair. The game director should stop the game when it becomes apparent that the squares have abused their power and the other groups show signs of resentment. This takes some judgment and the director must be constantly alert to responses of individuals and the groups.

Maintaining an atmosphere that protects the participants against undue abrasion of personal feelings is important. During the discussion that follows, there may be some need to air emotional reactions but it is important to insure that it does not become personal. The discussion should focus on the issues rather than personalities; cultural differences in the perception of power, authority and competition, the importance of the social system in determining individual behavior and how interpersonal relationships evolve under these conditions.

Star Power provides an objective medium for exploring conditions that exist in the participants' organizational or social life. By focusing on the issues involved, it is possible to analyze intergroup conflict, group decision making and problem solving, interpersonal communication, the dynamics of power, the frustrations and pressures experienced in minority groups and a host of other topics. As the name implies, it is about power, it can also be a relatively powerful experience.

## ROLE PLAY

Role plays are far less complex than simulations but, properly handled, can involve the student intensely and provide a strong stimulus to learning. The purpose is much the same -- to offer an experience that stimulates thoughts and feelings which then can be related to concepts and built into a framework for understanding and personally dealing more effectively with cross-cultural relations.

Some people are uncomfortable with role playing, either as participants or instructors, though often the discomfort passes once they're involved in the activity. Those who continue to be uncomfortable should avoid role plays. Also, no one should be required to participate. Observing is often as valuable as involvement anyway.

Included here are both several role plays and a guide to constructing your own.

# CONSTRUCTING A CROSS-CULTURAL ROLE PLAY

OBJECTIVE

To provide a classroom experience of cross-cultural interaction in a form offering depth involvement.

PARTICIPANTS

Two or three volunteer "actors."

MATERIALS

Instructions for actors; scenarios for actors and observers; props (dress, artifacts, etc.) if appropriate.

SETTING

Appropriate to scenario.

TIME

Variable. At least forty-five minutes.

PROCEDURE

For this role play the instructor needs an incident or an encounter between persons from two of the culture groups on which the course focuses or which are represented among the students in the class. It may take place in school, in an office, on the playground, in the home, in a store, on the street, or in any other natural setting. Just so that people of two different cultures encounter each other in some significant way. This incident is then turned into a scenario for the students to act out.

Next, the instructor defines the objectives of the role play. These may be based on the subject of the course or may be derived uniquely from the role play. Example objectives:

a. Demonstrate an understanding of the importance of conformity and tradition

b. Demonstrate an understanding of the value of status and respect for authority

c. Show an awareness of different attitudes toward change and other cultural values

d. Show skill in dealing with an official from another culture group

e. Show awareness of certain family pressures faced by the other person

f.  Demonstrate the ability to control the tendency to push one's own point of view, finding a thoughtful compromise and controling one's frustration during the process.

From the incident and the objectives the instructor builds the event or events which constitute the scenario. It should be a short encounter which can be played out in 15 or 20 minutes. The scenario should be described briefly on a sheet of paper separate from the "instructions" (see next item).

The aim is to provide a core event which the students can act out adding their own words and elaborations according to their individual personal responses to it. Written instructions are prepared for each of the "actors" which establish each character's point of view or role. The instructions for each role should be on separate pieces of paper. Actors should see instructions for only their own role. The role should be culturally logical and consistent and should give the student a clear guide as to how in general to behave. The roles, however, should be <u>directed toward conflicting ends</u> or <u>should use incompatible means of achieving a common end</u>.

At the beginning of the session everyone should be given a copy of the scenario. Actors should be selected in whatever way is most comfortable for the teacher. The rest of the class are then considered "observers" and are asked to watch for the following:

a.  Sources of conflict between the characters

b.  Differences in motivation, approach and perspective

c.  Kinds of feelings exhibited

d.  Types of non-verbal communication

e.  The influence of real or pretended culture in the encounter.

After the scene has been played, allow twenty to thirty minutes for discussion of it.

DISCUSSION

First ask the observers what they saw and how they reacted. Then ask the actors to describe (1) how they felt during the session and (2) what it meant to them.

Be sure to relate the role play, by way of summary, to other intercultural issues. All the students should be asked to take a few minutes to record what they learned from the session.

NOTES:

If the facilities are available, you might try video taping the role play. Watching the video tape can be both fun and a reinforcement to the learning experience.

Care must be taken in writing the situation so it is believable
-- and performable.  You might have to try several situations before
you get the right one.  Be sure that the scenario is written as
non-value-laden as possible.  It should be a simple description of the
facts and should not bias the reader or the actors one way or the
other.  Make sure the roles are clear and descriptive, but do not make
them so rigid that the participants have no freedom of action.

Check the accuracy or believability of the exercise <u>before</u>
conducting it so as to avoid stereotyping and loss of credibility.

Source:  Adapted from "Role Plays" in <u>A Manual of Teaching Techniques
for Intercultural Education</u> (UNESCO).  Henry Holmes and Stephen Guild,
eds., 1971.

# A TUTORING PROJECT

## OBJECTIVE

To practice resolving a cross-cultural conflict situation by using skills in communication and analysis to reach a solution.

## PARTICIPANTS

There is no particular group size but it should not be so large as to intimidate the actors.

## MATERIAL

1. Scenario.  2. Individual Roles.  3. Props (dress, artifacts, etc.).

## SETTING

Any standard classroom, preferably with moveable chairs.

## TIME

Variable.  One class period should be sufficient.

## PROCEDURE

1.  Distribute copies of the scenario to the entire class, who will be observers.  This is the only information they will receive.

2.  Distribute the roles and a scenario to the "actors" being careful not to expose one role to the other.

3.  Set the stage both physically -- with props, furniture, etc. -- and educationally by preparing the observers and participants for what they are going to do.  (There is a tendency, especially at first, to treat role plays and situational exercises lightly, so the instructor's role is very important in setting the right mood.)

4.  When all are clear on their parts, start the exercise.  Let it run as long as you feel is productive.  When the action begins to lag, it should be stopped.

5.  Follow with discussion, perhaps 20-30 minutes, organized around these suggested topics:

     a.    What was each of the individuals trying to accomplish?

     b.    What were the problems?

     c.    What differences did you notice in each individual's behavior?  What non-verbal differences did you observe?

     d.    How do you think each felt during the scene?

6. After observers have shared their ideas on these, allow the participants to give their own reactions to the same points.

When selecting students for the exercise, do not necessarily choose ones who will "perform" the best, but those who can benefit personally from the experience.

The role play can be run again with other students playing the roles. It makes an interesting comparison.

If video-tape equipment is available, the entire exercise can be recorded and then played back immediately or at a later time.

## SCENARIO

The Situation: A Tutoring Project. Because it is a large urban school serving a somewhat unstable population, Bourdin School has found it difficult to maintain close relations with members of the community. One particular aspect of this problem is the increasing number in immigrants to the community from different ethnic and racial backgrounds whose children are often very unprepared -- from a cultural and language standpoint -- for the academic and social expectations of the school.

The principal, in an effort to improve the school's service to the communmity, set to work with members of the English department and student leaders to introduce a program in which older student volunteers would offer tutoring to younger children from immigrant families. These lessons would be given in the family's home. The school hoped that the service would result in more rapid adjustment to school life for the new student and increased confidence in the school on the part of the new parents. It might also offer a good cultural experience for the tutor.

Mee Loon is 15. Her parents have very recently emigrated from Hong Kong. Her English teacher at Bourdin, observing her difficulty with English, recommended to her the student tutoring service, and suggested she explain it to her parents. If they agreed to the sessions, the school would select a student to come to the house and arrange a tutoring schedule suitable to the family.

Juan, an older student, was told yesterday that the parents of a Chinese girl, Mee Loon, were interested in someone to tutor her in English. Miss Smith, Mee Loon's English teacher agreed to accompany Juan to an initial meeting at the Chow's home in the Chinese community in order to introduce him and help get the tutoring started.

### Individual Roles

Mr. Chow (Father). You are the absolute head of the family in the traditional manner. Although you had little opportunity for formal education yourself, you are quite happy that your daughter, Mee Loon, is getting educated. You try to bring up your daughter according to tradional ways. You have had very little contact with Bourdin School yourself.

-184-

It made you apprehensive to learn that the school was going to send instead of a teacher, a young man -- a student -- to teach your daughter. It was also uncomfortable for you to have this young man coming to your house. You were worried about neighbors might make of it.

When the young man arrives, you will be further concerned about the length of his hair, his clothes, and perhaps his unusual manners. You are also surprised and distressed to find that he is of Hispanic rather than native English speaking background.

Mrs. Chow (Mother). You have observed with keen interest the developments concerning these English lessons since they concern your daughter. You are a sympathetic person although you are relatively unexposed. Your husband is usually the spokesman for the family to the outside world and you are therefore not outspoken with important matters. You would, of course, abide by any decision your husband makes. You are always courteous.

Mee Loon (New Student). You are rather quiet, particulary in the presence of a teacher or your parents. You have been having a difficult time with several subjects at Bourdin School, in large part because of the need for English lessons. Your English teacher seems to want you to start taking lessons but you do not feel strongly one way or the other. You have been brought up to respect authority.

Juan (Tutor). You are a fluently bi-lingual student of Puerto Rican background and the top student in your English class. You are eager to begin this new project. Besides the tutoring, you look forward to learning about Chinese culture. Although you have studied about a number of other cultures, you know little about Chinese customs and traditions. You surmise that Mee Loon and her parents will welcome you as someone who can intoduce her to this country, its customs and its cultural diversity.

Miss Smith (Teacher). You are an outspoken direct person, deeply concerned with the education of your students. You are not sure assigning Juan to Mee Loon was the right decision but his English teacher had insisted. You know little about Chinese or Puerto Rican cultures. Your Chinese students have always been hardworking but much too reserved in class.

Source: Adapted from A Manual of Teaching Techniques for Intercultural Education, UNESCO. Henry Holmes and Stephen Guild, eds., 1971.

# WASHINGTONVILLE

## OBJECTIVE

To enable trainees to explore (or 'check') the assumptions they make about other people and how these people assess issues of common concern. To demonstrate how differing cultural perceptions and perspectives influence those assumptions.

## PARTICIPANTS

Any size group in which open discussion can easily be conducted.

## MATERIALS

Copies of the roles and the situation; copies of the Superintendent's memo.

## SETTING

No special requirements.

## TIME

To be fully effective, the Washingtonville simulation requires at least two hours. The first hour is spent role playing and the second hour is devoted to clarifying and discussing the cultural assumptions that were observed to surface during the role play.

## PROCEDURE

The four individuals who have volunteered to play the roles are provided with materials and allowed some time to think about how they would like to play their roles. During this period, the leader will explain the situation to the other members of the group who will be observing and will provide them with copies of the Superintendent's memo. This should take about 10 minutes.

Clearly, there is no predetermined, correct way to play a given role. The actors should simply play them as they see them.

## ROLES

Melissa Cathers - 31 years old Black female. Four years as social science teacher, two years at Washingtonville Junior High.

William Anderson - 47 year old White male. Language arts teacher for 14 years, ten years at Washingtonville Junior High. Tenured.

Maria Del Fuego - 37 years old Hispanic female. Entering second year as math teacher at Washingtonville Junior High.

Lou Chen - 25 year old Oriental male. First year teacher in science.

The cultural identification of the role players may be changed according to the cultural make-up of the participant group.

SITUATION

Poll-takers and realtors refer to Washingtonville as "a transition area." The population is 1% Oriental, 22% Black, 13% Spanish speaking, and 65% White. Every year more Whites move away. The school reflects the population distribution of the area.

WJH comprises 424 students in grades 7 and 8. Your team is responsible for 106 students, from both grades. You are meeting for the first time as a team; although Bill and Melissa worked together on the same team last year. The agenda is to deal with the Superintendent's memo of August 30, 1972.

At the end of the role play period the players will be asked to comment upon the assumptions they brought to their roles and the feelings and difficulties they experienced in playing the roles. The players will also be asked to describe the assumptions they felt the other role players were making toward them in their roles. Then the observers will comment on the assumptions they felt were revealed in the role play.

In reporting observations each commentator will use the role players role name rather than actual name.

Source: Adapted from an exercise developed by Terry Whaling, University of Massachusetts.

HIGHVIEW
SCHOOLS 1374 Gray, Lincoln, PR.


MEMORANDUM

FROM: _____ Office of the Superintendent _____

TO: _____ Teaching Teams _____

RE: _____ Your Team's Learning Concerns _____


August 30, 1972


As part of its summer agenda, the Curriculum Task Group developed the attached list of Learning Concerns for consideration by each teaching team.

I request that each team use the attached list to develop its own list of Learning Concerns at its pre-opening planning session. Specifically, I am asking you to:

1) cross out the listed concerns which do not apply to your team or students

2) expand into several items those items on the guideline list which you feel are too general

3) add items which you feel are appropriate to your team or students

4) once your team's concerns have been established, prioritize the items by assigning to each a number from 1 to 10 -- ten indicating the highest priority.

HIGHVIEW
SCHOOLS  1374 Gray, Lincoln, PR.


Learning Concerns identified by the Curriculum Task Group

____ 1   community relations          ____ 21   scheduling

____ 2   black wall                   ____ 22   materials

____ 3   sex education                ____ 23   drug education

____ 4   three R's                    ____ 24   Spanish

____ 5   school calendar              ____ 25   vocational training

____ 6   parent-teacher liason        ____ 26   ethnic studies

____ 7   grading                      ____ 27   nutrition

____ 8   grouping                     ____ 28   hall passes

____ 9   student rights

____ 10  teacher rights

____ 11  parent rights

____ 12  discipline

____ 13  homework

____ 14  dress code

____ 15  field trips

____ 16  establishing basic values

____ 17  interpersonal relations

____ 18  learning contracts

____ 19  survival

____ 20  testing

# CASE STUDIES/CRITICAL INCIDENTS

Case studies involve the participants in problem-solving. They provide an excellent, brief and easy way of generating substantive discussion. If properly prepared, case studies are especially useful because they can focus on real life issues experienced by the students themselves, by people similar to them or by people in comparable situations.

Briefly, case studies are analogues of actual situations written as close to reality as possible. The advantage of the case study lies not within the described case, in which there may be more or less descriptive material than the individual or group might like to have, but in the almost unlimited potential for thinking about, talking about and deciding about the many ways of solving the problem, discussing the human and organizational interactions described, and analyzing both organizational and human successes and failures. Case studies open up the opportunity to think carefully, analytically, and understandingly about the experiences that the cases describe. None of the situations set forth in the cases is simple or capable of easy solution; many of the situations depend upon the attitudes, the sentiments, and the prejudices of the people involved rather than upon the actual events. Hence, these cases engender the need for careful thought about:

1. one's own personal reactions to the situation and to the people coping with it;

2. the points of view of each of the characters involved; and

3. the possible outcomes of such situations and their effects upon the various protagonists.

In other words, the case studies are designed to develop a method of approaching situations that will facilitate maximum understanding of those situations, of the people in them, and of the several outcomes that might result when one or another of the people emphasizes certain values rather than others. Furthermore, the case studies afford students an opportunity to practice this method of tackling problems before they are personally involved in situations that may be confusing, frightening or overwhelming.

To think carefully, analytically and understandingly as mentioned above is not as easy as it seems. In using case studies, seemingly simple situations when analyzed carefully are in reality complex and open-ended, amenable to resolution only over a long span of time.

What then is the case method?

1. It is a description of a specific situation, as near to reality as analogy permits (with names changed to protect the innocent).

2.   The focus is on experience, therefore an actual situations where action/decisions can be made.

3.   The discussion centers on an actual, multi-faceted situation.

4.   As much as possible, case studies emphasize the particular rather than the general.

5.   The participants should feel that they have had the experience that the case study describes.

6.   The case study must be interesting.

7.   The decision-making is done by the individual reader or the group. There are no observers or spectators.

8.   The decision-making process itself can be dissected and analyzed as the group moves toward solutions.

9.   Ideally, the case study method, when used well, gets the participant in the habit of making decisions.

10.  If a time-frame is established, i.e. 60 minutes, 2 hours, etc., decision-making includes use of time. We _have_ to decide, and "not to decide is to decide."

11.  To make good decisions, all the factual material in the case study should be used.

12.  Case studies are best when they come as close to reality as possible; therefore, they should reflect day-to-day and run-of-the-mill decision-making with opportunity for differences of opinion. Resolving those differences of opinion into consensus, or majority-minority decisions, is part of the task.

Critical incidents are shorter case studies, usually no more than a few paragraphs long, which present the bare outlines of an event. They are designed more as a trigger for discussion than as the focus of substantive analysis.

An interesting video taped series of critical incidents has been produced by the Human Relations Research Organization in cooperation with the Illinois Office of Education. Included in the series are brief encounters between Anglos and Hispanics in a school setting. These encounters are designed to show differences in values, perceptions and behaviors between the two culture groups. In it's current form, the series is intended to be used in cultural awareness training programs for Anglo school personnel. (Further information may be obtained from Dr. Alfred Kraemer, HUMMRO, 300 N. Washington Street, Alexandria, VA.)

# BILINGUAL EDUCATION COMES TO LONGFELLOW

Angrily waiving a stack of papers in front of the principal's face, the president of the local school advisory council demanded, "You have twenty minutes to explain THIS!"

The place was the St. Demetrios Greek Orthodox Church. The occasion, a regular meeting of the Longfellow Elementary School Local Advisory Council. The date, March 21, 1973. The papers in question were mimeographed copies of the school's first preliminary proposal requesting state bilingual education funds to implement a program designed to meet the special needs of, according to the proposal, a large number of Greek immigrant children living in the district.

Highly emotional questions and statements were articulated at this meeting:

"We are not involved in planning this program!" said one member of the council.

"You and the Hellenic Council are trying to cram this program down our throats."

"The Greek classes at St. Demetrios will suffer if Longfellow begins teaching Greek."

"Teaching Greek is a home and church responsibility, not the responsibility of the public school."

"If we start running programs for immigrant children the word will get around and Greek immigrants will flood Longfellow."

"The bilingual program goal of giving Greek surnamed children a positive self-image of their heritage insults the Greek home, the Greek church, and Greek community in this city. It also insults Greece since it implies that Greece as a country has failed to establish a culture of any worth, and its citizens when they leave Greece have to hunt for some kind of identity."

"This program asks for a handout from the state. It's really for poor Spanish-speaking people, not for hard-working Greeks who know how to take care of their own."

"There are only two Greek children in Longfellow who don't know any English."

Not all of the comments attacked the proposal. Some members of the council defended it.

"There is a definite need for the program. There are over 400 children at Longfellow who don't know enough English to get along in school."

-192-

"We were involved in the planning of the program. The principal was asked by this council three months ago to look into both state and federal funding for bilingual education."

"The bilingual program planning committee included representatives from the faculty, council, and the PCA, and all helped draft the proposal."

Within one month of this meeting the battle lines were clearly drawn with only few people in the community remaining neutral. The most common reason people gave for supporting the bilingual proposal was the large numbers of children who needed it. But other reasons were offered too. One woman said that the opponents to the program complained that it would just attract poor immigrants, and she had been in the U.S. just nine years and already had bought a $65,000 home and resented anyone calling Greek immigrants poor and ignorant.

It is harder to pinpoint the central issue among the program opponents. A sample of their comments follows.

"The school principal tells us lies."

"The Church opposes the program. They (the Church) provide the services already."

"I've been here in the Longfellow community for 22 years and people regard me as an American, not a Greek. Now this bilingual program is stirring everybody up and reminding them that we are Greeks."

"With more immigrants moving in, property values will go down."

"We've made a good life for ourselves here, now the immigrants want to spoil it. They don't know how to get ahead; they want charity."

"Our people aren't like some other groups. Greeks are smart and hardworking."

"These children need to learn more English, not hear Greek, all day in school."

From this point out, few people changed sides on the issue in spite of considerable efforts to "explain" the bilingual proposal. Petitions supporting either side could and did appear from time to time with anywhere from 600 to 2,000 signatures gathered over two or three days. Both sides actively lobbied to influence state and local officials and public opinion amidst a backdrop of charged emotionalism. Police were called to ewject dissidents at several meetings: a three-day boycott of the school was 45% effective. Neither side was willing to compromise any point.

The two opposing groups did not differ much in terms of ethnic background. Both were largely Greek with a minority membership of non-Greeks. The opposition tended to be middle class, while the program supporters were heavily working class. The opposition tended to be assimilated Greeks with both prestige and political connections, while the program supports tended to be recent arrivals to the U.S. Longfellow teachers were equally divided on the issue of whether to initiate a bilingual program.

The program, with some compromises insisted by the state, was funded in September, 1973. The community remains divided. Attack has shifted somewhat from the bilingual program specifically, to all of the school policies and its administrators.

Source:  Prepared by H. Ned Seelye for the Annual Conference of the Society for Intercultural Education, Training and Research in Phoenix, Arizona, February, 1978.  Based on a real incident; name of the school has been changed.

# CRITICAL INCIDENTS

## OBJECTIVE

To uncover and analyze the cultural components of an incident in which misunderstanding or conflict has occurred.

## PARTICIPANTS

Any number.

## MATERIALS

Copies of incidents for each participant.

## SETTING

No special requirements but it is best if people can sit in a circle or around a table.

## TIME

Variable.

## PROCEDURE

1. Copies of all the incidents you plan to discuss are distributed to the participants. It is useful to have a set of ten or twelve from which to choose.

2. Divide the participants into small groups and ask each group to discuss one incident (assigned by the instructor), answering the following questions:

      a.   What is the problem?

      b.   How can it be resolved?

3. Have small groups reconvene after about twenty minutes of discussion (or whenever the instructor notices people have finished) and report on the results of their discussion.

4. The instructor should assist participants in identifying the cross-cultural issues involved and use those issues to illustrate the basic concepts and processes of intercultural communicaton and cross-cultural relations.

# SAMPLE CRITICAL INCIDENTS

1. Lu Chen Chang applied for a scholarship to assist her with her educational expenses. In an interview with the scholarship committee she explained that her father had recently suffered a stroke and was no longer able to assist her financially. Since her grades were good the interviewing committee sought primarily to determine the extent of her financial need. Lu Chen indicated to the committee that she had taken a part-time job but was unwilling to say anything about the job. When questioned about her part-time work she answered only, "I'd rather not say."

   Afterwards during the committee review of her application several members remarked that it was strange that Lu Chen refused to discuss her part-time job. One member remarked that perhaps she was afraid to disclose her wage earnings because they might disqualify her for the scholarship. Another member hinted that she might be involved in some illegal or immoral activity.

2. Maria Gonzalez, a Puerto Rican student who had been getting excellent grades during the first half of her sophomore year, began to have trouble. When her advisor asked about it, she said she was upset at having broken up with her boyfriend, Bob Williams. The advisor tried to help her gain perspective, but it didn't seem to do any good.

   Maria said the problem was that she couldn't understand what had happened. They had already talked of marriage. She had gone with him to visit his home in Ohio, and had liked his mother and father. They had been kind and friendly. In New York her family took to Bob at once and welcomed him fully.

   After that he grew cool toward her and finally stopped seeing her. The only reason he would give was that he didn't want to be smothered.

3. Raphael Garcia and Alfredo Perez started out as close friends in college. They had grown up together in the Chicano section of the city, gone to high school together, worked for Chicano civil rights, and gone on to the city's major university.

   Once in college, however, they began to grow apart. Raphael found the stimulus of an academic education exciting and turned his attention heavily to his books. He also made new friends among Anglos as well as Chicanos. At about the same time his family moved to another city and he took up residence in a dorm.

   Alfredo, on the other hand, continued to be more committed to his community, his old friends, and the cause.

When they got to their senior year, Raphael was elected student body president and Alfredo led a sit-in protesting the anti-Chicano statements of one of the Anglo vice-Presidents of the university.

Each opposed the action of the other and their friendship ended in a bitter quarrel, with Raphael claiming he could do more for Chicanos within the system and Alfredo arguing that the only way to help Chicanos was in opposition to the system.

Source:  Used in workshops by the Intercultural Network, Inc.

# FORCE FIELD ANALYSIS

Force Field Analysis is a basic process designed to help groups clarify issues and explore their feelings about them. It is frequently used at a point in a discussion when the group is stymied and needs to understand better what it is discussing and whether or not to continue. It is also an exercise that can clarify ideas that are both complex and emotion-laden but which are important for the group to look at and deal with. It is particularly useful as an aid to decision-making since it presents graphically the pros and cons.

Basically, Force Field Analysis asks participants to look at the forces working for and the forces working against the achievement of some defined goal. An analysis of these "forces in the field that surrounds the issue" reveals a great deal about the subject that is being considered and about the people who are engaged in analyzing it.

# FORCE FIELD ANALYSIS EXERCISE

## OBJECTIVE

To isolate forces that contribute to clarification and decision-making behavior in a cross-culture setting, and to acquire an appreciation of the complexity of those forces.

## PARTICIPANTS

Moderate to large size groups with members of diverse cultural backgrounds.

## MATERIALS

Paper and pencils, blackboard and chalk.

## SETTING

No special requirements.

## TIME

At least thirty to forty-five minutes.

## PROCEDURE

1. The instructor and/or students select an issue which is important to the instructional objectives of the course. Example: "Can a program be established that facilitates learning between children of different cultural backgrounds at _____ school."

Issues selected can be broad or more narrowly focused. Broad issues (such as "multicultural education, improving intercultural relations among ethnic groups, the advantages of cultural pluralism") may be more useful at the outset of a program to give the students a quick overview of what they will be discussing. More specific issues (such as non-evaluative feedback in intercultural communication, overcoming the 'remedial' image of bilingual programs, changes in curriculum design) may be more effectively used later in the program when participants are ready to come to grips with the issues in greater detail.

2. Students may remain in a full group or break into subgroups which may be culturally diverse or homogeneous.

3. Each group is asked to brainstorm a list of "forces working for" and "forces working against" the subject selected. One member of the group is asked to record suggestions under the respective headings. One member is asked to record the list.

4. The lists (if participants are in subgroups) are then shared and a final list is compiled on the board.

5.   Discussion includes:  clarification of the forces listed
and why they were identified, exploration of cultural dimensions of
the forces and how they can be dealt with (if against) or reinforced
(if for), and evaluation of the relative 'weight' of the forces on
either side.

6.   The group may continue to deal with the issue by systematically considering ways in which each obstacle can be overcome and
each advantage exploited to meet the objectives of the group.

Source:   Adapted by the Intercultural Network, Inc. from a commonly
used workshop exercise.

SUGGESTIONS FOR THE DISCUSSION OF FILMS

EXAMPLE: CHAIRY TALE

I. General Suggestions

    A. Content Questions for Discussion

        1. What is the theme or moral in this film for you? Is it universal?

        2. If the setting of this film was your cultural environment, how similar/different would events and personal relationships have been than to those in the film?

        3. If the film involved resolution of a problem, what are other alternatives to the course of action taken in this film?

        4. With which character do you identify the most? Why?

        5. How real was this film for you? How does it relate directly to any experiences you have had?

        6. What feelings did you experience during the film? When did these occur, and why?

        7. What does this film suggest to you about behaviors, thoughts, feelings to strive for or avoid when communicating with someone from another culture?

        8. What values lay behind the main character's actions in the film? If someone from your country was in a similar situation, would the same values be in operation? If so, would the same behaviors follow from such values?

Any or all of the above questions might be used according to their appropriateness to the context of the film and to the audience.

    B. Process Issues During Discussing

During the discussion following the film you should be alert to cultural issues or biases which arise as the audience shares reactions to the film. The following thoughts may be helpful:

        1. There is no culturally universal way of behaving in a small group. Be conscious of group members who are silent or hesitant to speak up. These members may need structure provided by a leader's direct question in order to feel comfortable participating.

2. Although everyone in the discussion group may speak English, none will share identical meanings for words -- particularly if the words in question are emotion-laden. Past experiences to which meanings of words are tied will also differ from person to person. If several group members appear to misunderstand each other or if an argument should occur, it is often very helpful to ask these group members to define the terms or concepts which they misunderstood or about which they disagree. Rather than being ignored, the presence of such unclear communication can be the basis for clarifying how cultural experience determines communicative behavior. Out of this clarification may come a model for behavior which facilitates communication.

3. Sometimes one person, representative of a particular culture, is asked to respond to a question as if his or her experiences could represent all members of that culture. This not only puts an undue responsibility on this person, but obscures the context of individual variation within cultural parameters. Speaking for "my culture" instead of "my experience within my culture" also ignores regional, religious, occupational, age, sex and other differences which exist within a culture. Thus, group members should be encouraged to speak only for themselves. Their cultures will be sufficiently manifest to those who listen carefully. It may be appropriate, at times, to point up differences within a culture by asking how a woman, an older person, or "someone from the North" would respond to a particular question.

II. Specific Suggestions Relevant to A Chairy Tale

A. Content Questions

1. How does the film illustrate the role that expectations play in determining the nature of an interpersonal encounter? What feelings are aroused when expectations are not met? Can you personalize this to a time when your expectations were not met when interacting with a particular person or when entering an unfamiliar culture or environment? How does our cultural membership help to set up our expectations?

2. How does this film illustrate the process of stereotyping? How is your culture group stereotyped by others? Do you feel you have ever been reacted to as a stereotype in a one-to-one situation? How did you react . . . in any way similar to the chair?

3.    Did you personify the chair? How? A man, a woman, a
      child? <u>Why?</u> What in the chair's behavior led you to
      your personification? What about the relationship
      between the man and the chair led you to your
      personification?

      In discussing the answer to question 3, it is vital to
      point out that what we see is "partly what is there
      and partly who we are." Although we always project
      meaning into any stimulus based on our own cultural
      experience, this is particularly true as the stimulus
      becomes more ambiguous.

      These points about the perceptual process, as
      illustrated by this film, are extremely relevant to
      the process of giving meanings to behaviors of others
      in an unfamiliar cultural setting.

4.    The man and the chair seemed to go through stages in
      their relationship. Can you separate out and name
      them. How do these stages relate to the stages of an
      interpersonal intercultural encounter?

"A Chairy Tale" is available from Film Bureau, Inc., 332 S. Michigan
Avenue, Chicago, ILL., 60604 or Syracuse University Film Rental
Service, 1455 E. Colvin Street, Syracuse, N.Y., 13210.


Note: A list of films appropriate for cross-cultural training follows
the bibliography in the full manual.

Source:   Sheila Ramsey and Toby S. Frank

# REFERENCE LIST

Batchelder, Donald and Elizabeth G. Warner (eds.) Beyond Experience. Brattleboro, Vt.: Experiment in International Living, 1977.

Holmes, Henry and Stephen Guild. A Manual of Teaching Techniques for Intercultural Education. Amherst, MA: UNESCO, 1971.

Hoopes, David S. and Paul Ventura. Intercultural Sourcebook: Cross-Cultural Training Methodologies. Washington, D.C.: Society for Intercultural Education, Training and Research, 1979.

Hoopes, Davis S. (ed.) Readings in Intercultural Communication, Volume V, Intercultural Programming. Pittsburgh, PA.: Intercultural Communications Network, 1976.

Ruben, Brent D. and Richard W. Budd. Human Communication Handbook: Simulations and Games. Rochelle Park, N.Y.: Hayden Book Co., Inc., 1975.

Weeks, William H., Paul B. Peterson and Richard W. Brislin (eds.) A Manual of Structured Experiences for Cross-Cultural Learning. Washington, D.C.: Society for Intercultural Education, Training and Research, 1977.

Wright, Albert R. and Mary Anne Hammons. Guidelines for Peace Corps Cross-Cultural Training. Estes Park, CO.: Center for Research and Education, 1970.

CHAPTER 7

EVALUATION:  SOME PRACTICAL GUIDELINES

CONTENTS

CHAPTER 7

EVALUATION:

SOME PRACTICAL GUIDELINES

George W. Renwick

Has there actually been any learning? If so, what kind of learning? Is it what we intended? If our best efforts have resulted in some learning, how much learning has there been? For whom? And how long will the learning be retained? Does it become the basis and means for still further learning over time, or is it quickly extinguished?

As is true with most questions in the social sciences, it is difficult to come up with conclusive answers. When dealing with people, especially changes within and between people, proof is elusive. Evidence, however, is available; indications, clues and signals can be obtained; they suggest answers to these fundamental questions and are therefore indispensable.

Evidence is gathered through evaluation. Revealing evaluation does require some thought and effort, but it can be done with less technical knowledge than many teachers and trainers realize. For some kinds of evaluation, for example, a knowledge of statistics is not necessary. A rather simple, carefully designed evaluation of a carefully designed course or program can yield surprising insights and suggest new, very promising directions. Evaluation can become, in other words, the primary channel through which the teacher learns. What is learned through this channel is often extremely interesting. Further, of course, what the teacher learns enables the teacher to increase what the student learns.

Let's be more specific. We are not concerned with all kinds of learning; we are concerned, much concerned, about learning how to function and grow within, and contribute to, pluralistic societies. Multicultural education and cross-cultural training have been defined as a structured process designed to foster understanding, acceptance and effective interaction among people of many different cultures. The question we must now ask is: How do we know, in the midst of this process, whether we are actually fostering understanding, acceptance and effective interaction?

Still more specifically, through multicultural education and cross-cultural training we attempt to build an awareness of one's own cultural heritage, and to build those skills in analysis and communication that contribute to an ability to function effectively in multicultural environments. The question now: How do we know that students and program participants, as a result of our efforts, have developed more cultural self-awareness and more competence (and confidence) in intercultural analysis and intercultural communication? We know this, or can at least estimate this, through basic evaluation procedures.

Fortunately, there is now much work in the field of evaluation to draw upon. During recent years, as the number of institutions and projects competing for limited financial resources has rapidly increased, the requirements for systematic evaluation have become more frequent and more stringent. Project directors, educators and others are now held more accountable for what they do (and fail to do). More attention has therefore been given to the purposes and especially the methods of evaluation. Numerous organizations and several journals specializing in evaluation have been established (some of these are listed with the resources at the end of this text). Evaluation has now become a distinct and very lively field.

Our purpose here is to explain some of the basic procedures of sound evaluation and some of the methods of measurement which are now being used. We have selected those which are most helpful to those involved in multicultural education, and especially helpful to teachers and trainers who are experimenting with the cross-cultural training approach.

How, then, does the teacher or the trainer become a responsible evaluator? The first step, of course, is to recognize the importance of evaluation to oneself and one's students or program participants, and to commit oneself to doing evaluation. Next, a number of basic questions must be considered:

1. Who does the evaluation
2. For whom is it done
3. When is it done
4. What is to be measured
5. How is the measurement to be made
6. How can the tabulation of results be enjoyable
7. What is the appropriate format for the findings
8. How are the findings to be interpreted and used

We will consider each of these questions in the remainder of this chapter and will outline some of the alternatives within each.

# WHO DOES THE EVALUATION

There are a number of reasons why it is sometimes best to have the evaluation done by someone who is not involved in the course or program, someone in another part of the school or the organization, or perhaps better, someone from outside. Such a person brings object- ivity to the task and may bring special expertise. There are several organizations which evaluate intercultural teaching and training activities; information on these is included in the list of resources.

There are also reasons, however, why it may be best for teachers and trainers to do the evaluation themselves. Although it may be difficult for them to be objective, they are certainly the ones most thoroughly acquainted with the goals, content and methods of the courses they teach and the programs they conduct, as well as the needs, learning styles and aspirations of the students and program participants. Furthermore, there is seldom time or funding to enlist someone else. If there is to be an evaluation, therefore, there is normally little room for choice. It is usually the teacher or trainer who must do it. In the remaining areas, however, there is a great deal of room for choice.

# FOR WHOM THE EVALUATION IS DONE

This decision will influence significantly all subsequent decisions relative to evaluation. The choice of the "consumer" of the evaluation - the person or group for whom it is being done - will influence the purpose of the evaluation, when it is done, what is measured, how the measurement is done and how the findings are used.

There are several possible consumers. At the beginning of any evaluation effort, the evaluator should choose the one to which priority will be given:

THE STUDENTS AND PROGRAM PARTICIPANTS: In some of their evalu- ation efforts, teachers and trainers will probably want the findings, and in fact the evaluation process itself, to be of primary and most direct benefit to their students and participants. In this case, the evaluation is designed to provide pertinent information to them for their consideration and discussion, or to give them periodic check points and readings on their progress.

Evaluation designed primarily for the student or participants can serve another important purpose, perhaps the most important purpose. It can enable them, through the questions it asks or thought it stimulates, to continue to evaluate their learning after the formal evaluation in a particular course or program is completed. Through their structured practice in the classroom, students and participants can learn habits of constructive self-evaluation which will be used and developed further during later education and later experiences in life. Of greatest benefit to them, therefore, may be the process of the evaluation which serves as a stimulus to further learning. The design of this process is therefore extremely important, both for the information it yields and the patterns it imparts.

-209-

THE TEACHER AND THE TRAINER: Certain times during the year (or during their careers), teachers and trainers may want or need a reading on themselves and on their courses or programs. Evaluation can provide them with information on how they come across and how the subject matter they choose and the methods they use are being received. The end in mind is to increase their professional growth and effectiveness and to enable them to modify where indicated some of their strategies.

All conscientious teachers and trainers, of course, try to pick up indications of learners' responses (and others' responses) every day. A more systematic procedure, however, can be more accurate and can be a very valuable supplement. Because the person to gain most directly from this kind of evaluation are teachers and trainers themselves, the findings are often not given to others (students, administrators, etc.).

ADMINISTRATORS: In their attempts to determine the quality of their school's curriculum, administrators may periodically ask teachers for reports on their intercultural courses. Or an administrator may call upon them to justify the continuation of a course, the introduction of a new course or special intensive program, or the introduction of a major new approach within existing course. In each case, the evaluation is done primarily for the administrator. The administrator's interests and questions must therefore be the ones clarified at the outset and addressed in the evaluation design.

COLLEAGUES: Teachers and trainers often work quite isolated from one another. The approaches and strategies of each, and the consequences of these for the students or participants, are seldom known to one's colleagues. This lack of communication, of course, limits the learning of everyone in a field and retards the development of multicultural education and cross-cultural training.

Both teacher and students, as well as trainers and participants, stand to benefit from the experiences and experiments of others. Teachers and trainers can begin to provide some of this benefit by conducting careful evaluation designed primarily to assist themselves and their colleagues in their common endeavor and to advance their developing field. Such evaluation efforts are usually most helpful if they are designed cooperatively by several colleagues. The evaluation can then be conducted in several classes and programs, the findings can be jointly analyzed and the conclusions jointly drawn. Perhaps, occasionally, articles can then be written. Evaluation of courses and programs, and cooperative analysis of their effects, are especially important where new intercultural techniques are being tried, modified and integrated with regular curricula and training sequences.

OUTSIDERS: Teachers and administrators, trainers and managers, sometimes find it advantageous (or even necessary) to describe their courses and programs in a clear, convincing way to particular individuals and institutions outside their schools and organizations. These would include state and federal government agencies, accreditation units, potential funding sources, professional societies, school boards, other schools, and other organizations. If the teachers and trainers are to represent their efforts in a credible manner, they must base their presentations on sound evaluation. In such cases, it is the requirements of this outside party that must be kept in mind while designing the evaluation. The subsequent choices will be shaped accordingly.

The basic purpose of evaluation in academic and professional education, then, is to provide for learners, evaluators, administrators, colleagues and outside parties the specific information on courses and programs which will be directly related to their concerns and immediately useful in their work.

In determining what will be most useful to the one to whom priority has geen given, it is helfpul to look especially at the decisions the person or group must make. Once their major decisions have been clarified, the evaluator will be able to specify what information is necessary in order to help them make a sound decision. Knowing the kind of information needed, the evaluator is then better able to make subsequent choices regarding when to do the evaluation, what to measure, the methods to be used and the format in which the findings are to be presented.

## WHEN THE EVALUATION IS DONE

Courses and programs are seldom evaluated at all. When they are, the evaluation is usually looked upon as a means for finding out generally how things went and is tacked on at the end.

Evaluation, however, is also a very valuable means for finding out how things are going. It should therefore be done during the course or program.

In addition, evaluation is the most useful means for finding out how things should go. It is therefore important to begin asking questions about the evaluation, using evaluation methods (and studying the findings from previous evaluations) before the course or program, that is, during the planning phase.

In order to contribute all it is capable of, evaluation must be built into the entire teaching and training process and should inform each phase of the process. It is, in fact, a primary means through which the different phases of a course or program can be integrated with one another. Next to the teacher or trainer himself, evaluation can be the major source of course integrity.

A diagram is presented below. It clarifies the purposes of evaluation and identifies the phases of the teaching and training process at which evaluation can be most productive.

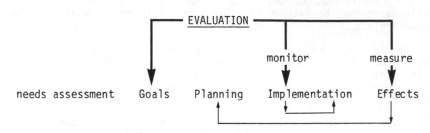

As illustrated in the diagram, the first step in preparing a course or program is the needs assessment. The specific needs of students and of participants in training programs, if estimated at all, are often estimated on the basis of hunches. In non-technical learning (involving, for example, cultural self-awareness and communicative competence), as in technical learning, systematic assessment is essential in ensuring that the course or program meets the real needs of the learners. It is upon the precise definition of their needs that the goals of the course are formulated and the course itself is designed. Also, it is (partially) in terms of students' specific needs that the goals, implementation and effects of the course are later evaluated.

It is helpful to think of assessment and evaluation as somewhat different activities. Assessment looks more at given conditions and then describes those conditions. Evaluation looks more at processes and then determines their worth and their consequences. The procedures and methods for assessment and evaluation, however, are often the same. In preparing their needs assessment, therefore, the teachers and trainers can choose from the alternatives outlined later those which are most appropriate to their particular students and to their particular purposes. The teacher assessment phase is usually necessary whether the evaluation is to be done primarily for the students, the teacher, an administrator, colleagues or an outside party.

Looking now at the rest of the diagram, the reader can see that it assumes the evaluation is to be used primarily by the teacher or trainer. The monitoring function of evaluation, for example, feeds back immediately into the course itself in order that the teacher can make the indicated adjustments as the course goes along. Similarly, the measuring function does not feed directly into the discussions of the learners or the decisions of an administrator (although, of course, with some different choices it could). Rather, the measuring function feeds back into the planning phase for which the teacher or trainer is responsible and during which fundamental decisions must be made.

The effects which are identified and measured in the diagram are those which are evident at the close of the course or program. The longer-term effects, those which are measured during a follow-up evaluation, are not represented. Needless to say, however, they are crucial. A follow-up evaluation is seldom done but is usually essential if accurate conclusions are to be drawn regarding the impact of the teaching or training effort--and if confident planning is to be done for the next one. The follow-up evaluation can be done one month, three months, six months or longer after the course or program, or it can be done at each of these points (thereby tracing multiplying or diminishing effects). Care must be taken in interpreting the findings, of course, because there are inevitably many other factors during the post-course period which can influence students' and participants' learning and therefore their responses during the follow-up evaluation (this influence is mentioned again in our discussion of methods of measurement). The findings from the follow-up evaluation, as with the findings at the close of the course, feed into the planning phase for the next course.

## WHAT IS TO BE MEASURED

As with the choices in each area, the choices regarding what one should measure will be influenced by the choices which have already been made in other areas. If the findings are primarly for the students, for example, what is measured will sometimes be different from what would be measured for an administrator. Similarly, the choices made in this area will influence choices made in subsequent areas; what is to be measured influences especially the next area: how the measurement is to be done.

The choices here, as elsewhere, are also influenced by the culture and preferences of the teacher, and especially by the cultures and preferences of the students. Investigation of certain subjects is inappropriate for people from some cultures. Investigation of other subjects is not only appropriate but expected. Fundamental cultural characteristics must therefore be kept in mind during the design (and the introduction and administration) of an evaluation, not only out of consideration for the people but also out of concern for the accuracy of their responses. Their responses to a question which is inappropriate, for example, may reflect their resentment toward the question itself (or toward the questioner) rather than their judgment (which is actually being sought).

What, then is to be measured? Lets take teachers and their intercultural courses as an example. There are three basic alternatives: we can measure the teachers, their course, or the consequences of the teachers and their course - the effects upon the learner. Once this choice has been made, there are further alternatives to consider. With regard first to the teachers, one might want to look at their knowledge of their subject, their control over their classes, their ability to interest and motivate students, and so forth. If one is working with multicultural classes, especially if the teachers are trying to develop the students' abilities as intercultural communicators, an evaluation might measure the teachers abilities as role models: their own cultural self-awareness, their appreciation of the contrasting values, goals and learning styles of the students, their ability to act as cultural interpreters or brokers, their ability to identify the cultural sources of conflict among the students and deal creatively with these, or their capacity to communicate their ideas (and perhaps feelings) to all of their students in a clear, receivable manner.

With regard to the course or program, if this is to be the focus of the evaluation, one might look at the goals, components, sequencing (does one component build upon another?), pace, atmosphere, organization, facilities, and so forth. If there are a number of cultures represented in the course, or program, one of the questions an evaluator might ask is this: Are the demands which the structure and strategies make upon the learners (for participation, initiation, or self-disclosure, for example) compatible with their customary ways of learning and relating in formal settings?

With regard now to the effects upon the learners, it is with these that this and the next area are primarily concerned. Measurement of effects sometimes takes more thought, and it is in specific effects that teachers and trainers in multicultural education are usually most interested. Furthermore, a careful study of the effects of a course or program will produce findings which, at least indirectly, provide some critique of both the teacher and the course.

A course or program has effects upon both the individual learner and upon the group of learners as a whole. We will outline first some of the possible effects upon the individuals, then the effects upon the group.

There are five major categories of possible effects upon the individual. An evaluation of effects measures changes which occur within one or more of them. The categories are:

1. knowledge
2. perceptions
3. attitudes
4. skills
5. patterns of behavior

Each of these, of course, is related to the others. Each is integrated with the others in the individual student. Looking at the way a student handles intercultural conflict, for example, we might find the following: the student has studied and learned about the fundamental characteristics of both his own culture and the culture of the person with whom he is now in conflict (knowledge). Given this knowledge, the student's images of the other person, especially his images of the other background, are rather accurate perceptions. Because of his knowledge and his perceptions, the student may be open toward the other person, willing to deal with the conflict and confident as he begins to do so (attitudes). Given his knowledge, perceptions and attitudes, the student may be able to explain his own position in a

-214-

way that the other person can understand, and may be able to analyze for the other person the cultural differences which caused or contributed to their conflict (skills). As the student explains, analyzes, and interprets with this person and then with others, as he conveys his attitudes to this person and then to others, and as he responds to others, he practices and develops new modes of relating and communicating (patterns of behavior).

If the student or participant is in a multicultural setting, of course, he has an excellent opportunity to gain his knowledge of other cultures directly from representatives of those cultures. Given that the cross-cultural training approach is designed to take maximum advantage of this opportunity through the structured interaction, the individual's knowledge about other cultures and persons is significantly enhanced--and his perceptions and attitudes are often shaped accordingly.

Intercultural courses and training programs are also designed to enable persons from contrasting cultures to learn about the process of perceiving -- about the process itself -- and about the process of communicating; the student is then given opportunities to engage in both. Intercultural approaches, therefore, contribute to an additional, and fundamental, kind of knowledge -- a knowledge of process (which can be measured), as well as contributing to the development of specific perceptual and communication skills (which can also be measured).

A word about feelings. A variety of feelings emerge during an intercultural course or program, especially feelings among the students for the teacher and for the other students. These feelings may be some of the most significant effects of the course: affection between an Anglo and a Chicano, rapport between a Black and a White, frustration between a Puerto Rican and a Chinese, and so forth. Such feelings are usually not addressed directly in an evaluation. The reasons are that direct investigation of feelings is sometimes inappropriate, and feelings are assumed to be reflected in attitudes and patterns of behavior, both of which are usually more easily (and more appropriately) measured.

Carefully designed and integrated intercultural teaching and training strategies, therefore, will probably produce all five measurable effects -- some more than others, perhaps, but all five will usually be present. The question is, Which of the five should be measured? It is probably best if teachers begin evaluation efforts by choosing just one, and perhaps just a few of the alternatives within that one. Let's look at some of the alternatives within each. The reader will undoubtedly think of (and perhaps choose) others.

KNOWLEDGE: If it is knowledge that is chosen, one might want to examine some of the following and may want to ascertain any changes in these as a result of the course or program. These include the learner's knowledge of:

1. His own culture, his own distinctive values, goals and patterns of learning and behaving.

2. Other cultures studied or represented in the class (Puerto Rican, Nigerian, Mexican, etc); in other words, his "cultural literacy."
3. The influence of culture upon personality and behavior.
4. The process of perception.
5. The process of communication.
6. The sources of intercultural conflict.
7. Stresses unique to, or augmented in, multicultural environments.
8. Culture shock, culture fatigue, role shock and role fatigue, and what to do about them.
9. His own resources to be mobilized when he is isolated in a new environment.

PERCEPTIONS: Courses and programs also influence perceptions. Perceptions are sometimes, in fact, the major focus of a course or selected strategies within a course. The evaluation may want to get a reading on the learners' perceptions and trace changes in them. An evaluation designed to do this might measure the learners':

1. Images of themselves.
2. Images of people from their own culture.
3. Images of people from other cultures studied or represented in class (Chinese, Germans, Vietnamese, English, etc.).
4. Perceptions (attributions) of the causes of their own and others' behavior.
5. Perceptions of the intentions of culturally different persons toward them.

ATTITUDES: The teacher may be primarily interested in the effect of the course upon the students' attitudes. As an evaluator, then, he or she should measure some of the learners' attitudes toward:

1. Themselves (cultural self-affirmation, self-esteem).
2. People from their culture.
3. Strangers in general (ethnocentrism).
4. People from another particular culture.
5. Initiating contact with people from different cultures.
6. Assisting individuals from a different culture.
7. Being assisted by individuals from a different culture.
8. Being involved in a close relationship with someone from a different culture (a Black, an Italian, a Native American, etc.).

Other possible attitudes include the learners':

9. Curiosity about different cultures, their values, priorities, lifestyles, etc.
10. Motivation to pursue relationships with individuals from different cultures.
11. Confidence before and during intercultural interaction.
12. Comfort during, and enjoyment of, interaction with individuals and groups which are distinctly different.

SKILLS: Most teachers want their courses and their other efforts for their students to have practical consequences. They want to develop in their students certain skills and abilities which will result in clear understanding and constructive behavior during intercultural interaction. An evaluation designed specifically to measure such skills and abilities would concentrate on one or a few of them. In making a choice, the teacher should consider the learners' ability to do the following:

1. Read, write and especially speak the appropriate second language. (Because of the number of methods and tests available for measuring language ability, this chapter does not consider this kind of evaluation.)
2. Learn about their own and other cultures (information gathering skills).
3. Analyze systematically basic characteristics of their own culture, especially those which influence most directly their interaction with individuals and groups from different cultures.
4. Learn from individuals from other cultures.
5. Explore the basic characteristics of a different culture, especially those which influence most directly the interaction of people from that culture with them.
6. Analyze quickly and accurately a given intercultural exchange.
7. Understand both the words and the meaning of a person during an intercultural exchange.
8. Withhold judgment while getting to know an individual or group from a different culture.
9. See and sustain conflicting viewpoints.
10. Tolerate ambiguity and ambivalence (in themselves, in others and in relationships).
11. Anticipate specific points of potential difficulty in intercultural relations.
12. Recognize and clarify value, perceptual and other culturally-based conflicts.
13. Put themselves in the position of someone from a different culture.
14. Accept, respect and accommodate major cultural differences.
15. Find common ground and common objectives with someone whose values and preferences are, for the most part, quite different from their own.
16. Motivate an individual or group whose priorities are quite different from their own.
17. Adjust their images of individuals and groups from different cultures so as to make them more accurate (cognitive flexibility vs. rigidity).
18. Analyze accurately and respond constructively to prejudice and discrimination against them.
19. Cope with the particular stresses inherent in multicultural environments.

PATTERNS OF BEHAVIOR: The students' and participants' knowledge, perceptions, attitudes and skills will, to some extent, result
in particular patterns of behavior. Conversely, their patterns of
behavior will, to some extent, result in particular skills, attitudes,
perceptions and knowledge. Some courses and programs, therefore, are
designed primarily to bring about specific, directy observable, patterns of behavior. Because behavior can often be directly observed,
it is often more easily measured. Teachers and trainers, therefore,
may want to design their evaluation in such a way that it will locate,
record and measure specified patterns of behavior in and between
individual students. Some of the patterns for which they might look
are the following:

1. Listening "actively" with individuals from contrasting
   cultures.
2. Giving constructive feedback to someone from a different
   culture.
3. Receiving feedback, perhaps given in an unfamiliar way,
   from someone from an unfamiliar culture.
4. Checking their own perceptions during an intercultural
   exchange with an individual or group.
5. Clarifying their own and others' intentions during
   intercultural interaction.
6. Shifting their behavior when one pattern is no longer
   appropriate to the situation or the person (behavioral
   flexibility vs. rigidity).
7. Taking specific, appropriate steps to reduce intercultural
   conflict.
8. Negotiating the misunderstandings and tensions inherent in
   intercultural interaction.
9. Taking specific, constructive action in the midst of
   culture fatigue or role shock.

We have been considering in the above an evaluation of the
effects upon individual students and participants. As mentioned
earlier, courses and programs also, of course, have definite effects
upon groups. The particular groups with which we are primarily
concerned here is the teacher with his (or her) students who comprise
a given class. The effects upon the group can be quite significant if
the members represent contrasting cultures. Some measurement of these
effects is often important, especially if the approach being used with
the group is experientially based, as is much intercultural education
and training. Listed below are some of the characteristics of a group
which may be directly affected by a course or program, especially if
it is a multicultural group. Teachers and trainers should choose
particular ones which they want to anticipate, design for, work toward
and then (of course) measure (perhaps at different points):

1. Level of trust between different sub-groups and within the
   class or program group as a whole.
2. Patterns of communication (e.g., who is included and
   excluded, by whom and why; development of vocabulary
   and non-verbal expressions unique to the group).
3. Extent to which the group agrees on common objectives.

4.  Clarity with which their objectives are defined and the degree to which the students or participants are included in the defining process.
5.  Emergence of leaders; extent to which support for them, cooperation with them, divides along cultural lines.
6.  Development or dissolution of cliques; their number and solidarity.
7.  Degree of discrimination against one sub-group by another.
8.  Degree of conflict and the lines along which the conflicts are drawn.
9.  Level of tension and suspicion.
10. How the group handles a crisis or challenge.
11. Degree of competition within the group, and between the group and other groups.
12. The extent to which the group contributes to other groups, school projects, organization-wide efforts, etc.
13. The extent to which the members of the group have a sense of group identity.

We have now considered a variety of things which the teacher and the trainer may want to evaluate: the teacher or trainer himself, the course or program, and the consequences of each -- the effects (upon both the individual and the group). The effects chosen should become the teachers' and the trainers' general objectives and the objectives of the course. These then shape the design of the course and become a primary basis for the evaluation.

## HOW THE MEASUREMENT IS TO BE DONE

How the measuring is actually done, of course, depends upon the choice of subject, when it occurs and what is being measured. Some methods, for example, are suitable when measuring attitudes whereas others are suitable for measuring specific patterns of behavior. The reader may select from the alternatives below the particular methods of data collection and measurement which are most consistent with his or her situation and preference.

Several general principles should be considered as selection is made. The first, of course, is that the methods must be as compatible as possible with the values, preferences and customary modes of response of the students. The effect of certain kinds of questions upon the students, for example, given their cultural backgrounds, should be anticipated. Some questions may be appropriate only if written; others only if oral. How the questions are worded can influence significantly how they are answered. Perhaps no direct questions at all should be asked.

Responses of any kind -- written, oral or enacted -- are influenced by the extent to which the student, for example, wants to please, compliment, show respect for or "level with" the evaluator and the other students. What is socially desirable for students from one culture is likely to be different for students from another. Attitudes toward candor, politeness, cautiousness and critiquing those in authority differ, as do attitudes toward expressing oneself or performing in front of others. The feelings of students about being rated by their peers (as well as by their teacher) are deeper for some students than for others, depending in part on the cultures from which they come. Anonymity is very important to some when they are expressing reactions and criticisms; others strongly want their names associated with their opinions.

Because modes of responding differ (as do modes of learning), a variety of methods, carefully selected and limited, is often best for a multicultural class or program, especially if the cultures represented are quite diverse and the evaluation is to be a rather thorough one.

Clarity is essential in any evaluation, but it becomes particularly important when the respondents come from different cultural, educational and language backgrounds. The format, instructions and composition of the evaluation must be very precise, consistent and simple. Examples and demonstrations of what is expected are often helpful for the students, as is an opportunity to ask questions regarding procedure, meaning and so forth. Clarity and consistency are critical when the evaluation requires translation (as, of course, are equivalence and accuracy); pretesting and practicing, which are important for all methods, are especially important where they require translation or bilingual interpretation.

In addition to the cultural compatibility of particular methods, the teacher should carefully consider their effect upon the students' learning. Methods of data collection often affect directy and deeply the outcomes of a course or training program -- sometimes very positively, sometimes negatively. As the teachers and trainers build their methods into their course design, care must be taken to ensure that the methods are consistent with the purposes of the course or program and complementary to the other components in the design. The thinking, acting and interacting required of students, for example, in order to come up with the desired data can, if the methods are chosen properly, contribute substantially to the students' learning. The needs assessment helps to establish expectations; monitoring during the course can increase motiviation by demonstrating teacher concern and responsiveness; evaluation at the close can serve as an opportunity for systematic review and valuable integration; the follow-up evaluation can provide necessary reinforcement.

Most of the methods below can be more revealing, and the results they yield more credible, if they are applied to both the class in which experimentation is being done and to another (and similar)control group. The point here, of course, if to compare the results from the two groups. If changes are identified in the group in which new intercultural techniques are used, for example, but the same changes do not occur in the other group (in which the techniques were not used), then the teacher or trainer can conclude with more confidence that the changes are the result of the techniques and not the result of other factors. When the use of control groups is not possible, as is often the case in multicultural education and training, more thorough evaluation is called for and more caution is necessary in interpreting the results.

If the teacher or trainer has decided to measure a number of effects, or if he is measuring just one but has chosen a number of methods, it is sometimes advantageous to divide a large class or program group into several groups and measure just one effect or use just one method with each group. Each group, of course, must be as representative as possible of the larger group if inferences are to be drawn regarding the larger group.

In choosing and using the method(s), it is essential that the teacher and trainer be very clear as to what exactly he or she is looking for. Every method must be selected and tailored to focus on the effects to which priority has been given. One helpful way to ensure clarity and pertinence of data is to ask oneself, "Given the purposes, format and content of this course or program, and given the particular individuals in it, what specific questions do I want to be able to answer through my evaluation?" Once the questions are formulated (and preferably written down) choosing the appropriate methods will be easier.

Once the methods have been chosen, the responses of the students and participants will be easier, probably more on target and probably more eagerly given, if the teacher or trainer explains why the evaluation is being done, how the results are to be used and who is to benefit from their joint efforts. As is often true in intercultural communication, we assist others in responding to us if we let them know "where we are coming from."

We have suggested a number of general principles: methods must be compatible with the cultures represented, a variety of methods are often more appropriate and more productive than a single one, precision and simplicity are essential, methods of evaluation enhance or hinder learning, control groups are desirable although not necessary, the teachers and trainers must be clear as to their own objectives in doing the evaluation and can encourage the cooperation of students by explaining the objectives to them. If teachers keep these principles in mind, and keep their own students in mind, they can select from the following alternatives the methods that will serve their purposes most fully. An example or two is given with each alternative; each example is preceded by an asterisk(*). The examples are only suggestive, of course; teachers should construct their own questions.

## PAPER AND PENCIL (SELF-REPORT)

Methods of this kind usually require students and participants to reflect upon and respond to items which are written down, recording their responses on the same or separate sheets. The respondent usually does this alone. The results are analyzed later. The alternatives include the following:

1. Check Lists: These are usually lists of single words (often adjectives or short descriptive phrases); the respondent simply checks the particular ones which apply. This method can be used for numerous purposes, one of which is to obtain a reading of the respondents' perceptions of their own and other culture groups:

-221-

*Generally speaking, Chicanos are:
(please check as many as apply):

_____ warm                    _____ aggressive
_____ critical                _____ tolerant
_____ confident               _____ dishonest
_____ insensitive             _____ generous
_____ sincere                 _____ superficial
_____ cold                    _____ respectful
_____ friendly                _____ idealistic
                                        etc.

This kind of question can become the basis for evaluation by asking it before the course or program, at the close and perhaps again some months later. If the course has brought about changes in learners' perceptions, some of these would probably be indicated by the different adjectives (or short descriptive phrases) chosen at the different points. For further consideration of this method, see the section on the Adjective Check List in the most recent Mental Measurements Yearbook.

This method can also be used to evaluate the course or program more directly (rather than the effects) by asking the students or participants which adjectives (or short phrases) they would choose to describe the activity:

*For me, this course has been (check as many as apply):

_____ informative             _____ frustrating
_____ boring                  _____ enjoyable
_____ motivating              _____ tedious
_____ confusing               _____ easy
_____ encouraging             _____ unorganized
_____ competitive             _____ one of the best
_____ useful                  _____ a waste of time
_____ too theoretical         _____ exciting
_____ engaging                _____ too demanding
_____ tiring                  _____ cooperative
_____ confidence-building     _____ challenging

2. Rank Ordering: In this method the respondent is given a small number of items (perhaps three to six), asked to compare them to one another, then decide which items are more preferable and which are less preferable. The respondent usually indicates the order of preference by writing the appropriate numbers on a questionnaire:

*Listed below are several groups of people. Please decide which groups you would prefer to live next door to and spend a lot of time with. Then write a "1" beside the group you would most prefer, a "2" beside the one you would prefer somewhat less, and so forth, ending by writing a "5" beside the group you would least prefer:

|            |                |            |              |
|------------|----------------|------------|--------------|
| _____     | White Americans | _____    | Nigerians    |
| _____     | Puerto Ricans   | _____    | East Indians |
| _____     | Black Americans | _____    | Japanese     |
| _____     | Chinese         | _____    | Latinos      |
| _____     | Chicanos        | _____    | Italians     |

By asking such questions before a course or program (perhaps during the needs assessment), teachers can gain useful information about those who would learn from them. Such questions can also become the basis for an evaluation when they are asked again at the close of the course and perhaps several months later. If student attitudes toward some of the groups have changed during the course or program, this change may be reflected in the average ranking for each of the groups after the learning sequence (especially if the alternative groups included in the question are carefully chosen by their evaluator).

The rank ordering method can also be used quite productively to compare and evaluate different components of the course or training program. The subjects covered can be isolated and compared, or the teaching methods can be isolated and compared, or both can be combined:

*How helpful (or interesting, or valuable, or useful, or new, etc.) have the following parts of the course been for you? (Please write a "1" beside the part which was most helpful, a "2" beside the part which was less helpful, and a "3" beside the part which was least helpful):

_____ lecture on communication
_____ lecture on perception
_____ lecture on cultural adjustment

*How helpful have the following parts of the course been for you? (Please write . . .etc.):

_____ discussion of cultural conflict
_____ film on cultural conflict
_____ role playing of cultural conflict

*How helpful have the following parts of the course been for you? (Please write. . .etc.):

_____ lecture on communication
_____ film on cultural conflict
_____ simulation of cultural adjustment

The results of such questions can become valuable guidelines as the next course or training program is being designed. When the teacher, for example, then compares these results with the results from the same questionnaires administered for subsequent courses, still more valuable feedback can be obtained on the subjects and teaching methods and on the teacher, himself (on the relative effectiveness of a lecture given repeatedly, for example). Furthermore, suggestive information can be obtained on the particular students in each class (students from certain cultures may respond very positively to a given teaching method in one class, for example, whereas students from another culture in the next class may respond to the same method very negatively).

C. Scales: A variety of scales are used in evaluation, especially where the evaluator wishes to measure perceptions and attitudes. Two basic kinds of scales will be outlined here. The first is based on lines, usually horizontal lines with a sequence of positions located along the lines:

*Please indicate how strongly you agree (SA) or disagree (SD) with each of the following statements by putting a check at the appropriate place on each line:

| | SD | D | A | SA |
|---|---|---|---|---|

The reasons for a culturally different
person's behavior are easy to understand

I can learn a lot from foreigners

I really enjoy meeting Black Americans

People in other countries would be better
off if they adopted more American ways

Although questions dealing with different subjects (self-esteem, ethnocentrism, curiosity, etc.) are usually mixed on the questionnaire, they are grouped according to subject during the design (so as to ensure adequate coverage for each subject) and during the tabulation (in order that the results can be broken down into each subject and compared).

The desired response is decided upon by the evaluator (or a small group of "objective" informed individuals). Asking the same questions (or closely comparable questions -- as determined by similar results from repeated tests with different groups) before and after the course or program will probably reflect some of the shifts in perceptions and attitudes which occurred during the activity. For purposes of tabulation, numbers can be assigned to each of the response categories (SD = -2, D = -1, A = 1, SA = 2, assuming "strongly disagree" is the least desirable response. If it is the most desirable response, then the numbers assigned would be reversed (SD = 2, D = 1, A = -1, SA = -2). An average of -1.5 then, at the beginning of the class, for a given student (or for the whole class) would be a low rating. An average of 1.8 at the close of the class would suggest considerable improvement.

A second kind of scale is based on numbers. The series of numbers can include polar opposite positions (with a central position), or it can progress from a minimum to a maximum position. An example of the first, a series providing opposite alternatives, is the following:

*Please indicate how strongly you agree or disagree with the following statement by circling the appropriate number:

This training program has been valuable for me:
strongly disagree - 3 2 1 0 1 2 3 - strongly agree

In tabulating this kind of question, the numbers to the left of zero can be entered on the tabulation sheets as negative numbers. In presenting and interpreting the results, both the range of responses (from -2 to +3, for example) and the average (2.5, for example) are useful.

As mentioned above, a series of numbers can also progress from a minimum to a maximum position. Examples of a series providing progressive alternatives are the following:

*To what extent has this course been valuable for you? (Please circle the appropriate number):

    not at all - 0 1 2 3 4 5 - extremely

*To what extent has this course increased your understanding of different (perhaps specified) cultures:

    not at all - 0 1 2 3 4 5 - a great deal

*As a result of this course, how much increase has there been in your motivation to get to know individuals from different (perhaps specified) cultures?

    none - 0 1 2 3 4 5 - a great deal

*How valuable have the following parts of this course been for you? (Please circle the appropriate number for each part):

| | | |
|---|---|---|
| lecture on communication | not at all - 0 1 2 3 4 5 - extremely | |
| lecture on perception | 0 1 2 3 4 5 | |
| self assessment of skills | 0 1 2 3 4 5 | |
| inventory of prejudices | 0 1 2 3 4 5 | |
| exercise on intercultural learning | 0 1 2 3 4 5 | |
| status game | 0 1 2 3 4 5 | |
| | | |
| assumptions & values checklist | 0 1 2 3 4 5 | |
| exercise on listening | 0 1 2 3 4 5 | |
| BAFA BAFA | 0 1 2 3 4 5 | |
| case study on conflict | 0 1 2 3 4 5 | |
| film on perceptions | 0 1 2 3 4 5 | |
| role playing(Washingtonville) | 0 1 2 3 4 5 | |

Once the tabulation has been completed, the value of each part can be compared with the value of the other parts. Furthermore, by calculating the average of all of the parts, the overall value of the course or program can be estimated.

Somewhat different scales based on numbers can be designed and used when it is judged to be appropriate. They can serve both learning and evaluation purposes when the scale is built into an exercise used in the course or program. One example would be the exercise "We and You." It uses a scale of 1 to 9. By having the students participate in such an exercise early in a course, and then again (in at least the relevant parts of the exercise) at the close of the course,

-225-

the teacher can trace shifts in their perceptions of themselves and others during the course.

4. Written Training Exercises: As pointed out above, when the teacher or trainer uses exercises which involve the recording on paper of perceptions, attitudes, etc., these can easily become the basis for an evaluation. If the student or participant knows about the evaluation, this may, of course, alter somewhat his responses (though not necessarily reduce his learning). It is often best to make provisions whereby the results of the exercise, when given to the teacher or trainer afterwards for evaluation, are anonymous.

Another example of the kind of exercise which would be suitable for the purposes of an evaluation is the "Inventory on my Prejudices." In the exercise the student answers a series of questions regarding the frequency with which he feels or displays prejudice. By putting the responses of all the students together, the teacher can prepare an overall summary of their prejudices (as they have -- anonymously -- reported them). By doing the exercise both at the beginning of the course and then again at the end, the teacher can obtain an estimate of the changes in their prejudices during the course.

A third example is the "Profile of Attitudes and Feelings." In this exercise the student places tabs, each with a different word on it, at any point he wishes along a continuum from positive to nega- tive, the particular place representing his feelings regarding the word on the tab. By putting the responses of all the students togeth- er, the teacher can draw up a rough profile of his students' feelings regarding,. say "foreigners," "Blacks," "my neighbors," "Chinese," etc. If this exercise is done twice, once at the beginning of the course and again at the close, an estimate can be made for example, on how much more positively the students may now feel toward "Blacks." By combining all of the results from the second time, and comparing these with the first, the teacher can get an idea as to the amount and kind of overall shift during the course. In order to do this, the teacher would probably find it easiest to assign numbers to different points along the continuum before making a tabulation and then enter on the tabulation sheet the number for the location at which each word was placed. These would be handled, in other words, in a way similar to the scales above using lines along which the students indicate their positions. Specific ways to illustrate the results will be suggested later in the section on formats.

Using particular training exercises for learning purposes, and then using the exercise recording sheets for evaluation pruposes, is one of the best ways in which learning and evaluation can be integrated.

5. Critical Incidents: The teacher or trainer can also integrate learning and evaluation by using appropriate critical incidents. These can be selected from incidents which have already been written, or which the teacher constructs, or which the students construct with the teacher's guidance. Once selected, the incidents are presented to each student individually, the purpose usually being to evaluate some of the student's intercultural skills and abilities.

-226-

The primary focus is usually upon the student's ability to uncover and analyze the cultural components of a specific situation in which misunderstanding or conflict has occurred:

*(A concise description of an appropriate critical incident)

There are four major cultural factors in the incident described above.  What are they?
1._____
2._____
3._____
4._____

Which one of these factors is the primary cause for the misunderstanding in the incident?
#_____.

Please explain specifically how this factor contributed to the misunderstanding:

_____
_____
_____

What specifically should be done to clarify this misunderstanding?

_____
_____

Given their cultural differences, what is the most significant difficulty likely to be in the future between the people involved in the incident?

_____
_____

Having decided beforehand what the best answers are to these questions, the teacher can then evaluate the adequacy of the students' answers, thereby obtaining an estimate of the student's ability to recognize, analyze, resolve and anticipate.  If the same exercise is done at the close of the course with comparable critical incidents, an estimate of the increase in the student's abilities can be obtained.

Once the students have each written their answers, the learning purposes of the exercise can more fully be realized if they discuss their answers with one another.  Having thought through the incident individually, and having actually written down their analysis, they will probably have a much more productive discussion.

6. Case Studies, Films, Photographs:  The purpose of case studies, films and photographs is much the same as that of critical incidents:  to present to the student or participants a carefully structured, provocative, intercultural situation with a specific setting, identifiable individuals and groups, and pertinent details, to which the student can react, and on which he can sharpen his skills. The particular skills with which we are usually most concerned are his

skills in isolating the cultural forces present in the situation, analyzing their effects, deciding what to do, and anticipating subsequent difficulties and possibilities.

The questions to the student after having read the case study or seen the film can be similar to those for the critical incidents. The requirement for <u>specific</u> responses is equally important. The teacher's decisions as to the best responses must, of course, be equally accurate, for these become the criteria in terms of which the students' responses are evaluated. The teacher should also be open to the possibility, of course, that the student may come up with some insights which the teacher had not.

As is true with critical incidents when they are used for evaluation, the student or participant usually studies the case or reflects upon the film or photographs privately, then prepares a written reaction. Having done this, discussion of the case may be very informative. After the discussion, the case may be read or the film viewed again thereby stimulating motiviation and reinforcing learning.

If the case study or film is used more strictly for purposes of evaluation, the film, say, would be shown early in the course or program and the student would answer the integrated series of questions which guide his analysis of it. There would be <u>no</u> discussion. At the close of the course, the film would be shown <u>again</u> and the questions would be answered again (discussion afterward might then be very beneficial). Seeing the film a second time at the close of the course can be rewarding for students (and, of course, teachers) because they realize how much more can be seen in the film having taken the course. New awareness and skills will be reflected in responses to the questions at the close of the course. The increase in awareness and skills can be demonstrated to the student (and perhaps to others) by contrasting these responses (privately or anonymously) to the ones written down early in the course.

A thought on who is being evaluated: we have been assuming that evaluation would focus on the individual student or participant. Given their highly individualistic orientation, this is usually the way most Americans do their evaluating. There is an alternative, however, to which some careful attention should be given. A group or a team can be evaluated. A small group, for example, would study a case, discuss it, arrive at some consensus on the answers to the questions, then record their consensus on the questionnaire. The teacher or trainer then evaluates the <u>group's</u> answers. This approach can strongly influence the interaction within the class or program and the cohesiveness of the group, of course, and it can increase the opportunities for learning, especially if two or more cultures are represented in the group (if, in other words, members of the group engage in intercultural interaction as they are cooperatively analyzing an intercultural interaction). Relations within the group can be further developed if, after providing the more formal questions on the questionnaire, the teacher or trainer asks the members of the group more personal questions and then discusses their responses with them. One question might be, "How would you feel if you were Lu Chen Chang in the situation we have been discussing?"

If the class or program group is divided into several sub-groups (as a large group would have to be), if each sub-group is evaluated on its combined awareness and skills, and if the evaluations are then reported to the whole group, this will, of course, further influence relations within the group. As each sub-group compares its "grade" to that of the other sub-groups, some intergroup rivalry may develop. If the teacher's or trainer's attitudes and methods are appropriate, however, intergroup competition can be more constructive than the interpersonal competition stimulated by individual evaluation. Intergroup competition can be especially constructive, and is sometimes preferable, where there are a number of cultures represented in the group. In a multicultural class or program, if the individuals are evaluated separately, the individual's isolation and inclination to return to his own culture group may be intensified.

If discussion is to take place within small groups in a multicultural class or program, and if an evaluation is to be done of these groups, each group should itself be multicultural. If each group is composed of only one culture (Chicanos in one, for example, and Anglos in another), intercultural interaction is reduced and stereotypes may be reinforced.

7. Sentence Completion: The first part of each sentence (like the method above but in a much abbreviated form) sets a certain situation or identifies particular individuals (often including the student or participannt himself). The respondent then finishes the sentence in whatever way he wishes. This method can be used to estimate the present level of, and subsequent learning in, all areas: knowledge, perceptions, attitutdes, skills and patterns of behavior:

*When a traditional Japanses woman attends her first American cocktail party, she is likely to feel

_____

*What Native Americans probably want most in life is

_____

When I am with a group of Anglos I feel

_____

*When I find I am in strong disagreement with a Chicano, I usually

_____

*While I am listening to a male Anglo friend who is telling me about a personal problem he has, I can show him I am actively listening to him by

_____

When the evaluator has decided specifically what he is looking for and has constructed the first part of each sentence, the specific criteria for completing each sentence can be established (against which he will compare and assess the responses of the students). In addition to determining the adequacy of each response (and perhaps calculating the overall adequacy of all the responses), the pattern of the responses can be determined; this can be done by putting each response into one of several categories and then examing their frequency. Some of the questions that may then be asked are: What kinds of responses do Blacks usually give? What kinds do Puerto Ricans usually give? What do their different responses imply for the relations between them? For my teaching of them? My evaluating of them?

If the sentences are completed by the students early in the course, and if the same (or comparable) sentences are completed at the close of the course, the teacher can demonstrate changes in the patterns of the responses and can estimate the increase in the adequacy of the responses (i.e., the increase in the students' knowledge, etc.).

8. Questions: This is the method with which people are most familiar. If the method is to be effective and the results accurate, each question must be very carefully constructed. Each must have a clear and specific purpose. The words must be carefully chosen and the order of the words must be deliberately arranged; such care is especially important in multicultural groups. The order of the questions themselves must also be thoughtfully arranged; each must build upon the ones preceding it, providing logical sequence and development throughout. Students and participants learn not only from the questions they think about but also from the order in which they think about them. Integrated questions can help integrate knowledge, integrate experience, and integrate knowledge with experience.

There are two basic kinds of questions: structured and open-ended (or free response). With regard to structured questions, the multiple choice format is the standard one; it is sometimes the best and (for the respondent, at least) often the simplest. It is normally used to test specific knowledge but it can be used more broadly. The examples below cover the areas of knowledge, attitudes, skills and patterns of behavior:

*When a White American first meets a Black American, the primary non-verbal difficulty they are likely to experience is (please circle the letter beside the correct answer):

   a.  personal space
   b.  kind of physical contact
   c.  eye contact.
   d.  none of the above would cause any difficulty

*How willing would you be to spend time assisting a new student who has just arrived from a foreign country?

   _____  very willing
   _____  willing
   _____  not very willing
   _____  not at all willing

*If you have recently moved to an Asian country and are having serious difficulty getting along with an Asian in your organization, what should you do?

-230-

a. Be polite to him and avoid him whenever possible.
b. Confront him directly and discuss the difficulties with him.
c. Express your frustrations to him, but do it in a light, humorous manner.
d. Select someone to be your interpreter and discuss the situation with him.

(These three kinds of questions, especially the second, can become the basis for more revealing evaluation by asking them before the course or program (perhaps during the needs analysis), then again at the close, and then contrasting the results.)

*During the last two months, how often have you initiated contact with a student from a different (perhaps specified) culture?

_____ as often as possible
_____ frequently
_____ sometimes
_____ seldom
_____ never

This same kind of question can then be asked again two months after the course or program; the results may suggest that some of the students or participants are initiating contact more often than before their learning sequence. It is usually better to get the same information through someone's direct observation or recording of the contacts but this, of course, is seldom possible. The learner's own reports must therefore be used and an assumption of consistency in his reporting must be made.

The same kind of information can be sought in another way during the follow-up evaluation; one example:

*We are interested in knowing whether or not this course has encouraged you to initiate contacts with people from different cultures during the two months since the course ended. During these last two months, how many people (not from your culture) have you started a conversation with, people whom you probably would not have approached had you not taken this course?

_____ none
_____ 1 or 2
_____ 3 or 4
_____ 5 or 6
_____ more than 6

With regard now to the second basic kind of question, the open-ended question calling for a free or essay response, this can also be used to gather information in all five areas (knowledge perceptions, attitutdes, skills and patterns of behavior). This is the kind of question used above in the examples for Critical Incidents (although structured questions can also be used, of course, with Critical Incidents, as well as with case studies, films and photographs). One of

-231-

the essential student or participant skills which open-ended questions can help to measure, which structured questions and other methods usually cannot, is skill in synthesizing, criticizing and applying what has been learned in the course or program.

One variable which the evaluator should keep in mind as the open-ended questions are being constructed is the extent to which each question guides and limits the student's or participant's response. More specific questions, and usually longer questions, restrict more the range of possible responses. Whether this is desirable or not depends largely upon the backgrounds and expectations of the students or participants, the purpose of the course or program and the purpose of the particular question.

Some examples of open-ended questions are the following:

*What are your two major objectives in taking this course?

1. _____
2. _____

(By asking a question regarding their objectives during the needs assessment or early in the course, the teacher can assist the students in clarifying their objectives and assist himself in designing the course. Their objectives, once established, can then become a basis for monitoring the relevance of the course as it proceeds and for evaluating the course as it closes. The questions at the close of the course would ask the students to what extent their objectives had been met and which parts of the course contributed the most toward meeting their objectives.)

At the close of the course or training program the following kinds of questions might also be asked:

*In what specific ways has this course itself been a product of North American Mainstream culture, reflecting basic values and procedures of that culture?

_____
_____
_____

*In what specific ways has your own culture influenced your participation in this course?

_____
_____
_____

*Please list and describe briefly the seven phases of the intercultural learning process:

1. _____
2. _____
3. _____
4. _____
5. _____
6. _____
7. _____

*What, specifically, is effective feedback?

_____
_____
_____

*Please describe briefly how you gave (or could have given) verbal feedback during the course to a particular person from another culture:

_____
_____
_____

*Describe briefly how you gave (or could have given) non-verbal feedback during the course to a particular person from another culture:

_____
_____
_____

*"Sterotypes are necessary and very constructive in intercultural relations." Discuss this statement:

_____
_____
_____
_____
_____

*Assume you are going to move to Peking next week. You will live alone and will be there two years. What specifically will you do during the first two months to orient yourself and facilitate your adjustment to life in Peking?

_____
_____
_____
_____
_____

-233-

*In what specific ways is your own approach to cultural adjustment consistent with the basic values and patterns of behavior in the culture from which you come?

_____
_____
_____
_____

*What are the two most significant things which you have learned from this course?

1. _____
2. _____

In deciding upon the appropriate order for the questions, it is often best to put questions asking for an overall evaluation of the course, like the last one above, at the end (after the student has thought through and evaluated the particular parts of the course in the preceding questions). If scales and structured questions are used, the student's thoughts and feelings about these will probably influence his responses to any open-ended questions which follow. This influence is sometimes desirable; the structured questions can prepare the student to respond to the unstructured questions. If the teacher does not want to take advantage of this influence, the open-ended questions can be put first. As mentioned above, students' responses can be even less channeled by making the first open-ended questions brief and rather general. As the teacher moves away from structured, specific questions, of course there is a greater reliance upon more "subjective" means for rating the responses, less upon "objectve" and quantifiable means.

9. Journals: Diaries and journals are the least structured method of evaluation used in intercultural courses and training programs. The instructions to the student, for example, are usually:

*During this course, write down in a special notebook after each class your thoughts and feelings about the class, about intercultural relations, and about your pariticpation in both. Be sure to include the most important things you are learning from the class and the things you have done (or plan to do) differently because of what you are learning.

The Journal can be read by the student only, or by the student and the teacher; the student should be told which. If the teacher is to read it, the student should also be told the teacher's purpose in reading it (interest, evaluation, discussion with the student, etc.).

If only the students are to read their Journals, frequent review of what has been written will be helpful. The reviews will provide opportunities to reinforce and consolidate their learning. Furthermore, each time they look back and see what they have learned, they will probably be more motivated when they enter class next time.

If the teacher reads the Journals and uses them simply as a basis for discussions with the students, the students' expectations will influence what is put into them. If the teacher evaluates the students' learning on the basis of the Journals, this will probably influence even more what the student puts into them. The teacher can determine to some extent the kind of influence by specifying the particular criteria to be used in doing the evaluation. Exactly what the student writes down, of course, will also be partly determined by the amount of rapport between him and the teacher. From the Journal, especially if the rapport and trust are high, the teacher will be able to draw information on changes in all five areas: the student's knowledge, perceptions, attitudes, skills and patterns of behavior.

## DISCUSSION (SELF-REPORT)

The method which combines paper and pencil procedures with discussion is interviewing. An interview schedule (containing instructions to the interviewer and the questions to be asked during the interview) must be constructed as carefully as a questionnaire. Decisions regarding the subjects to be investigated, the word order in the questions (either structured or open-ended), and the sequence of the questions are as important on schedules as they are on questionnaires. Also important is the decision regarding who is to do the interviewing; the age, sex, nationality, role and appearance of the interviewer, as well as interviewing skill, will influence considerably the results of the interview -- especially in a multicultural situation. During a course, if the students interview one another, they will probably learn a great deal (especially in a multicultural class) but the teacher may learn less. Teachers who do the interviewing have more control and more opportunity to clarify responses; also they get to know the students better. On the other hand, interviewing takes time and the teacher's presence will probably influence, and perhaps inhibit, the student's response (the presence of a peer interviewer will also influence the response, of course, but the kind of influence will usually be different from that of the teacher). Regardless of who does the interviewing, the schedule can be constructed so as to enable the teacher to evaluate knowledge, perceptions and attitudes, and obtain the student's descriptions at least of skills and patterns of behavior.

Less structured discussion can also be used in evaluation. During a course, for example, the students can discuss with one another what they are learning (at these points, as demonstrated in the diagram, the evaluation would monitor the students' progress and the course's appropriateness); at the end of the course the students can discuss with one another what they have learned (at this point the evaluation would measure the effects of the course). One advantage of this kind of discussion is that the students learn from what the other students have learned. Other kinds of discussion which can also be analyzed would be discussions of case studies, films and so forth.

In order to base a course or program evaluation on rather unstructured discussion, the discussion should be recorded mechanically (on audio or video tape or by a court recorder) so that the contents may be analyzed. If mechanical recording is not feasible than an observer (or the teacher or trainer) should be appointed to take systematic notes (methods of observation will be described below). Like open-ended questions, discussion allows for some evaluation of the student's and participant's ability to synthesize, criticize and apply what has been learned.

## ENACTMENT (TEACHER-REPORT, PERHAPS PEER-REPORT)

When using the paper and pencil and discussion methods described above, the person who reports on attitudes, what has been learned, etc., is usually the student or participant himself. Beginning with this section on enactment and in the following sections, the person who reports is often the teacher and trainer or the student's participant's peers.

An enactment situation in the classroom, if it is carefully prepared by the teacher (or by the students themselves with the guidance of the teacher), will provide for the students an opportunity to demonstrate what they have learned, thereby reinforcing their learning and presenting to an observer (the teacher, colleague or other students) behavior which can become the basis for an evaluation. If an attempt to enact a situation reveals that students have not learned what they were expected to, not only should the student's motivation and ability be reconsidered but the design and methods of the course should also be re-evaluated (the evaluation serves here a feedback function, suggesting points at which changes in the course should be made). If, on the other hand, the enactment reveals that the students have learned what they were supposed to, the teacher can be reasonably confident that the course is on target.

The variety of situations which can be enacted in courses and programs is wide: role plays (and reverse role plays), simulations, skits, plays, critical incidents (where, before discussing the incident, it is acted out), debates (where, for example, the students must argue a position contrary to their own and do so on the basis of values very different from their own), or common tasks for the class or small groups within the class (which require that the students plan, decide and cooperate with others from different cultures).

If any of these situations (a particular role play, for example) is enacted early in the course and then again at the close, the students can more clearly recognize and appreciate how much they have learned, and the teacher, by contrasting the students' performance during the first with their performances during the second, will be able to estimate the degree of improvement.

The method of enactment makes possible, more than the other methods above, the direct and precise observation and analysis of the student's interactive skills and patterns of behavior. Data on these are usually gathered through the teacher's and sometimes the students' observations (methods of observation are described below). In deciding what to enact, and in deciding exactly what to observe, the teacher or trainer must, of course, have established specific criteria for effective performance in each situation. These criteria must also be consistent with (in fact are best derived from) the goals and objectives of the course or training program.

## PRODUCTION (TEACHER-REPORT, PERHAPS PEER-REPORT)

This method involves the construction of a tangible product. In intercultural courses the construction can be undertaken by the individual student or by a small group. Possible kinds of products are limited only by the goals of the course and the imagination of the teacher and students. The alternatives include photographs, poems, drawings, sculptures, short stories, essays, conceptual models, case studies, critical incidents, scripts, video tapes, films and so forth.

What exactly is to be evaluated? In the previous section where we described situations which can be enacted, the primary focus was upon the <u>process</u>, usually the process of interaction among the students. Here, however, because there is a specific product, <u>either the prduct or the process</u> can be evaluated -- or both. (In deciding between them, it is well to bear in mind that, contrary to some American assumptions, it is possible to have a splendid process and a worthless product; furthermore, an unacceptable process can result in a superior product.) In multicultural education priority is often given to the process, but the teacher and the students often learn much if some attention is given to both.

If it is the product which is to be evaluated, anticipation of the evaluation can increase the motivation of an individual or consolidation of a group (which, of course, will influence the process). From an analysis of the products, depending upon what kinds of products they are, some inferences can usually be drawn regarding all areas: knowledge, perceptions, attitudes, skills and patterns of behavior. Some estimates of the last two, for example (the student's intercultural skills and patterns of behavior), can be made through an analysis of the student's portrayal of these in the characters he creates in his short story or script.

From an analysis of the process, sometimes regardless of the product, some inferences can be drawn, again, regarding all five areas. As is true during the enactment of a situation, the construction of a product by a multicultural group makes more possible than do most other methods the direct and precise observaton of the student's or the participant's interactive skills and patterns of behavior.

As was also true during the enactment of a situation (as well as during an unstructured discussion), if it is the process which is to be evaluated, some means of recording must be provided. Because much that happens during the construction of a product is not verbal, video tape is usually preferable to other mechanical means. The alternative is systematic observation and notation by the teacher, selected colleagues or other students; some methods of observation are described in the next section.

If the individual student or small group constructs a product (a conceptual model or a critical incident with an analysis, for example) early in the course, and then constructs the same kind of product toward the end of the course, the teacher and the students can compare the content of the products  and the quality of the interaction

at the two points. They may also want to compare the relative importance of the process as opposed to the product (the process may have
become more important to the students during the course).

## OBSERVATION (TEACHER-REPORT, PERHAPS PEER-REPORT)

Observation is important to a number of other methods described
above, especially unstructured discussion, enactment and production.
As mentioned earlier, observation during intercultural courses may be
undertaken by the teacher, by one or more of his colleagues or by the
students (who would learn valuable observation and intercultural
analysis skills through the exercise -- especially if they compare and
discuss their observations afterward).

The presence and purposes of the observer (which should be
explained to the students) will probably influence the process and the
behavior of the people being observed. The influence of a teacher
will probably be different from the influence of a student. The
influence of five students will probably be greater than the influence
of one. The kind of influence which is likely to be exerted, and the
effect of this influence upon the results of the observation, must be
considered by the teacher as the observer is selected and instructed.

Observation is usually more penetrating and more useful for
evaluation if it done systematically. As with other methods, the
teacher and the trainer must first decide exactly what is being
sought. All five areas can be investigated. When it is knowledge,
perceptions and attitudes being evaluated, the teacher must specify
what forms of behavior will probably be associated with each ("If the
student has X piece of knowledge, he is likely to behave in Y and Z
ways"). Therefore, when certain forms of behavior are actually
observed, inferences can be made back to the knowledge, perceptions or
attitudes which the behavior presumably represents.

Observation is especially appropriate for the evaluation of
skills and patterns of behavior. Fewer intermediate steps are necessary than for the other areas. The best basis for an evaluation of
these two areas are the behavioral objectives of a course or program;
("By the close of this course, the student will be taking such and so
actions in this specified situation"). It is exactly these actions
(and consequent interaction) that the observer will look for.

In order to ensure that the observing itself is done systematically, and that the target patterns of behavior are actually recognized and recorded, it is helpful for the observer to have in front of
him a list of the specific patterns (an observation schedule). The
schedule should be set up in such a way that a given action or interaction can be quickly recorded by simply making a mark on the sheet.
The categories which can be marked for a given individual action can
include the frequency and appropriateness of the action. Categories
for a given interaction can include the frequency, quality (perhaps
constructiveness) and intensity of the interaction. Room should also
be provided for other kinds of notation which seem pertinent to the
observer and which may be important in interpreting the results.

An initial alternative, of course, is to use a mechanical means of recording. Notations are then made on the schedule while listening to, looking at or reading a transcript of the interaction. The advantage here, of course, is that the teacher or trainer can back up and listen again to sections or go through the whole recording again if he wishes. In deciding whether to use an observer or a mechanical recording device, one of the considerations is that the device, too, will probably influence the process being recorded, and it will probably do so in ways different from (though sometimes preferable to) an observer.

The performance of each individual, the interaction between two individuals, and the overall process of the group -- all three can be recorded in these ways and then evaluated. If all three are to be evaluated, it is usually best to have at least one observer for each (with a separate and appropriate schedule for each) in order to allow adequate concentration.

Once the actions, interactions or group processes have been recorded, inferences can be drawn regarding the students' knowledge, perceptions and attitutdes, and estimates can be made regarding the extent to which desired skills and patterns of behavior have been developed.

## UNOBTRUSIVE MEASURES (TEACHER-REPORT)

All of the methods which we have considered above require the student and participant to respond to what the teacher or trainer plans and prepares: writing, choosing, discussing, enacting, constructing, observing and recording. These methods enable the teacher and trainer to maintain considerable control and to conduct systematic, thorough evaluations.

There are three basic problems, however, with these methods. The first has to do with feasibility. In some situations it is simply not possible for the evaluator to have this much control. For the teacher or trainer, however, it usually is possible; they do have some jurisdiction over what the people involved do, how they do it and when they do it.

The second problem, a more serious one for the teacher or trainer, has to do with artificiality. Reading a critical incident is not the same as causing it. Role playing or simulating culture conflict for a few hours probaby evokes some different responses than living in the midst of the confict.

The third problem, which may be still more serious, is the possibility of "contamination." In doing an evaluation, it is difficult to determine exactly what the student is responding to. The student may be responding to the teacher, the classroom setting, the methods of measurement, or a combination of these -- as well as to the subjects the teacher wants to investigate. The results may reveal to the teacher more about the effects of his methods of measurement than the effects of his course.

The problems of artificiality and contamination can be dealt with in two ways. First, the teacher and the trainer can anticipate and minimize in a number of ways the effects of extraneous factors. Some of these ways have been suggested in the descriptions of the methods above (deciding carefully who is to record observations and how they are to do it, for example, and minimizing the discrepancy between the methods used and those to which the student or participant is accustomed). What extraneous effects remain can be somewhat clarified and compensated for in the interpretation of the results.

The second way to deal with these problems is to use methods which avoid them, methods which in no way interfere with what the learner would normally be doing, methods of which the learner is completey unaware. Much attention has been given such "unobtrusive" methods during recent years. They usually focus upon the learner's behavior and patterns of behavior; they are therefore most appropriate to a course or program with behavioral objectives and should be consistent with these objectives.

If unobtrusive measures are to be used, the teacher might look at such things as library records (which students check out which titles for how long), attendance records for the class and how these change during the course, participation in voluntary activities (multicultural events, clubs, orientations for foreign students, etc.) and how this changes before and after the course, the number of times disciplinary action is required and the kind of action required, the composition of cluster groups during free time, enrollment in subsequent courses also related to multicultural education, the degree of cultural awareness represented in a small school newspaper, the kinds of summer jobs taken and careers chosen, and so forth.

Coming up with all the alternative indicators of learning and indicators of other effects of a course or program which can be unobtrusively measured requires much thought and imagination. Actually studying the indicators requires a lot of planning. Because it often means going through other people's records and files, it requires time and patience: if the records have been kept at all they are usually designed for other purposes, they are often difficult to find and some of the critical ones have inevitably been lost. Patience is also called for on the part of the other person whose files are being searched (who usually has no idea what the evaluator is after). It is therefore especially important here, as with every method, that the evaluator know beforehand exactly what he or she is looking for.

When using unobtrusive measures, therefore, suitable data are often difficult to come by. Also, once they have been collected, inferences regarding course or program effects and learner characteristics are difficult to make. When a teacher finds, for example, that 30% of his students go on to careers in multicultural education, he may conclude that one reason they do is his excellent course. In fact, however, the reason most of them took his course may have been their intention, previously formed, to pursue such a career. They may have continued on into this career in spite of the course. Perhaps without the course another 10% of the students would have pursued such a career.

Unobtrusive measures, therefore, although they can have some advantages, can also have some serious disadvantages. The other methods described above, the more obtrusive ones, although they do present several problems, have some definite advantages. One major advantage, possible in an integrated course or program, is that their effects upon the students can be very constructive and therefore very desirable; these methods, in fact, can be so selected and so designed as to have particular effects, effects which further realize the objectives of the course.

The conclusion is clear: because of their different advantages and disadvantages, the teacher should use, whenever possible, both kinds of methods, then see to what extent (and at what points) they corroborate each other.

## HOW THE TABULATION OF THE RESULTS CAN BE ENJOYED

Many teachers and trainers who could do evaluation, and learn a lot from it, don't. The reasons are often that they do not know how to do it and they are fearful of the time it may take. The preceding sections explain how an evaluation can be done. If the teacher and trainer follows the procedures outlined, the amount of time required can be minimized -- including the time required for tabulation. When the evaluator starts off knowing exactly what is wanted, then select the methods accordingly and constructs the questionnaires and schedules accordingly, the tabulation follows easily. In other words, if the data collection is focused and systematic, the tabulation can be done very efficiently. And enjoyably. Seeing the results emerge can be exciting. One starts with definite questions to which answers are really wanted and then goes step by step through the process of getting them. They emerge ready for incorporation into the final format and for interpretation. For many people, doing a tabulation is more enjoyable (and sometimes more efficient) if it is done with someone else. One person can read the responses to the structured questions, for example, while the other records them on the tabulation sheets; after awhile, they can switch.

The sheets on which the tabulation is done can be designed in a variety of ways. Teachers and trainers should set up those which are quickest and simplest for them. Some possible designs are suggested below.

CHECKLISTS

## ANGLO PERCEPTIONS OF CHICANOS

# of students:  32

|  | | total responses | % of total students |
|---|---|---|---|
| sincere | / / / / / | 5 | 16 |
| aggressive | / / / / / / / / / / / / / / / / / / / / / / | 22 | 69 |
| etc. | | | |

If this kind of question is asked after the course as well as before the course, the number of Anglo students who perceive Chicanos as being sincere, for example, may have increased considerably.

SCALES

|  | 0 | 1 | 2 | 3 | 4 | 5 | average rating |
|---|---|---|---|---|---|---|---|
| Question #1 | | | / | // | //////// | ///// | 4.1 |
| 2 | / | ///// | ///////// | // | | | 1.7 |
| 3 | | | | | | | |
| | | | | | | | 2.9 |

In order to figure the average rating for each question, multiply the number of responses in each column times the rating number at the top of the column, then add these products together, then divide by the total number of responses for that question; with a little practice it goes very quickly.  For Question #1:

$$(1 \times 2) + (2 \times 3) + (9 \times 4) + (5 \times 5) =$$
$$2 + 6 + 36 + 25 = 69$$

This is then divided by the total number of responses (17) to the question:

$$69 - 17 = 4.1$$

After the rating for each question has been determined, they can be compared with one another.  Also, the ratings for all the questions of a particular kind (those evaluating parts of the course, for example) can be added up, then divided by the number of questions, thus providing an average rating for the whole course.  The ratings for each part of the course and for the whole course become especially interesting when compared with the ratings for the next course.

## MULTIPLE CHOICE QUESTIONS

In multiple choice questions the alternatives from which the respondents choose are not numbers, therefore an average rating is not possible; instead, the percentage of respondents who chose each alternative is determined:

### QUESTION # 4

|  | | total responses | % of total students |
|---|---|---|---|
| as often as possible | / | 1 | 1 |
| frequently | // | 2 | 12 |
| sometimes | /// | 3 | 18 |
| seldom | /// | 3 | 18 |
| never | //////// | 8 | 47 |

This question for an intercultural course might ask, "How often would you be willing to spend time assisting a new student who has just arrived from a foreign country?" If the question were asked before the course and the above responses were given, it could be asked again at the close of the course, by which time the students might be willing to spend much more time with new foreign students.

## ESSAY RESPONSES

The evaluation and tabulation of essay or free responses, given to incomplete sentences and open-ended questions, is sometimes more difficult and less precise. The several ways of doing it divide into two basic approaches: those that compare the students' responses to one another and those that compare their responses to a general standard or specific set of criteria. When using the first approach, the teacher (or his willing and perhaps more "objective" colleague) consid- ers all of the responses to a given question, then decides which responses are better and which are worse than the others. This can be done by arranging them on a table or in a pile such that the best response is on the top and the poorest on the bottom. The teacher decides what he wants the highest and lowest ratings to be, then assigns them to the top and bottom responses and distributes the rat- ings in between to the rest of the responses. Having done this the teacher will have ranked and rated the students' responses, but not the course.

When using the second approach, one alternative the teacher or trainer has is to keep in mind a general notion as to what an excellent response would be, then rate each response according to how closely it approximates his standard of excellence. The rating suggests how much a given student has learned on that point; an average of all the students' ratings suggests how effectively the course has covered that point. If all of the responses are poor in terms of the standard, and assuming the question was clear, perhaps the teacher should go into the point more extensively or use different methods to convey it.

Another alternative: the teacher or trainer can more easily and more precisely quantify essay responses by establishing specific criteria for each set of responses to a given question. He can say, for example, that if the student refers to such and so, which is most important, he will get the highest score, perhaps 20. If the student deals with another particular point, which is also important but less so, he will get a score of 15, and so forth.

A variation on the above: the teacher establishes that four points (or five, or two, etc.) should be covered (or four particular attitudes revealed, etc.) in an excellent essay response. If the student covers all four, he gets a 20; if he covers three, he gets a 15, and so forth. The tabulation sheet for this kind of rating procedure could be the following (the numbers entered are each student's score; the scores assume each response should contain five points, four points, two points or one point respectively, and that the maximum score for each response is 20):

QUESTIONS #7, 8, 9 and 14

|  | #7 | #8 | #9 | #14 | student's average |
|---|---|---|---|---|---|
| Mary | 20 | 15 | 0 | 20 | 14 |
| Juan | 8 | 5 | 0 | 0 | 3 |
| Aaron, etc. |  |  |  |  |  |
| CLASS AVERAGE | 14 | 10 | 0 | 10 | 9 |

The tabulation sheet therefore shows each student's average score on all of the essay responses written; it also shows the class' average score on each question and (in the box in the lower right hand corner) the class' average score on all the questions; it is these scores which take on more meaning when obtained before and at the close of the course or program, and then compared, and when compared from one year to the next.

A third alternative: the teacher or trainer can establish very specifically what he or she is looking for, as above, but then simply record whether or not it appears on the essay rather than deciding upon a score. This method is valuable when the teacher is more interested in discerning patterns in the students' responses than rating their responses. This kind of analysis is a form of observation (what is being observed here is an essay passage rather than an actual behavioral sequence). The tab sheet, therefore, is similar to an observation schedule.

In setting up this kind of tabulation sheet, the teacher or trainer decides specifically what will be looked for (a particular attitude, for instance), then lists these on the sheet. Next, all of the phrases which would indicate each particular attitude are written down. As the response are read, marks are made on the sheet whenever the kinds of phrases and attitudes sought are encountered. The frequency of each is then calculated.

Responses pertaining to all five areas can be recorded; patterns of behavior, of course, are those reported by the student or participant. A comprehensive tab sheet of this kind might look like the one on the following page.

| AVERAGE % | % OF TOTAL STUDENTS | FREQUENCY | | etc. | Aaron | Mary | Juan | | |
|---|---|---|---|---|---|---|---|---|---|
| | | | | | | | ✓ | about Anglo American culture | KNOWLEDGE |
| | | | | | | | ✓ | about Black American culture | |
| | | | | | ✓ | | | patterns of cultural adjustment | |
| | | | | | | | | etc. | |
| | | | | | | | ✓ | of self | PERCEPTIONS — Positive |
| | | | | | ✓ | | | of Japanese | |
| | | | | | | | | etc. | |
| | | | | | | | | (same) | PERCEPTIONS — Negative |
| | | | | | ✓ | | | curiosity | ATTITUDES — Constructive |
| | | | | | | ✓ | | motivation | |
| | | | | | | | ✓ | confidence | |
| | | | | | | | | etc. | |
| | | | | | | | ✓ | exploitation | ATTITUDES — Obstructive |
| | | | | | | | | suspicion | |
| | | | | | ✓ | | | rejection | |
| | | | | | | | | etc. | |
| | | | | | ✓ | | | cultural analysis | SKILLS |
| | | | | | ✓ | | | interaction analysis | |
| | | | | | ✓ | ✓ | | conflict clarification | |
| | | | | | | | | etc. | |
| | | | | | | | ✓ | listening | BEHAVIOR — Constructive |
| | | | | | | | ✓ | helping | |
| | | | | | | | ✓ | learning | |
| | | | | | | | | etc. | |
| | | | | | ✓ | | | judging | BEHAVIOR — Obstructive |
| | | | | | | | ✓ | dominating | |
| | | | | | | | ✓ | ridiculing | |
| | | | | | | | | etc. | |

From the patterns which emerge during this kind of analysis, the teacher can learn much about the students and the course. If the analysis is done at the close of the course, the results may suggest which areas have been neglected (or those areas to which the students have been least receptive). If the analysis is done both before and after, the changes in the patterns (perhaps as a result of the course) can be traced. If then the same analysis is done of the students' essay responses in subsequent courses, changes in the patterns from one course to the next can be traced. The teacher may find, for example, that each year for the last three years the percentage of students who manifest constructive attitudes has increased sharply, while the percentage who manifest specific knowledge has decreased sharply. In attempting to account for these changes, the teacher will begin an interpretation which will consider changes in the course and methods during these years, changes in the backgrounds of the students enrolling in his course, and so forth. Having done this, there will be a very sound basis for re-designing the course. By sharing his findings with his students, colleagues and administrators, the teacher can help others clarify their own understanding of and planning for multicultural education courses. Whether or not these people will listen and assimilate the information, will depend in large part upon the format in which the findings are presented.

## THE APPROPRIATE FORMAT FOR THE FINDINGS

Once the tab sheets are completed, the teacher or trainer can decide which is the best format in which to display the findings. Sometimes the tab sheet itself is best. Often, however, it contains more data than are needed. Furthermore, if the findings are to be clear and easily grasped, a format is usually needed which is more visually representative, one which presents the data in lines, bars, graphs and contrasting locations on the page. Such a simplified, easily assimilated format is especially important when the results are to be presented to someone else (the students or participants, administrators, etc.).

Some formats tend to be more suitable for the results obtained through certain methods, other formats for the results from other methods. Several of these formats are illustrated below. Often, however, a given set of results can be displayed in a variety of formats. The teacher can therefore select the one which is most appropriate to him, his class, his methods and his audience. Regardless of the format chosen, it is usually best to present the question or the instructions in order that the person looking at the results can know exactly to what the students were responding.

<u>CHECK LISTS</u>

ANGLO PERCEPTIONS OF CHICANOS

number of respondents: 32

15.  Generally speaking, Chicanos are (please check <u>as many as apply</u>):

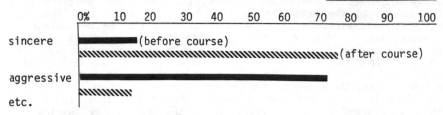

When using this method and format, the teacher can estimate (or
better, have the students judge -- <u>after</u> responding to the question)
which adjectives (or short phrases) are positive, which negative and
which neutral or mixed.  In the graph, then, the positive ones can be
displayed separately; an increase in most or all of the positive ones
can be demonstrated, as perhaps can a decrease in most or all of the
negative ones.

        The results of check lists can also be clearly displayed by
showing them in rank order with the number of respondents choosing
each alternative shown as a percentage of the total number of
respondents:

STUDENTS'DESCRIPTION OF COURSE

number of respondents: 32

17.  For me, this course has been (check <u>as many as apply</u>):

|     |                  |
|-----|------------------|
| 82% | exciting         |
| 80  | engaging         |
| 76  | motivating       |
| 68  | one of the best  |
| 65  | challenging      |
| 65  | informative      |
| 61  | useful           |
| 35  | frustrating      |
| 22  | tiring           |
| 14  | too theoretical  |
| 9   | confusing        |
| 0   | tedious          |
| 0   | boring           |
|     | etc.             |

When changes are made in the course the next time it is offered, the
teacher can ask this question again and see if there are any changes
in these responses; it may be found, for example, that in describing
the revised course, 14% of the students found it exciting and 82%
found it too theoretical.

## SCALES

Methods which provide lines on which the student locates his or her position can provide very interesting finds. These can be illustrated in a variety of ways, one of which is the following (this assumes the positions have been converted into numbers during tabulation):

### ETHNOCENTRISM, CURIOSITY AND MOTIVATION

number of respondents: 32
(-2 = very unacceptable; 2 = very acceptable)

questions 1, 4, 7 (ethnocentrism)

3, 5, 9 (curiosity)

2, 6, 8 (motivation)

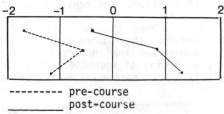

--------- pre-course
_____ post-course

Scales from which the student or participant selects a number can be equally interesting. One format appropriate for them is the following:

### EVALUATION OF COURSE GOALS

number of respondents: 33

18.     As a result of this course, to what extent do you now recognize <u>more clearly</u> the influence of your own culture upon your particular values, goals, expectations and patterns of relating to other people?
          (not at all - 0 1 2 3 4 5 - much more clearly)

          AVERAGE:  4.1                    RANGE:  1-5

When several short items have been rated with a numerical scale, the results can be clearly displayed by rank ordering them. These results, of course, are extremely useful in designing the next course or training program:

### EVALUATION OF COURSE COMPONENTS

          4.9  exercise on intercultural learning
          4.7  film on perceptions
          4.7  lecture on communication
          4.3  exercise on listening
          3.8  case study on conflict
          3.1  role playing (Washingtonville)
          2.0  Self assesment of skills
          1.8  status game
          1.0  lecture on perception

-249-

An average of all of these would give the teacher an overall evaluation of the course.

## ESSAY RESPONSES AND OBSERVATION

With regard to essay responses (elicited through critical incidents, case studies, films, photographs, sentence completion, open-ended questions and Journals), when these have been analyzed by means of tabulation sheets, the results can be presented in graphs, tables or other formats illustrated above. These same formats can also be used for the results from methods involving observation schedules and other systematic, quantifiable means of recording (discussion, enactment, production and unobtrusive measures).

When the tabulation of essay responses is not feasible or desired, the responses can be presented in a narrative which carefully summarizes the answers to each question and points out frequency of each kind of response. This narrative can be more clear and engaging if a few representative responses are actually quoted.

## INTERPRETATION OF THE FINDINGS

The teacher knows better than anyone else the purpose and content of his course, the backgrounds of the students in it and the appropriate methods of evaluation. The teacher, therefore, is in the best position to explain the meaning of his findings. For similar reasons, the trainer is in the best position to explain the significance of his findings. It is the teacher's and the trainer's obligation (and opportunity) to see that the results are interpreted responsibly.

The best time to do the interpretation is immediately after the tabulation. In fact, the evaluator will probably find irresistible the making of interpretative notes in the midst of the tabulation because questions, ideas and possibilities inevitably occur to an alert tabulator.

When the results of an evaluation are going to be presented to someone other than the evaluator, it is helpful to the other person if the interpretation begins with a brief description of the purposes and methods of the evaluation, the purposes and methods of the course or program in which it was done and the backgrounds of the students or participants involved.

The next step, whether the interpretation is being done for oneself alone or for others too, is to study all of the results and select those which are most important -- important in that they are most <u>unexpected, revealing</u> or <u>useful.</u> Care must be taken in selecting these results and caution must be exercised in interpreting them. What seems to have been a change in perceptions or attitudes, for example, may not have been. In the absence of statistical tests of significance, small changes should not be the basis for conclusions.

An increase of 10% in positive perceptions after a course, for example, probably demonstrates little one way or another about the course. An increase of 30% or more would probably be more suggestive and should be taken more seriously.

Caution is also called for in interpretation because the methods of social science are not precise, nor are the numbers which result; the numbers often suggest an accuracy which they do not possess. It is therefore with substantial changes, basic contradictions and consistent patterns over time that the interpreter is concerned.

Having selected the most important results, the evaluator tries to account for them. If a change in a particular perception is indicated, for example, everything to which the student has been exposed which might have brought that change about is considered: a particular series of exercises in this (or another) course, a major unplanned event in the course, the instructor's teaching style, the students' participation in certain methods of evaluation, relevant experiences the student or his friends have had outside the school in the community and their families and so forth. The teacher then reviews all the other results and recalls his own observations of the class in order to pick up any further clues. The most plausible explanation for the change can be identified and then incorporated into the interpretation. Again, caution is appropriate: cause and effect relationships are difficult to establish in the social sciences. (The connection between cause and effect is sometimes especially tenuous when using unobtrusive measures.)

The final step in the interpretation: the teacher or the trainer answers the basic question, So what? Given these data, given these important findings, what specifically should I do? What changes should be made in the course or program. What should be kept, what modified, what eliminated? What should be created? It is here, at this point, that evaluation can begin to make a profound difference in the nature and depth of intercultual learning offered to students and program participants.

Responsible interpretation, then calls for thinking carefully into the results and making judgments which are backed up by explicit rationales. Repetition is also extremely important. As the evaluation of the course with different students in different years is conducted and carefully interpreted, fundamental patterns begin to emerge. The teacher's and administrator's knowledge of these patterns becomes the basis for more accurate, more confident interpretation -- and for more effective multicultural education and intercultural training.

# CONCLUSIONS

Particular perspectives on learning and methods used by teachers and trainers usually develop within, and become increasingly reinforcing to, a single culture. These perspectives and methods are therefore uniquely suited to students and participants who were themselves brought up in that culture. They are usually inappropriate, and can even be damaging, in multicultural classrooms. Teachers in multicultural education and trainers in intercultural programs therefore have a responsibility to explore new perspectives and create alternative teaching styles and methods. In the midst of their experiments, they must measure the effects of each. The results of their measurement can then become the basis for selecting those approaches which are most effective. Having more fully and confidently implemented these approaches, further evaluation becomes the basis for improving and refining them.

As we do our designing, measuring and interpreting, it is well to recognize that the assumptions and methods of evaluation have themselves developed within particular -- for the most part Western -- cultures. Many assumptions and methods are distinctly American. This does not mean we should not do evaluation within multicultural groups. It means that we should do it as carefully as possible, being sensitive to the diverse backgrounds of our students and participants, and working toward those perspectives and methods which will respect and accommodate contrasting, even contradictory, expectations and preferences.

In addition to being limited by our culture, our methods are limited by our subject -- learning. Because of the complexity of any learning, and because it occurs within a human being (not a machine), we can measure only some of what some of our students and participants learn. If, for example, we would like to measure the amount of a certain kind of change in their knowledge, perceptions, attitudes, skills or patterns of behavior, we can measure only part of that change. Looking at the diagram "Measuring Amount of Change," let's assume that their knowledge has increased from point A to point D. We then do our evaluation. The area in the triangle represents the area

## MEASURING AMOUNT OF CHANGE

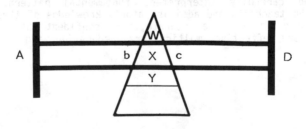

-252-

of knowledge revealed by the evaluation. We can see that the evaluation will reveal only the increase from b to c. As our selection of methods becomes more informed, and as we improve upon these methods, this area can be increased. As both our methods and our interpretations become more precise, we can be increasingly confident that it is in fact X that we are describing, rather than W (old knowledge) or Y.

In evaluating the effects of courses and training programs, as explained earlier, it is often desirable to distinguish between old knowledge or previous perceptions (what the student brings to the course) and new knowledge or altered perceptions (what the student takes from the course, presumably as a result of having been in it). The means for making this evaluation were explained in the sections above. The complexity of our subject however, and the lack of precision in our instruments continue to limit what we can discover. Looking at the next diagram, "Differentiating Old from New", we can

### DIFFERENTIATING OLD AND NEW

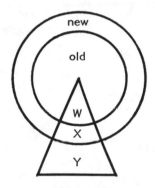

see that our evaluation can distinguish between old and new, but it reveals only parts of each. In our methods, in the formats for displaying the results, and in our interpretations, we must be careful that we measure and demonstrate the differences between W and X. As above, we must also be careful to differentiate both of these target areas from Y.

To whom should we show our results and interpretations? The individuals or organizations for whom we may have done th evaluation, of course, will want to see them. Our colleagues will probably be very interested in seeing and discussing them. And our students and participants would probably appreciate seeing them. In fact, some evaluators believe that we are ethically responsible to our students and participants to show them the results of our -- and their -- efforts. Because they cooperated in the evaluation, and because they were themselves the ones studied, they may have a right to see and discuss the results.

There are additional reasons for going over the results with our students. In doing so, they learn more about the topics of the course, about their teacher and, especially, about themselves. They also learn more, sometimes a great deal more, about evaluation. This is constructive, as mentioned earlier, in that they will then be better able to continue some self-evaluation on their own after the course and, one hopes, after their graduation.

Learning about the purposes and procedures of evaluation, and especially about its capacity to provide very revealing results, is constructive for a further reason. Some of our students wil soon be the ones making the decisions and designing the courses which determine the quality of, and the support for, multicultural education. In learning more about evaluation, which is essential for strengthening quality and demonstrating consequences, our students will be able to contribute substantially to our common concern.

# BOOKS

Abt, Clark C., ed.   The Evaluation of Social Programs.  Beverly Hills,
        California:  Sage Publications, 1977, 504 pages, $25.00

Cook, Thomas D. and Charles S. Reichardt, eds.   Qualitative and
        Quantitative Methods in Evaluation Research.  Beverly Hills,
        California:  Sage  Publications,  1979,  160  pages,  $12.50
        hardcover, $5.95 softcover

Handbook of Evaluation Research.  Beverly Hills, California:  Sage Pub-
        lications, two volumes, 1,400 pages, $50.00

Improving Cross-Cultural Training and Measurement of Cross-Cultural
        Learning.  Denver, Colorado; Center for Research and Education,
        1973, $6.00

Improving the Evaluation of Peace Corps Training Activities.  Denver,
        Colorado:  Center for Research and Education, 1973, $3.00

Rich, Robert F., ed.  Translating Evaluation into Policy.  Beverly
        Hills, California:  Sage Publications, 1979, 160 pages, $12.50
        hardcover, $5.95 softcover

Schulberg, Herbert C. and Jeanette M. Jerrell, eds.  The Evaluator and
        Management.  Beverly  Hills,  California:  Sage  Publications,
        1979, 159 pages, $12.50 hardcover, $5.95 softcover


# JOURNALS

Evaluation Review.  Beverly Hills, California:  Sage Publications,
        six issues per year, one year $40.00 Institutional, $20.00
        Individual

Evaluation Studies:  Review Annual.  Beverly Hills, California:  Sage
        Publications, 1976, 1977, 1978, 1979

# BIBLIOGRAPHY

When organizing a bibliography for a manual of this nature, concern for the usefulness, quality and ready availability of the items included is primary. In an effort to keep it manageable about fifty entries were selected that are representative of the considerable number of existing publications that relate to intercultural communication, multicultural education, pluralism and methodologies that can be adapted to teacher training programs. They were selected because they provide a theoretical framework or methodologies that can be applied directly or adapted easily to the process of training teachers to work in multicultural situations and to the development of a multicultural approach to education. (References cited for some of the early chapters in this manual provide additional unannotated bibliographic material.)

In a sense, the criteria employed for selection had conflicting elements. We felt the materials had to be broad enough to provide a set of general concepts and practices that could be used in a variety of situations and yet specific enough to provide connections between the general and those particular or concrete conditions that educators encounter. Most entries can pass this test. The few that do not meet both requirements have been described in a manner that indicates where they are most useful. Very few ethnic studies or culture-specific items are included and those listed were selected because they provided examples of approaches to learning about a culture in addition to information about one culture group. Finally, undergirding the entire selection process was a conscious attempt to bring together the conceptual and practical approach of intercultural communication and the ideal of building multicultural education programs.

Some readers may wish to pursue items not contained in this selected bibliography. They will find the two more extensive bibliographies listed here (Seelye and Tyler; Gollnick and Klassen) and those books whose annotations indicate the presence of notable reference lists especially helpful. Entries not readily available through bookstores or libraries include an address of the publisher from which they can be easily obtained.

We would like to express our appreciation to Ned Seelye and Lynn Tyler for permitting the use of several annotations from their publication, _Intercultural Communicator Resources_. Daisy deJesus provided printouts of ERIC abstracts from which we were able to construct other annotations. Wherever these sources were used, it is noted at the end of the annotation. All other annotations are the responsibility of the authors.

* * *

# BIBLIOGRAPHY

Allport, Gordon W.  The Nature of Prejudice.  Garden City, N.Y.: Doubleday & Co., Inc., 1954.

A study of the human phenomenon of prejudice, its roots in individual psychology and social structure.  The book is organized to provide an understandable analysis of each facet of prejudice as well as an understanding of the whole.  Prejudice is addressed in its generic form and through real life illustrations.  Race is but one facet of this extremely complete review.  (Seelye and Tyler)

Arizona University, Tucson.  The Cultural Literacy Laboratory: Multi-Cultural Teacher Education.  1973.

The goal of the Cultural Literacy Laboratory is to provide educators with cross-cultural adaptive skills needed to acclimate to different cultures and to reduce the effect of culture shock.  These skills are of particular importance to teachers working in bilingual and multicultural classrooms.  Based on social and scientific theory, the Laboratory incorporates and reinforces the participant's previous social science concepts and methodology and allows the practice of new skills and techniques in a variety of experience-based activities. Copies of instruments, Rokeach Scale E and the Cultural Literacy Inventory, are included as an appendix.  (ERIC abstract)

Banks, James A.  Teaching Strategies for Ethnic Studies.  Boston, Ma.:  Allyn and Bacon, 1975.

How to reach and teach Asians, blacks, Mexican-Americans, Puerto Ricans, and white ethnic groups.  (Seelye and Tyler)

Batchelder, Donald and Elizabeth G. Warner (eds.). Beyond Experience. Brattleboro, Vt.: Experiment in International Living, 1977.

Collection of materials used by the Experiment in International Living in their education and training programs. Focuses on concepts, processes and evaluation of cross-cultural learning in an international context but has application for domestic cross-cultural learning and training. Strong emphasis on experiential learning.

Blubaugh, Jon A. and Dorthy L. Pennington. Crossing Difference ... Interracial Communication. Columbus, Oh.: Charles E. Merrill Publishing Co., 1976.

This publication focuses on communication between people in different racial or culture groups within the U.S. They include Native American, Mexican American, Japanese American, and Chinese American cultures as well as the white and black culture groups usually associated with the "interracial" label. The authors state that, in the U.S. race is a difference to which "extra-ordinary significance" has been attached. Therefore, while other differences are considered, there is particular stress on race as a barrier to interpersonal communication. This book is organized into 8 chapters dealing with issues in interracial communication. Each chapter closes with a section of "Awareness Exercises" designed to engage students in exploring individual and group responses to each topic to reach a greater understanding of each issue. A useful "work book" for courses or workshops.

Brembeck, Cole S. and Walker H. Hill (eds.). Cultural Challenges to Education: The Influence of Cultural Factors in School Learning. Lexington, Ky.: Lexington Books, 1973.

A collection of addresses, essays and lectures, this work deals with topic of minority education in the U.S., intercultural education and educational anthropology.

California State Department of Education, Sacramento. Curriculum Materials: A Selected Bibliography, California Ethnic Heritage Program. Bureau of Intergroup Relations, 1975. California State Department of Education, Sacramento. Guide to an Analysis of Curriculum Materials for Ethnic Heritage Programs. Bureau of Intergroup Relations, 1976.

Procedures for the analysis of curriculum materials using a Preliminary Screening Form and Curriculum Analysis Questionnaire (included in the document) follow an introduction to the Ethnic Heritage Program in California and a discussion of assumptions about race and ethnicity that produce inadequate and, sometimes, unfortunate educational practices.

California State Department of Education, Sacramento. Guide for Multicultural Education Content and Context. Office of Intergroup Relations, 1977.

This guide provides a rationale for multicultural education focusing on needs and goals, the school setting and staff preparation and instructional planning. Also included are definitions of relevant terms and concepts, a procedure for the analysis of curriculum materials and a reference list.

California State Department of Education, Sacramento. Kit of Materials for Needs Assessment and Evaluation. Bureau of Intergroup Relations, 1974.

This kit includes a variety of needs assessment instruments and evaluation designs and methods for use by school districts in implementing school staff preparation in the history, culture and current problems of racial and ethnic minorities. They show diverse thinking about objectives and measurement. They deal variously with the assessment of staff needs, patterns of attituide and opinion, and the evaluation of content, presentation methods and outcomes. Samples of instruments used comprise the bulk of the kit. (ERIC abstract)

NOTE: Copies of California State Department of Education publications are available from Publication Sales, CA. State Dept. of Ed., P. O. Box 271, Sacramento, Ca. 95802.

Colangelo, Nicholas, Cecelia H. Foxley and Dick Dustin. Multicultural Nonsexist Education, A Human Relations Approach. Dubuque, Iowa: Kendall/Hunt Publishing Company, 1979.

A Collection of articles, exercises, discussion questions and projects and activities organized into four major sections: Human Relations Training, Multicultural Education, Nonsexist Education and Special Issues. The latter section deals with topics such as mainstreaming, age prejudice and counseling gays. The book is designed to incorporate the spirit and content of human relations education for teachers.

Condon, John C. and Fathi Yousef. An Introduction to Intercultural Communication, Indianapolis, 1975.

One of the most comprehensive introductions to the vast subject of interpersonal communication across cultures. Background is provided on the many issues which underpin the study of intercultural communication with theory illustrated by example. Major topics include: selected principles, intercultural encounters, values, value orientation, cultural beliefs, language in culture, translation and interpretation and rhetoric. It is a good introduction for beginners and a useful overview for professionals. Contains an extensive bibliography.

Curt, Carmen Judith Nine. Non-Verbal Communication in Puerto Rico. Fall River, Ma.: National Assessment and Dissemination Center for Bilingual Education, 1976.

Useful basic review of Puerto Rican non-verbal communication as contrasted with Anglo patterns. Based on two addresses focusing on non-verbal communication in teaching English as a second language followed by a series of chapters on special aspects of non-verbal communication, e.g. smiling, eye contact, greetings and farewells, etc.

Curt, Carmen Judith Nine. Teacher Training Pack for a Course on Cultural Awareness. Fall River, Ma.: National Assessment and Dissemination Center for Bilingual Education. 1976.

This is a guide to teaching a course in cultural awareness to pre-college students. Its aim is to help students affirm their own cultural roots and appreciate those of others. It is principally oriented, however, to Puerto Rican culture. It provides step by step instructions to carry the teacher through the two major foci of the course: cultural identity and non-verbal communication.

Darrow, Kenneth and Bradley Palmquist. The Transcultural Study Guide. Palo Alto, Ca.: Volunteers in Asia, 1975.

Practical guide for acquiring information in an unfamiliar cultural environment to assist in achieving an understanding of that culture. Provides, at length, specific questions the inquirer should ask. Considers the following areas: economics, politics, social structure, roles of men and women, religion and beliefs, music and art, food, education and communications. Although this guide was developed for people entering a foreign culture, it is easily adapted for domestic intercultural learning.

Educational Leadership. Vol. 32, No. 3, December, 1974:

This issue of the Journal of the Association for Supervision and Curriculum is totally devoted to articles on the implications of cultural pluralism for teachers, students and administrators in the schools. Entitled "Toward Cultural Pluralism," articles range from an outline of instructuional priorities for a culturally pluralistic school to a discussion on bicognitive development of students as an educational goal. Most articles are introductions to their topics and provide references for additional reading.

Ferguson, Henry, Ph.D. Manual for Multi-cultural and Ethnic Studies. Chicago, Ill.: Intercultural Press, Inc., 1977.

This manual is designed to assist educators in the development of cultural learning within the educational system. A discussion of the "philosophical and educational foundations of cultural learning" is followed by a "how to" guide for teacher training, curriculum development and evaluation techniques. Very practically oriented with an extensive collection of specific ethnic studies and cultural awareness exercises and activities for the teacher education classroom.

NOTE: Available from Intercultural Press, Inc., 70 W. Hubbard St., Chicago, Ill. 60610.

Fersh, Seymour (ed.). <u>Learning About Peoples and Cultures</u>. Evanston, Il.: McDougal, Littell and Co., 1974.

Text on cross-cultural perception and communication. Illustrates ideas of cultural sensitivity through culture-specific presentations. Also considers such topics as attitude formation, non-verbal communication, semantics, cultural differences within a culture and future prospects for cross-cultural understanding. Useful for informational reading or as a teaching tool. Illustrated with photographs and drawings from various cultures. Separate teachers guide is available. (Charles P. Pieper and Jacqueline H. Wasilewski from Seelye and Tyler)

Glazer, Nathan and Daniel Patrick Moynihan. <u>Beyond the Melting Pot: The Negroes, Puerto Ricans, Jews, Italians and Irish in New York City.</u> Cambridge, Ma.: MIT Press, 1970.

A study of the various racial and ethnic culture groups in New York city and their contributions to the community. The point of this book is that ethnic groups have a distinct identity which may change from one generation to another but is developed out of the maintenance of old values and forms and the creation of new patterns in a new country. The varying patterns of achievement in areas such as education, business and politics is considered in depth.

Gold, Milton J., Carl A. Grant and Harry N. Rivlin (eds.). <u>In Praise of Diversity: A Resource book for Multicultural Education.</u> Washington, D.C.: Teacher Corps, Association of Teacher Educators, 1977.

This collection of articles is organized into three sections. The introductory chapters, in Part I, discuss those considerations that are fundamental to multiculturalism, the dangers of stereotyping, areas of possible conflict and controversy and implications for schools. Part II contains "ethnic vignettes" that describe the experiences of nine major ethinic or racial groups in the United States. The final section is designed to "set the reader's thoughts in motion and spark the teacher's creativity" as the teacher's role in the process of affirming the advantages of cultural and individual diversity and in providing culture-learning opportunities in the classroom is discussed.

Gollnick, Donna, Frank H. Klassen and Joost Yff. <u>Multicultural Education and Ethnic Studies in the United States.</u> <u>An Analysis and Annotated Bibliography of Selected ERIC Documents.</u> Washington, D.C.: American Association of Colleges for Teacher Education, ERIC Clearinghouse on Teacher Education, 1976.

This book, an annotated bibliography and analysis, contains abstracts of documents from the ERIC System on multicultural education and ethnic studies. The main categories for document classification are concept materials, classroom materials, curriculum materials, and program materials. Each entry includes an abstract, the ERIC Ed Number, the availability of the document (microfiche or hardcopy), and identification of the ethnic group being described or discussed in the document. The bibliography itself is preceded by a section reviewing the literature on multicultural education and is followed by an explanation of how the ERIC search was conducted and an analysis of the bibliography. (ERIC abstract)

NOTE: Available from AACTE, Number One Dupont Circle, NW, Washington, D.C., 20036.

Gordon, Ray. Living in Latin America. Skokie, Il.: National Textbook Company, 1974.

Fascinating study of Americans living in Columbian homes and their interaction with primarily middle and upper-middle class Colombian families in Bogota. This interaction is analyzed for the purpose of showing the implications of this one cross-cultural case study for intercultural communication in general. Focuses on the use of various parts of the home to get at cultural differences.

Hall, Edward T. The Silent Language. Garden City, N.Y.: Anchor Press, 1963.

Classical study of communication, especially non-verbal communication, as it is affected by culture. Hall emphasizes that "out-of-awareness" aspects of human activity transmits messages that are easily misunderstood cross-culturally. He lists ten basic kinds of human activity, called Primary Message Systems, that can be used as reference points to analyze and better understand a culture group.

Hall, Edward T. The Hidden Dimension. Garden City, N.Y.: Doubleday & Co., Inc., 1966.

The central theme of this book is social and personal space (proxemics), man's cultural perception of it and the significance thereof for intercultural communication. Cross-cultural comparisons are included and explained.

Hall, Edward T. Beyond Culture. Garden City, N.Y.: Anchor Press, 1976.

The central theme of this book is that man needs the experience of other cultures to learn. To survive, all cultures need each other. Hall proposes a global shift toward what he calls "cultural literacy" that will enable the human race to escape the constraints of "covert culture" (which he describes as those aspects of cultures that one takes for granted -- the latent structures that undergird any society).

Herman, Judith (ed.). The Schools and Group Identity: Educating for a New Pluralism. New York, N.Y.: American Jewish Committee, Institute on Pluralism and Group Identity, 1974.

In the mid-1960's the American Jewish Committee published a report on suburban school's failure (or inability) to teach children about "human differences." Since then, there have been significant changes in some school systems but there are many ways school administrators, teachers and curriculum developers interpret "Ethnic Studies." Most of the materials reviewed in this publication were extensions of traditional educational methods. Yet, as the examples suggest, the area of ethnic studies offers many possibilities for innovation that go beyond adding textual content or new individual learning packets. One purpose of this paper is to point to useful examples so that each school or system does not feel compelled to "reinvent the wheel." (ERIC abstract)

Herskovits, Melville J. (edited by Frances Herskovits). Cultural Relativism Perspectives in Cultural Pluralism. New York, N.Y.: Vintage Books, 1973.

This book contains 15 essays, produced over 20 years by one of the leading anthropologists in the U.S., on cultural relativism and related topics. They are organized under four broad topics: 1) Culture, Definitions and Values, 2) Ethnocentrism, Racism and Peace, 3) Economics and Values: The Modern World and Tradition, and 4) Expressive Arts: A Cross-cultural Perspective.

Hoopes, David S. and Paul Ventura (eds.). Intercultural Sourcebook, "Cross Cultural Training Methodologies." Washington, D.C.: Society for Intercultural Education, Training and Research; Intercultural Press, Inc., 1979.

A systematic survey of the major methods used in cross-cultural training and education. Analysis, descriptions and examples of methods are grouped under ten headings including Contrast-American, Culture-Assimilator and Workbook Approaches.

Hoopes, David S. (ed.). Readings in Intercultural Communication, Vol II, "Selected Course Syllabi in Intercultural Communication." Pittsburgh, Pa.: Intercultural Press, Inc. and Society for Education, Training and Research, 1977.

A collection of syllabi of graduate and undergraduate courses in intercultural communication and in communication and development/ social change. Although this volume is largely international in focus, material contained therein can be applied and/or adapted for domestic intercultural learning and training.

NOTE: "Readings" and "Sourcebook" available from Intercultural Press, Inc., 70 W. Hubbard St., Chicago, Ill., 60610.

Hunter, William A. (ed.). Multicultural Education Through Compentency-Based Teacher Education. Washington, D.C.: American Association of Colleges for Teacher Education, 1974.

This publication is the result of a Multicultural Education/Competency Based Teacher Education project which, among other objectives, sought to bring together the findings of separate studies, projects and research efforts. The project proposed to take a broader approach to the overall problem of quality education by seeking to identify generic concerns and needs common to all ethnic groups and diverse cultural situations. The project at the same time sought to identify those needs felt to be unique or more relevant to certain cultural circumstances and situations than others. Various authors contribute to the following topics: antecedents to the development of an emphasis on multicultural education; multicultural education from a Black educator's perspective; from a Spanish-speaking American's perspective; a Native American's perspective; and a cross-cultural approach to multicultural education. Available from AACTE. (ERIC abstract)

Jain, Nemi and Richard L. Cummings (eds.). Proceedings of the Conference on Intercultural Communication and Teacher Education. Milwaukee, Wis.: Milwaukee Urban Observatory, University of Wisconsin - Milwaukee, 1975.

These proceedings provide a broad framework for the need of intercultural communication training for teachers, some discussion of concepts and techniques for such training and of the human relations training programs that are being conducted at several teacher education institutions.

Klassen, Frank H. and Donna M. Gollnick (eds.). Pluralism and The American Teacher. Washington, D.C.: Ethnic Heritage Center for Teacher Education of the American Association of Colleges for Teacher Education, 1977.

This publication is an important contribution to the translation of multicultural education goals into practical reality. Consideration of the major issues in the field are followed, in the text, by descriptions of several curricular approaches to multicultural teacher education currently in use and a list of multicultural resources recommended for educators. Available from the Ethnic Heritage Center for Teacher Education, AACTE, One Dupont Circle, Washington, D.C., 20036.

LeVine, Robert A. and Donald T. Campbell. Ethnocentricism: Theories of Conflict, Ethnic Attitudes, and Group Behavior. New York, N.Y.: John Wiley and Sons, 1972.

An inventory of the varied and contradictory social science theoretical literature for propositions about ethnocentricism that are testable in cross-cultural research. The theories are from many disciplines: anthropology, sociology, political science, psychology, psychoanalysis. (Jacqueline H. Wasilewski from Seelye and Tyler)

Nichols, Margaret S. and Peggy O'Neill. Multicultural Materials. Stanford, CA: Multicultural Resources, 1974.

A selective bibliography of adult materials about human relations and the history, culture and current social issues of Black, Chicano, Asian American and Native American peoples.

Ramirez, Manuel and Alfredo Castaneda. Cultural Democracy, Bicognitive Development, and Education. New York, N.Y.: Academic Press, 1974.

Argues for an expansion of educational techniques to fit the thinking patterns of children of differing cultural backgrounds. Each chapter is followed by a list of references: books, monographs, articles, journals, films, filmstrips, videotapes, and elementary curriculum materials. (Jacqueline H. Wasilewski from Seelye and Tyler)

Rich, Andrea L. Interracial Communication. New York, N.Y.: Harper and Row, 1974.

Bringing together findings from the fields of anthropology, psychiatry, sociology, psychology, speech and linguistics, this book provides a framework in which to view and define the diverse factors at work during interracial and interethnic communication.

Ruben, Brent D. and Richard W. Budd. Human Communication Handbook: Simulations and Games. Rochelle Park, N.Y.: Hayden Book Company, Inc., 1975.

This book consists of a collection of games, simulations and exercises organized under four topics: 1) personal communication 2) social communication 3) communication systems and 4) communication, observation and recording guides, well suited for adaptation to multi-cultural learning groups.

Samovar, Larry A. and Richard E. Porter (eds.). Intercultural Communication: A Reader. Belmont, Ca.: Wadsworth Publishing Co., Inc., 1980 Third Edition.

A collection of articles and essays by many authors that cover both domestic and international intercultural communication issues. The 1972 edition was one of the first and best commercially published readers on the subject. This second edition contains many new articles, some written especially for it, as well as the most useful essays from the earlier edition. The book is divided into four parts: Intercultural Communications: An Introduction; Socio-cultural Influences: What We Bring to Intercultural Communication; Intercultural Interaction: Taking Part in Intercultural Communication and Intercultural Communication: Becoming More Effective. At the close of each section, there are annotated reading lists followed by other suggested readings and a series of study questions.

Saville-Troike, Muriel. A Guide to Culture In The Classroom. Rosslyn, VA.: National Clearinghouse for Bilingual Education, 1978.

Considers the role of culture in the bilingual classroom; provides recommendations for designing in-service and pre-service training programs to develop the cultural competencies of bilingual educators and for applying cultural information to classroom practices, curriculum development and evaluation. Although directed toward bilingual educators, this publication is useful for anyone concerned with culture learning and intercultural relations.

Seelye, H. Ned. Teaching Culture: Strategies for Foreign Language Educators. Skokie, Ill.: National Textbook Co., 1974.

A how-to-do-it approach to helping foreign language students develop empathy and learn cross-cultural communication skills. Designed primarily for foreign language teachers who wonder how and when culture ought to be taught. Focuses on student attitude and other resulting behavior. Outlines instructional objectives, curriculum design, tests and applied activities. (Peggy Burch from Seelye and Tyler)

Seelye, H. Ned and V. Lynn Tyler (eds.). Intercultural Communicator Resources. Brigham Young University Language and Intercultural Research Center and Bilingual Education Dept. of the Illinois Office of Education, 1977.

An annotated resource list that includes books, other print and media sources, fugitive materials and other resources such as films, systems and collections. The primary focus of the resource report is intercultural communication but materials from related areas that are applicable to this field are included. Available from BYU Language and Intercultural Research Center, 250 B-34, Provo, Utah, 84602.

Sikkema, Mildred and Agnes M. Niyekawa Howard. Cross-Cultural Learning and Self-Growth. New York, N.Y.: International Association of Schools of Social Work, 1977.

Describes an experimental cross-cultural education program in the School of Social Work at the University of Hawaii. Students were trained in intercultural communication and cross-cultural analysis, sent to Guam for two non-directed months of experience and then returned to campus to examine their experience in light of the concepts learned before going. Illuminates the process of cross-cultural learning. Very suggestive for the whole intercultural field.

Smith, Gary R. and George G. Otero. Teaching About Cultural Awareness. Denver, CO.: Center for Teaching International Relations, University of Denver, 1977.

Twenty-five activities to develop middle and high school students' cultural awareness by participation in experiences which stimulate constructive attitudes about cultural differences while examining the role of values, attitudes and beliefs in fostering and inhibiting cultural interaction and awareness.

Smith, Gary R. and George G. Otero. <u>Teaching About Ethnic Heritage</u>. Denver, CO.: Center for Teaching International Relations, University of Denver, 1977.

Eighteen activities to develop middle and high school students' ability to link their ethnicity, identity and heritage. The activities are designed to reach objectives in discovery skills, values and values analysis, and knowledge and recognition of ethnic heritage within a framework of five key concepts: perception, identity, ethnicity, heritage and human diversity.

Spindler, George (ed.). <u>Education and Cultural Process</u>. New York, N.Y.: Holt, Rinehart & Winston, 1974.

This work contains useful chapters on (1) cultural transmission; (2) culture and cognition; (3) some discontinuities in the enculturation of Mistassini Cree children; and (4) an interesting section on transcultural sensitization.

Stewart, Edward C. <u>American Cultural Patterns: A Cross-Cultural Perspective</u>. Chicago, Ill.: Intercultural Press, Inc., 1971.

Cross-cultural analysis of American cultural assumptions and values and a comparision of cultural patterns of thinking and behaving. Stewart defines differences in broad terms along dimensions of dominant patterns rather than providing a laundry list of explicit, particular items of specific cultural contrast. Used as a text in college level courses in intercultural communication and cross-cultural education.

NOTE: Available from Intercultural Press, Inc., 70 W. Hubbard St., Chicago, Ill., 60525.

Stone, James and Donald deNevi. <u>Teaching Multi-Cultural Populations: Five Heritages</u>. New York, N.Y.: Van Nostrand Co., 1971.

A book dealing with the subject of education in a multi-cultural context, this work is comprised of readings designed to sensitize teachers to the "needs and opportunities created by cultural pluralism in the classroom."

Weeks, William H., Paul B. Peterson and Richard W. Brislin. <u>A Manual of Structured Experiences for Cross-Cultural Learning</u>. Washington, D.C.: Society for Intercultural Education, Training and Research, 1977.

A collection of exercises, role plays, case studies etc., aimed at stimulating learning in multicultural groups. Available from Interculture Press, Inc., 70 W. Hubbard St., Chicago, Ill., 60610.

# FILM LIST

The film list that follows contains those films that the authors consider to be particularly useful as discussion starters or illustrations of particular aspects of communicaion and interaction between people who are culturally different. They are annotated to indicate which topics they are intended to address.

We would like to refer the reader to a short discussion on the use of films that is included in the strategy section of the manual. It contains some general suggestions on discussing films and specific questions that can be applied to the film "Chairy Tale."

These films usually can be rented for a nominal fee. Those fees have not been listed because they tend to change as the expense of maintaining films and mailing them increases. Most of the rental agencies will provide a cataloque with fee schedules on request. Additional sources of film listings is Films In A Changing World: A Critical International Guide by Jean Marie Ackerman, Published by The Society For International Development, Washington, D.C. in 1972, and The National Film Board of Canada, P.O. Box 6100, Montreal 101, Quebec, Canada.

Most cross-cultural trainers have found that films are not as useful in training programs as one might expect given our strong orientation to visual aids. There are very few good films that even adequately deal with intercultural relations. One major weakness of the films listed here is that they do not engage participants in the exploration of cross-cultural interaction as effectively as experience-based strategies. Those films listed here are, we feel, the best we've seen but strongly recommend that any film be reviewed before it is used in a classroom or workshop.

FILMS ON INTERCULTURAL COMMUNICATION AND
CROSS-CULTURAL HUMAN RELATIONS

ALL FILMS MADE IN U.S.A. OR CANADA UNLESS OTHERWISE NOTED.

## Balablock

An animated illustration of how we react to differences in others. The whole arena of human conflict is reduced to its simplest dimensions in a manner that is both amusing and penetrating. 1975  Sr. High through adult.  7-1/2 minutes, color.

> Available from:  Encyclopedia Britannica Films
> 425 North Michigan Avenue
> Chicago, Illinois  60611

## Boundary Lines

An animated film examining the numerous "boundaries" which keep people apart.  Some of the boundaries that are considered are wealth, religion, color and national origin.  Jr. High through adult. 13 minutes, color.

> Available from:  McGraw-Hill Films
> 330 West 43rd Street
> New York, New York, 10036

## Bwana Toshi                                               (Japan)

The story of a Japanese engineer's encounter with a group of East African villagers and their struggle for mutual understanding. Beautiful, sensitive film that illustrates how misperception and lack of knowledge about the values and communicaton style in a culture causes difficulty for the "outsider" even when there are the best of intentions.  Also illustrates how one's own "cultural blinders" make it hard to discover what one needs to know to function effectively in another culture and, in this case, complete a specific task.  1965. Sr. High through adult.  115 minutes, color.

> Available from:  Audio-Brandon Films
> 34 MacQueston Parkway South
> Mount Vernon, New York, 10550

## Chairy Tale

Man meets chair.  Man attempts to sit on chair.  Chair revolts.  The ensuing struggle, first for mastery and then for understanding, forms the story.  The classic film on the need for empathy. 1957.  Jr. High through adult.  10 minutes, black and white.

> Available from:  Syracuse University Film Rental Center
> 1455 East Colvin Street
> Syracuse, New York, 13210
>
> International Film BUreau, Inc.
> 332 South Michigan Avenue
> Chicago, Illinois,  60604

## Differences

An American Chippewa Indian, two Blacks, a Mexican-American and a longhaired bearded White relate their experiences and difficulties in learning to live within the unwritten rules of white, middle-class America. They discuss stereotypes, individual differences, family traditions, cultural heritage, biased history books, value of minority cultures and reasons why minority cultures play a significant part in American society. Central message emerges as "aren't you glad we are not the same?" 1974 Sr. High through adult. 25 minutes, color.

> Available from:  Syracuse University Film Rental Center
> 1455 East Colvin Street
> Syracuse, New York, 13210

## Eye of the Beholder

A small drama that demonstrates how people can perceive the same event differently. Amusing and good discussion starter. However, made in the 1950's, the clothing and other "dating" aspects may be a distraction and this should be discussed when the film is used. 1955. Adult. 30 minutes, black and white.

> Available from:  Syracuse University Film Rental Center and
> Allegheny Intermediate Unit,
> Instructional Materials Services
> 5-B, One Allegheny Square
> Pittsburgh, Pennsylvania, 15212

## Eye of the Storm

A unique two-day simulation conducted by a 3rd grade teacher in the Midwest. On the first day the teacher separated her class into "superior" and "inferior" groups based on eye color. On the second day the roles were reversed. Primary school through adult. 25 minutes, color.

> Available from:  Order Department, Program Division
> Anti-Defamation League of B'nai B'rith
> 315 Lexington Avenue
> New York, New York, 10016

## Four Families

A classic film which depicts scenes from everyday life of typical farm families in India, France, Japan and Canada. Margaret Mead discusses the cultural differences demonstrated. 1965. Adult. 62 minutes, black and white.

> Available from:  Syracuse University Film Rental Center and
> McGraw-Hill Films
> 330 West 43rd Street
> New York, New York 10036

Frank Film

Useful for illustrating the assault on the senses that occurs when unfamiliar and even familiar sounds and signs are hurled at the viewer. There is a continuous flux of objects (chairs, t.v. sets, shoes, shirts, houses, stereos, hot dogs, cars, tires, batteries, etc.) which seem to flow and merge into one another..."an eyeblower and an ear-blower and consequently a mind blower." 1973. Secondary school and adult. 9 minutes, color.

Available from:  Syracuse University Film Rental Center
1455 East Colvin Street
Syracuse, New York 13210

Invisible Walls

Demonstration of proxemic-behavior and how individuals react when their personal space is violated. Focuses on common American beliefs about personal space. 1969. Secondary school and adult. 12 minutes, black and white.

Available from:  Syracuse University Film Rental Center
1455 East Colvin Street
Syracuse, New York 13210

Latino:  Cultural Conflict

A film about cultural conflicts between Spanish speaking people and the Anglo community. Features a Latino high school student and how basic cultural differences lead to misunderstandings between him and his Anglo teachers. 1972. Jr. High through adult. 21 minutes, black and white.

Available from:  Syracuse University Film Rental Center
1455 East Colvin Street
Syracuse, New York, 13210

Majority Minority

Documents the life style, attitudes and aspirations of a statistically "average" American and his family. The Anglo bricklayer featured in this film has all the "credentials" to qualify him as a member of the majority. However, the groups from which he is excluded constitute an even larger section of the population than the group to which he belongs. Good discussion stimulator. 1975. Jr. High through adult. 23 minutes, color.

Available from:  Syracuse University Film Rental Center
1455 East Colvin Street
Syracuse, New York 13210

## Neighbors

A parable of interpersonal conflict which breaks out between two formerly friendly neighbors who come to blows over the possession of a flower. 1952. Jr. High through adult. 9 minutes, color.

> Available from: International Film Bureau, Inc.
> 332 South Michigan Avenue
> Chicago, Illinois, 60604
>
> Syracuse University Film Rental Center
> 1455 East Colvin Street
> Syracuse, New York, 13210

## Picture in Your Mind

Animated commentary on the significance of cultural and perceptual differences in human relations and the background and growth of prejudice. 1950. Secondary school through adult. 16 minutes, color.

> Available from: McGraw Hill Films
> 330 West 43rd Street
> New York, New York, 10036.
>
> Order Department Program Division
> Anti-Defamation League of B'nai B'rith
> 315 Lexington Avenue
> New York, New York, 10016

## The Wall                                              (Yugoslavia)

An amusing animated film about differences in values as reflected in different approaches to problem-solving. Jr. High through Adult. 4 minutes, color.

> Available from: Contemporary Films
> McGraw-Hill
> 1221 Avenue of the Americas
> New York, New York, 10020

## Walls and Walls

Emphasizes how we wall others out but ourselves in by dealing with literal walls that have been built against physical dangers, symbolic walls such as flags and "personal walls" erected as protection from being hurt. Also concentrates on walls represented by prejudice and stereotypes. 1973. Jr. High through adult. 10 minutes, color.

> Available from: Syracuse University Film Rental Center
> 1455 East Colvin Street
> Syracuse, New York, 13210

## Where is Prejudice

Ethnically diverse group of young liberal Americans gather at Cape Cod to explore the nature of prejudice. They are shocked to find it is deeply imbedded within themselves. Powerful, disturbing film. Adult. 60 minutes, black and white.

        Available from:   Indiana University Audiovisual Center
                            Field Services Department
                            Bloomington, Indiana, 47401